Gita
According to
Gandhi

BESTSELLING NON-FICTION

- Gravity by George Gamow
  Sciences/Physics, ISBN: 9789388118705

- How to Develop Self-Confi. and Pub. Speaking by Dale Carnegie
  Mind, Body & Spirit, ISBN: 9789388118286

- How to Stop Worrying and Start Living by Dale Carnegie
  Mind, Body & Spirit, ISBN: 9789387669161

- How to Win Friends and Influence People by Dale Carnegie
  Self Help/General, ISBN: 9789387669178

- Mein Kampf by Adolf Hitler
  Autobiographies/Leaders, ISBN: 9789387669260

- My Experiments with Truth by Mahatma Gandhi
  Autobiographies/Leaders, ISBN: 9789387669277

- Relativity by Albert Einstein
  Sciences/Physics, ISBN: 9789387669185

- The Art of War by Sun Tzu
  Self Help/Success, ISBN: 9789387669321

- The Diary of a Young Girl by Anne Frank
  Autobiographies/Memoirs, ISBN: 9789387669208

- The Magic of Believing by Claudie Bristol
  Religion/Christianity, ISBN: 9789388118217

- The Miracles of Your Mind by Joseph Murphy
  Mind, Body & Spirit, ISBN: 9789387669215

- The Power of Your Subconscious Mind by Joseph Murphy
  Mind, Body & Spirit, ISBN: 9789387669222

- The Richest Man in Babylon by George S. Clason
  Business & Economics, ISBN: 9789388118354

- Think and Grow Rich by Napoleon Hill
  Self Help/Success, ISBN: 9789387669352

Get 25% off on Amazon | Search the book by its ISBN

Gita
According
to
Gandhi

The Gospel of Selfless Action

Mahatma Gandhi

GENERAL PRESS

Published by
GENERAL PRESS
4805/24, Fourth Floor, Krishna House
Ansari Road, Daryaganj, New Delhi - 110002
Ph : 011-23282971, 45795759
E-mail : generalpressindia@gmail.com

www.generalpress.in

First Edition : 2019

ISBN : 9789389157888

Published by Azeem Ahmad Khan for General Press

Contents

Introduction

A sloka-by-sloka interpretation of one of the world's most enduring and influential spiritual texts of the twentieth century. Among the various interpretations of the Bhagavad Gita, the one by Mahatma Gandhi holds a unique position. Unlike other interpretations, Gandhi's commentary is direct and to the point, not offering an opinion on the meaning of the text, but fleshing out the message, often relating it to his own extraordinary experiences.

Gandhi interpreted the Bhagavad Gita, which he regarded as a gospel of selfless action, over a period of nine months from February 24th to November 27th, 1926 at Satyagrah Ashram, Ahmedabad. The morning prayer meetings were followed by his discourses and discussions on the Bhagavad Gita. During this time—a period when Gandhi had withdrawn from mass political activity—he devoted much of his time and energy to translating the *Gita* from Sanskrit into his native Gujarati. As a result, he met with his followers almost daily, after morning prayer sessions, to discuss the *Gita's* contents and meaning as it unfolded before him. This book is the transcription of those daily sessions.

Forward

The following pages by Mahadev Desai are an ambitious project. It represents his unremitting labours during his prison life in 1933-'34. Every page is evidence of his scholarship and exhaustive study of all he could lay hands upon regarding the *Bhagavad Gita*, poetically called the Song Celestial by Sir Edwin Arnold. The immediate cause of this labour of love was my translation in Gujarati of the divine book as I understood it. In trying to give a translation of my meaning of the *Gita*, he found himself writing an original commentary on the *Gita*.

The book might have been published during his lifetime, if I could have made time to go through the manuscript. I read some portions with him, but exigencies of my work had to interrupt the reading. Then followed the imprisonments of August 1942, and his sudden death within six days of our imprisonment. All of his immediate friends decided to give his reverent study of the *Gita* to the public. He had copies typed for his English friends who were impatient to see the commentary in print. And Pyarelal, who was collaborator with Mahadev Desai for many years, went through the whole manuscript and undertook to perform the difficult task of proof reading. Hence this publication.

Frankly, I do not pretend to any scholarship. I have, therefore, contended myself with showing the genesis of Mahadev Desai's effort. In so far as the translation part of the volume is concerned, I can vouch for its accuracy. He carried out the meaning of the original translation. I may add too that Pyarelal has interfered with the original only and in rare cases where it was considered to be essential, an interference which Mahadev Desai would, in my opinion, have gladly accepted, had he been alive.

On the train to Madras,

—**M.K. GANDHI**
20th January, 1946

My Submission

I. PRELIMINARY

I fear that it is an act of supererogation on my part to append a long supplementary introduction and fairly profuse notes to this translation of Gandhiji's *Anasaktiyoga*, because I know that the brief introduction by Gandhiji, written in his usual succinct and direct manner, leaves nothing to be desired so far as the central message of the *Gita* is concerned, and his brief notes are enough for the purpose. But, for several reasons I have thought it necessary to add both to his introduction and his notes. For one tiling, the *Anasaktiyoga* was written mainly for the Gujarati reading public, and especially the unsophisticated and even unlettered section of that public. Secondly, he wanted the book to be made available to the poorest in the country and, therefore, as small in size and as cheap as possible. These two ends necessarily limited the scope both of Gandhiji's introduction and notes. He studiously avoided all things that would make the little book in any way difficult for the unlettered reader, and deliberately kept out of his regard the studious or the curious who would need help or enlightenment on certain points in which the readers he had in view would not be interested. Thus, for instance, there is not one mention of even the word *Upanishad* in any one of his notes, or even in his introduction, not to speak of any points of interest to the scholar or to the student: for instance, the question of the date of the *Gita,* the text of the *Gita,* the question of the Krishna Vasudeva cult. His chief concern were his readers and the message he read in the *Gita.* Not only was his scope limited, but he disowns all claim to scholarship, and thinks that some of the subjects over which keen controversy has raged have no intimate bearing on the message of the *Gita.* Above all, he has, as everyone knows, too keen a sense of his limitations to be deflected out of the scope he sets to himself.

But this translation of his translation of the *Gita* is meant for a different, if not also a larger public. I hope and expect that a large number of English-knowing youths in India will like to have Gandhiji's interpretation of the *Gita.* I also feel that many outside India who are interested in a study of Gandhiji's life and thought may care to go in for this book. Furthermore, I have an impression that the bulk of the readers of the book will be students. It is with the needs of this public in view that I have appended additional notes to the *shlokas* (verses) and propose, by means of this "Submission" to cover a number of points that could not be dealt with in the notes, and were outside the scope of Gandhiji's book. Let me make it clear that I lay no more claim to scholarship than does Gandhiji, but I am myself a student—as I hope to remain until my dying day—and it is out of my sympathy for the needs of people of my kind that I have presumed to introduce this additional matter. I found that in the very nature of things some explanatory notes were necessary in a translation into a foreign language of a translation in an Indian language of a great Sanskrit work of philosophy and ethics; and as I read Gandhiji's translation over and over again I felt that certain doubts and difficulties that troubled me were likely to trouble other minds too, and that I should offer what explanation I could about them. In doing so I have steered clear of all matters of purely scholastic interest, but have referred again and again to the sources—the *Upanishads* which the Divine Cowherd is said to have turned into cows to draw the nectar-like milk of the *Gita.* I have also ventured to draw parallels from the Bible and the *Koran* and the words of great seers who drew their inspiration from those great books, in order to show how, in the deepest things of life, the Hindu and the Musalman and die Christian, the Indian and the European, in fact all who cared and endeavoured to read the truth of things, are so spiritually akin. This I thought would help, in however small a measure, to contribute to that "free sharing among religions which no longer stand in uncontaminated isolation", to the need of which Dr Radhakrishnan, that great interpreter of Hindu life and thought, has called attention in his *East and West in Religion.* Not that I went out of my way to hunt for those parallels, but I took them just as they came in the course of my quiet reading in my prison cell.

II. DATE, TEXT, AUTHOR ETC.

Let me warn the reader against expecting in this "Submission" a discussion of certain things usually discussed in such books. I have avoided them for precisely the same reason that Gandhiji would avoid them, even if he were writing for English-knowing readers. I would like to note, however, the results of research of scholars on certain points and my view regarding the bearing of some of them on the message of the *Gita.*

1. The first is the question of the date of the *Gita.* Whilst I have no fresh contribution to make on the subject, let me briefly record the results of the researches to date. Mr Hill thinks that the theory of a Christian influence to be traced in the *Gita* is "now almost universally discredited", and that "the internal evidence points to the second century B. G. as the period when the *Gita* in its present form appeared". This is the most conservative estimate. Dr Radhakrishnan summarizes the evidence on the point thus: "We shall not, I believe, be far wrong if we assign the *Gita* to the fifth century B.C.", "though if the references in the *Dharma Sutras* are regarded as interpolated texts, then the *Gita* may be assigned to the third or the second century B.C." Lokamanya Tilak has cited considerable evidence-7-that of Pali texts and other —to prove that the *Gita* existed before, and exercised considerable influence on, the growth of Mahayana Buddhism, and he has no doubt that the present text of the *Gita* must be assigned to the fifth century B.C.

2. The second is the question of the text of the *Gita.* There seems to be no doubt in the mind of the scholars that the present text of the *Gita* is a redaction of a much earlier original. The question about the scope of this earlier original must remain unsolved until something like a "Code Sinaiticus" for the *Gita* is discovered. One may, however, say that, even when this original is discovered, it will not make much difference to souls like Gandhiji, every moment of whose life is a conscious effort to live the message of the *Gita.* This does not mean that Gandhiji is indifferent to

the efforts of scholars in this direction. The smallest questions of historical detail interest him intensely as I can say from personal knowledge. In the quiet of the Yeravda Central Prison I have seen him spending hours discussing a reading or text. But his attitude is that in the last analysis it is the message that abides, and he is sure that no textual discovery is going to affect by a jot the essence or universality of the message.

3. The same thing may be said about questions of the historical Krishna and the genesis and history of the Krishna *Vasudeva* worship, i.e. the Bhagawat Dharma. While no labour and time spent on research in this connection would be ill-spent, for Gandhiji the quest of a historical Krishna has an entirely different meaning. As one may see from his intensely deep little introduction, he has already found Him, no matter whether the scholars prove him to be an inspired cowherd or an inspired charioteer driving Arjuna to victory. Substitute for "Christ" the" word "Krishna" in those beautiful words of Albert Schweitzer and you find Gandhiji's attitude described to the minutest precision: "Christ comes to us as one Unknown, without a name, just as by the lake side He came to those men who knew Him not. He speaks to us the same words, 'Follow thou Me', and sets to us those tasks which He has to fulfill for our time. He commands,, and to those who obey Him, whether they be wise or simple, He will reveal Himself in the toils, the conflicts, the sufferings which they shall pass through in His fellowship, and as an ineffable mystery they shall learn in their experience who He is." He has not the slightest doubt that Krishna is in every one of us, that we would feel and act on the influence of His presence if we were purged of all passion and pride and had ceased to run after the things of the earth, that He would listen to us if only we would seek refuge in Him, that He would claim us back as though we had never been away from Him. All questions of the quest for the historical Krishna become of subsidiary importance when we bear in mind the fact that the *Gita* preaches no exclusive doctrine and that when the author of the *Gita* introduces Krishna as speaking first person, it is no personal Krishna speaking but the Divine in Arjuna and in every one of us. Krishna is represented as speaking in the name of God, *Parmatman*, Supreme *Brahman*. The *Shvetashvatara Upanishad* is an unbroken praise of the Lord whom it names Siva or Rudra, but at no moment is the truth far from the seer who, composed the *Upanishad* that Siva or Rudra is

The one God, hidden in 'all things,
All-pervading, the Inner Soul of all things,
The Overseer of deeds, in all things abiding,
The witness, the Sole Thinker, devoid of all qualities,
The One Controller of the inactive many,
Who makes the one seed manifold—
The wise who perceive Him as standing in one's self
They, and no others, have eternal happiness.

It is the same thing with Krishna in the *Bhagawadgita,* He is the *Atman,* He is the *Purushotiama,* He is *Brahman.* He is the God of gods, the Lord of the Universe seated in the heart of all. Mr Hill calls the *Gita* "an uncompromising eirenicon" — uncompromising because the author of the *Gita* will "not abate one jot of Krishna's claim to be Supreme, to be the All." It is a mistake, I think, to talk of anything like "Krishna's claim". It is not so much the purpose of the author to advance the claim of a particular person, however divine, as the deity, as to direct the mind and the heart and the soul of man to the only abiding Reality. The name *Vasudeva* is defined in the *Mahabharata* thus: "Because I have my abode *(vasa)* in all creation, I am *Vasudeva.*" A person deified and described as *Vasudeva* was already being worshipped; no doubt the author of the *Gita* may or may not have seen him physically, but that his whole being was suffused with him is certain, and it is to that devotion that he gives name and form and reality. The characteristics of the ideal devotee — "in whom My soul delights" — quoted by Gandhiji in his introduction from the twelfth discourse, are not the characteristics of the devotee of a particular god. They are to be found — and must be found — in *any* true devotee of God, whether he calls Him Krishna or Christ or God or Allah. The 'ME' in "Abandon all duties and come to ME the only refuge" (XVIII. 66) does hot and cannot mean the person called Krishna — that person no longer exists — but it means the ever-abiding Lord in every one of us. "In Him alone take thy refuge, with all thy heart. By His grace thou shalt win to the eternal heaven of supreme peace" (XVIII. 62). The emphasis is not on ME as the Lord, but on the Lord speaking through ME, and further, as we shall see in the sequel, not on the profession of His name but on doing His work and His will: "He alone comes to Me, Panda va, who does My work, who makes Me his goal, who is My devotee, who has banished all attachment, who has ill-will towards none" (XI. 55). Did St. Paul mean an exclusive Jesus when he said: "That Christ may dwell in your hearts by faith; that ye, being rooted and grounded in love, may be able to comprehend with all saints what is the breadth and length, and depth, and height; and to know the love of Christ which passeth knowledge" (Eph. 3. 17-18-19); "As ye have received Christ Jesus, so walk in Him, rooted and built up in Him" (Col. 1. 6-7)? I submit not.

4. *Vyasa*, the reputed author of the *Mahabharata*, is believed to be the author of the *Gita*, as it forms part of the epic, but there is no conclusive evidence to prove this, nor have we any evidence on the facts regarding the life of *Vyasa*.

Evidence about Krishna *Vasudeva* cannot be said to be scanty, as references to a "Krishna" can be traced even in the early Vedic hymns. But there is no evidence of a conclusive nature to establish his identity or to prove that the *rishi* Krishna of the Vedic hymns and the pupil Krishna the son of Devaki, and the disciple of Ghora Angirasa, of whom the *Chhandogya Upanishad* speaks; and the Krishna of the *Mahabharata* now playing the role of a charioteer and warrior, now being described as worshipping Mahadeva, now being hailed as an incarnation of the Supreme Deity even by Dhritarashtra and Bhishma and now being decried by scoffers as built of common clay; and the Krishna of the *Puranas*—whether all these are one and the same. There can be no doubt, however, that an extraordinary personality combining in himself the qualities of a hero and a statesman, a warrior and a philosopher, did exist at a time of which we have no record, that he grew to enormous proportions in the race-memory of the Aryans, so much so that he came to be revered as an *avatara* and later on as the Incarnation, and countless traditions and legends grew up about "the ideal man", according to the varying psychological and spiritual levels of the ages that followed.

I would thus sum up my attitude — and perhaps Gandhiji's also — on this and similar questions. An aspirant will not make himself uneasy over the absence or uncertainty of evidence regarding the author of the *Gita* or the identity of Krishna. Let the scholars not tire of effort in this direction.

But for us laymen there is much comfort to be derived from the thought that the seers of old practised *anasakti* (detachment), which is the message of the *Gita,* to an extent that puzzles our sophisticated generation. The doctrine of detachment, or selflessness, or work in the spirit of sacrifice is as old as Creation, as Lord Krishna assures us in the *Gita*. It must have been practised to perfection by the seers who revealed the message to mankind It is delivered in a concentrated form in. the *Gita* and argued out in it as in no other scriptures. The author of the *Gita* felt and saw and knew and lived Krishna and left his experience as an abiding heritage for mankind.

III. THE BOOK AND THE THEME

Is not then the *Gita* anything in the nature of a historical narrative, forming as it does, part of the great War-epic? Gandhiji has challenged the description of the *Mahabharata* as a historical war-epic. In support of the challenge, I venture to enforce its argument by a few more considerations to show that the *Gita* can, in no sense of the term, be regarded as a historical dialogue. That a war named the *Mahabharata* War or some other took places need not be disputed, but that the author of the epic and the *Gita* had anything like the object of a historical narrative in mind is certainly disputed.

1. Look at the intensely significant artistry of the way in which the jewel of the *Gita* is set in the field of gold of the great epic. The reputed author *Vyasa* is supposed to be one of the deathless ones — *Chiranjivas* — and he is said to be the, progenitor of Pandu and Dhritarashtra whose sons fought on the field of Kurukshetra. It is this 'deathless one' who approaches Dhritarashtra, the blind king,, before the commencement of the fight and asks him if he would care to have his eyes opened in order to see the fighting. He is said to have declined the privilege, lest his heart should subside in him to see the fearful carnage,, but at a certain stage he evinces anxiety to know the happenings from day, to day. Sanjaya was endowed with divine vision and without being on the battlefield narrated, the happenings to the blind king. As though this much was not enough to open the eyes of the blind student trying to read history in a spiritual epic, *Vyasa* goes further and reassures the king that Sanjaya's divine vision would

serve him better than his natural vision, for "this Sanjaya will narrate the battle to you (in a unique way), for he shall know whatever happens, within the sight of or unknown to all, whether by day or by night, *whether actually or in the mind of any of the actors.* Weapons shall not touch Sanjaya and fatigue shall not tire him." It is Sanjaya thus endowed with supernatural vision who narrates the dialogue which is said to have taken place between Arjuna and Krishna. And how does he satisfy the old king's curiosity? The old king, in the only question that is put into his mouth in the whole poem, asks to know "what my Sons and Pandit's did, assetribled, on-battle intent, on the Field of Kuru". The reply is the narration of an intensely philosophical dialogue between Arjuna and Krishna through eighteen discourses, and at the end of the narration he describes not what the king's sons did or what Pandu's sons did, but that he was intensely exultant to have had the superb privilege of listening to that unique dialogue and that *'where is the Master of *Yoga* and where is Partha, the bowman, there, I am sure, are Fortune, Victory, Prosperity: and Eternal Right". Does it need any argument after this that it is riot a historical dialogue that we are reading, but a profoundly meaningful poem?

There is, therefore, no wonder, that to quite a considerable class of readers the *Gita* conveys an allegorical meaning : some likening the Pandayas to the forces of light and the Kauravas to the forces, of darkness, and making the human body the field of *dharma;* some putting various meanings on , the obviously meaningful names of the various characters of the epic and pressing allegory to distant lengths. To some Dhritarashtra, the blind king, is the individual ego blindly holding on to the flesh, as his name indicates, listening to the dialogue between Krishna, the Indweiler, and Arjuna, the humble and transparently pure intellect obeying His behest and fighting the forces of darkness and winning the victory. To use a phrase of Dr Carid, Dhritarashtra, to these interpreters, becomes "at once the combatants and the conflict and the field that is torn with strife". Some, on the other hand, would make Arjuna the individual ego torn with internal conflict and approaching Krishna, the Self for guidance.

2. Even if one assumes that the epic is a historical narrative, is it necessary that the *Gita* too must be the narration of a dialogue that took place on the field of battle? Instances are not wanting of genuine works of history containing imaginary dialogues. Thucydides, the most conscientious

historian known to antiquity, did not hesitate to introduce such imaginary dialogues between, and to invent speeches for, historical characters in order to elucidate situations, and has himself said that he had deliberately done so. As for poetical works, many poets of a transcendental vision have picked up historical or semi-historical incidents and used them for depicting imperishable visions of the soul of man struggling with grim facts of life. To take only, one instance — that of that master painter of human passions, Shakespeare. We see in his dramas men and women thrown into situations as profoundly tragic as that in which we find Arjuna in the first discourse of the *Gita*. See how Lady Blanch, in *King John,* feels herself torn between different interests, and talks almost in the language of Arjuna:

> Which is the side that I must go withal?
> I am with both : each army has a hand:
> And in their rage, I having hold of both,
> They whirl asunder and dismember me.
> Husband, I cannot pray that thou mayst win;
> Uncle, I needs must pray that thou must lose;
> Father, I may not wish the fortune thine;
> Whoever wins, on that side shall I lose;
> Assured loss before the match be played.

But Shakespeare simply describes her sad predicament and leaves her to her fate. We do not hear of her again. Macbeth he does not leave to his fate but puts in charge of the devil, who at one time as witches and at another as Lady Macbeth fans the flame of his ambition, dries up all the milk of human kindness in him, and drives him to the dire deed. Hamlet he tosses on the boisterous seas of a devastating indecision. Brutus loses his sleep, his mind suffers "the nature of an insurrection", he walks about "musing and sighing with arms across", avoids the counsel of his noble wife, lest she should cure him of the 4'sick offence within his mind", and finally decides to do what he thinks is for the "general good", not in the spirit of a butcher but that of a sacrificer:

> Let's kill him boldly, but not wrathfully;
> Let's carve him as a dish fit for the gods.

And throughout the drama he retains such a composed selflessness that it makes even his enemies declare him to be "the noblest Roman of them all". The author of the *Gita,* centuries before Shakespeare, made Arjuna's mind also suffer "the nature of an insurrection", but neither did he leave him to his fate nor fling him to the devil. He put him face to face with God — as Shakespeare put Brutus face to face with his self—and made God quell the insurrection and surround him with light and peace and bliss. We have not only the whole insurrection described, the delusion exposed, the doubter with his doubts fully depicted, but we have something more revealed to us—the Dispeller of doubts and the Bringer of Peace. It is this which to my mind makes the *Gita* the Bible of Humanity. The *Gita* says: When you are torn with doubt and despair and anguish, go to the Dweller in the Innermost, listen to His counsel, obey it implicitly and you will have no cause to grieve. Every mystic, burning with genuine aspiration, seeks comfort and solace from his God in matters of doubt, and Miss Underhill had referred to so many "internal conversations" between the contemplative soul of the mystic and his God. Is it any way unreasonable to imagine that the author of the *Gita* — one of the supreme mystics of the world — had himself a similar "internal conversation", and so visualized Arjuna, an aspirant, as having such "internal conversations" and left the picture as an inspiring heritage for all the spiritual aspirants of the world ? It may not be unreasonable, but it is heretical, someone might perhaps say. Heretical it is, I admit, but the heresy should in no way hurt one's faith. If it is an actual discourse between Krishna and Arjuna that is narrated by the author of the *Gita,* one can think of him as nothing more than a reporter. I for one should prefer to think of him as a *Kavi* (poet-seer, a word we often find applied to God Himself) who has given us God's authentic message as was revealed to him and as was believed by him. The *Gita,* seen in this light, becomes none the less adorable for me, than it would be if someone proved to me that it was an actual dialogue between Krishna and Arjuna that was reported therein.

3. The barest examination of the contents of the *Gita* shows that the author, saturated with the teachings of the *Upanishads,* and a devotee of Krishna, as he was, wanted to leave to mankind an expression of what he had felt and seen and lived. Hopkins' charge that the *Gita* is an "ill-assorted cabinet of primitive philosophical opinions" has value only in that

it proves that the poem is certainly not a historical narrative. But the charge betrays gross ignorance of philosophy and a most superficial reading of the *Gita*. Modern philosophical opinion has wellnigh accepted the *Upanishadic* philosophy or is at least coming near it. What appears to be a jumble is nothing more than a reflection of the state of things in the days when the poem was written. The Vedas with their apparently many gods and occasionally expressed monotheism were there; the *Upanishads* had raised a noble protest against the Vedic ritual which had still a hold on the people and in decrying paradise-seeking ritual had laid an excessive emphasis on the life of renunciation as the only means of salvation; the *Sankhya* and *Yoga* principles were there in the atmosphere not yet crystallized into definite systems; the Bhagawat cult of Krishna *Vasudeva* was also there. Whether Buddha and Buddhism were there it is not yet definitely established, but atheistic doctrines were certainly prevalent. It was the unique, though very uphill, task of the author of the *Gita* to pick up scattered and heterogeneous material, to sift the true from the false, to attenuate seeming contradictions, and to present a new philosophy and new art of life. There is *Sankhya*, there is *Yoga*, there is *Tajna*, there is *Bhakti*, and there are the gods too, everywhere in the *Gita*, but all in their proper place and setting and some with a connotation and meaning which they did not possess before. As regards the relation of the *Upanishads* to the *Gita*, I have already referred to the well-known metaphor of the cows, the milker and the milk. If I may venture to change the metaphor, without incurring the charge of heresy, I may say that the meadows of the *Upanishads* provided for the author of the *Gita* a rich verdure which was converted into the nectar-like milk of the *Gita*. For whilst one finds the influence of the *Upanishads* throughout the *Gita*, whilst one finds words and whole verses taken from them, they are so digested and assimilated that one can scarcely think that they went into the making of the rich product.

For what is there in the *Gita*, one may ask, that is not in the *Upanishads*? What Dr Radhakrishnan calls the "fundamental ultimates" are there borrowed bodily from j the *Upanishads;* the *Atman* (Self) and the *Brahman* are there in the very language of the *Upanishads*—in the seemingly mutually contradictory language of the evolving *Upanishads,* as my notes on II. 19, II. 20, II. 29, XIII. 12-17, and other verses will show; but whilst one has to trace the evolution and reconcile the contradictions in the *Upanishads* (as Prof. Ranade has ably done in his *Constructive Survey of Upanishadaic Philosophy*) the author of the *Gita* has woven them in with such consummate skill that they are all in their appropriate place on the pattern for which they are used and to which they seem to belong in a most vital manner. Where he has adopted a thought from the *Upanishads* it seems as though he had simply chosen a test to produce a most inspiring sermon.

I shall take just a few examples. Take this well-known text from that very brief *Upanishad* containing all the philosophy of the *Upanishads*, I mean the *Ishopanishad:* "Even while engaged in action here, a man may look forward to living a hundred years; for even thus and not otherwise the actions will not smear the man." As it is, it almost reads like a conundrum. But the author of the *Gita* related it to the preceding verse "renouncing that, thou must enjoy", and out of the two produced his whole philosophy of action that binds and action that does not bind but frees.

I have pointed out in detail in its proper place in my notes the way in which the author has summarized one whole section of the *Mundaka Upanishad* and clothed it with a new meaning (IV. 32-38). He had a lively sense of the essentials and had no hesitation in jettisoning the unessentials as we find in so many places in the *Gita*. For instance, he refers to the ancient eschatology, summarizes a string of verses from the *Chhandogya Upanishad* (5. 10. 1-6) in two neat *shlokas* and in a third gives us the significance of the belief (see my note on VIII. 24-26).

Take now the *Sankhyan* principles which we shall have occasion to study in some detail in the next section. The *Praskna Upanishad* (4.8) contains a full enumeration of them, and indeed the *Sankhyan Purusha* is already turned into the empirical self, the seer, toucher, taster, hearer, smeller, thinker, whose abode is the Supreme Imperishable *Atman* — *Paramatman* the Universal Self. The *gunas* also are there in the germ in other *Upanishads*. But the author of the *Gita* has constructed a whole philosophy and ethics out of these scattered elements and given them a new and rich meaning.

For the *Yoga* of meditation take the sections in the *Maitri Upanishad* 6. 18-22, on which one may say the whole of the sixth and part of the eighth discourses are based. I shall not enter into the comparison here, but the reader who will care to go to the sources in the pages of Hume will not fail to see that the *Gita* exposition of the method of meditative mysticism, shorn of the technical details described in the *Upanishad,*, is a vast development on the latter, and the final part of the sixth discourse containing the covenant of the Lord to the failed aspirant is the *Gita's* most original and inspiring contribution.

The gods of the Vedas are there, and the worshippers of different gods are also referred to, but each of these worshippers, whilst fully recognized, has been given his proper desert, and the gods are brought under the numerous manifestations of the one All-pervading God who is to be worshipped and adored, through those manifestations, if one will. The tenth discourse, read in this light, is a luminous commentary on the Vedas. I do not know how far Prpf. Ranade is justified in tracing the seeds of the full-grown tree of *bhakti* (devotion) to the instances of humble discipleship that we come across the *Upanishads:* Narada who approaches Sanatkumara with a broken and contrite heart 7—"I have heard from those like you, sir, that he who knows the *Atman* passes beyond sorrow. Such a sorrowing one I am; pray help me to pass beyond sorrow"; or Brihadrathai who in the same spirit begs his *guru to* "deliver" him from *sansara* wherein he was lying like a frog in a waterless well. Well, we must not forget that the *Gita* too is described as an *Upanishad*— though not counted as one —and the spirit of discipleship has been in India ever since the beginnings of philosophy. I would rather read in these and other instances of disciples going to their masters to learn *brahmavidya* (divine knowledge) a strong suggestion that Arjuna's is also a similar case, in a different background of course. The seeds of the tree of *bhakti* are to be looked for in the praises and prayers with which the Vedas are full — the *upasana* in which the Vedic seer "bows to God over and over again — God who is in fire and in water, who pervades the whole world, who is in the annual crops as well as in the perennial trees"; or in those glorious *Upanishadic* prayers where the soul implores the Nourisher (*Pushan*) to uncover for the votary of Truth its face hidden in a golden veil; or where the *Upanishad* prescribes for the sacrificer that sublime form of prayer for being led from the unreal to the Real, from darkness to Light, from death to Deathlessness. The atmosphere was there ready with the Krishna *Vasudeva* cult for the *upasana* of the Vedas to be systematized and converted into the life-giving farm of devotion to one God.

But Prof. Ranade is fully justified in seeing the description of the Universal form of the Lord (eleventh discourse) already in the germ in the *Mundaka Upanishad:* "When in the *Mundakopanishad* we find the description of the cosmic Person with fire as his head, the Sun and the Moon as his eyes, the quarters as his ears, the Vedas as his speech, air as his *prana,* the universe as his heart the earth as his feet, we have in embryo a description of the *vishvaroopa* which later became the theme of the famous eleventh chapter of the *Bhagawadgita* on the transfigured personality of Krishna."

But at this rate it is possible to trace almost everything in the *Gita* to the *Upanishads* likened to cows in the meditation versus preceding the *Gita.* If, without offending the susceptibilities of those who want to read in the *Gita* the actual words of the incarnate Lord, I might make a suggestion : I would say that the very idea of Krishna as charioteer and guide, philosopher and friend of Arjuna may be traced to the *Rathopanishad* which makes the *Atman* the master of the chariot of the body, the intellect the driver, the mind the reins, and the senses the horses. There are nearly a dozen places in which the *Gita* has actually borrowed from this great *Upanishad.* Why should not the master-artist use this beautiful image in his epic in order to weave out of the philosophy of the *Upanishad* the living religion of the *Bhagawadgita?*

I shall, however, not elaborate the point. Whoever would be a serious student of the *Gita* must go to these source books — the "revered *Upanishads*" as Hume has called them, and he will find die truth of the metaphors of the cow, and the meadow I have referred to above. But let no one therefore run away with the impression that the *Gita* is a highly poetic echo of the *Upanishads.* The *Gita* performs the unique function of making what was an esoteric doctrine a living reality for the unlettered, the lowly and the lost, and present the highest form of practical religion to enable each and all to realize his or her purpose in life. Above all, it blazons forth in an unmistakable manner the truth that life is worth living and teaches how it may be worth living. It is a unique synthesis and reconciliation of the two doctrines which were in those days held to be contradictory — *sannyasa* (renunciation of action) and *yoga* (performance of action).

Hinduism, remarks a Christian critic, has no New Testament, and hence no Gospel to offer to it adherents. Well, the critic did not know that the venerable Dr Deussen had already given the reply to him: "To every Indian *Brahmana* today the *Upanishads* are what the New Testament is to the Christians"; and if I may venture to extend Dr Deussen's comparison, I may say that if the *Upanishads* are the New Testament, the *Gita* may well be said to constitute therein the Gospels. The author of the *Gita* having lived the teaching of the *Upanishads* summed it up thus: "Performing action without attachment, man shall attain the Supreme" (III. 19), or if I may paraphrase the language of this and other similar verses, according to the *Gita,* 'Sacrifice is the fulfilling of the law.'

But there is nothing exclusive about the *Gita* which should make it a gospel only for the *Brahmana* or the Hindu. Having all the light and colour of the Indian atmosphere, it naturally must have the greatest fascination for the Hindu, but the central teaching should not have any the less appeal for a non-Hindu as the central teaching of the Bible or the *Koran* should not have' any the less appeal for a non-Christian or a non-Muslim.

In the verse I have just quoted is contained in a nutshell the teaching of the book. The *Gita* presents to its devotee a vision of the Supreme, tells him how to discover Him, how to recognize Him in His true nature and magnitude, how to enter Him and how to be one with Him— the End and the Means thereto as we might say in short. The colophon at the end of each discourse of the *Gita* is note-worthy. It has come down to us from an ancient date and though the title of each discourse given in this colophon differs in various editions, the colophon itself is the same in all editions: "Thus ends discourse (number) entitled (name) in the converse of Lord Krishna and Arjuna, on die science of *Yoga* as part of the knowledge of *brahman* in the *Upanishad* called the *Bhagawadgita* (Sung by the Lord)." *Upanishad* etymologically means what the pupil learns sitting at the feet of the master; it may also mean the knowledge which by taking one near the Supreme helps to cut off earthly ties. Thus, in one sense, *brahmavidya* and *upanishad* are synonymous. The *Gita* is, therefore, the science and art of *Yoga* — or shall we call it the Art of Life — for the attainment of the knowledge of *brahman*, or the Wisdom and the Art of Life! This phrase in the colophon may also be translated, "the science of *Yoga* rooted in *brahmavidya.*" It goes without saying that unless the Art of

Life is rooted in the Wisdom of Life it will never lead to it. There seems to be no doubt, however we may interpret it, that Wisdom, as leading to the *summum bonum*, is the goal for the attainment of which the Art of Life or *Yoga* is the means. The *Gita* is the *Upanishad* of the *Mahabharata*.

IV. THE FUNDAMENTALS

We shall now turn to a study of that Wisdom and that Art as revealed in the *Gita*. Perhaps the best way to do so is to present a brief interpretative analysis of the various discourses. But before we start with the analysis, it would not be out of place to indicate what we might call the permanent background of the *Gita*. It starts with accepting certain "unanalysable ultimates" — the Self, the Absolute, God, and the Universe and certain fundamental postulates. It presents no philosophical treatment, as it is really addressed to those who assume these ultimates, for the simple reason that the author's purpose was to expound the ordinary man's mission in life rather than to present a philosophical system. Thus, when Arjuna approaches Krishna with an appeal which recalls, 'What in me is dark, illumine,' He does so by a sudden flash light revelation of the Unborn, Ageless, Deathless, Everlasting, Indemonstrable *Atman* or Self. He uses the epithet 'Indemonstrable' indicating in a word his whole meaning. How will one demonstrate or measure Him who is the proof of all proofs and measure of all measures? As the *Kena Upanishad* puts it: "He is the very hearing of the ear, the very mind of the mind, the very voice of speech, the very breath of breath and the very vision of the eye." Or as the modern philosopher Dr Radhakrishnan puts it: "The ultimate assumption of all life is the spirit in us, the Divine in man. Life is God and the proof of it is life itself. If somewhere in ourselves we did not know with absolute certainty that God is, we could not live. Even the sun and the moon would go out if they began to doubt. Our lives are not lived within their own limits. We are not ourselves alone; we are God-men."

About the composition of the Universe, the *Gita* takes up the theory then in vogue, as any modern-thinker would start with assuming the theory of evolution. The Shankhyan cosmology was then in vogue; it was, as we have already seen, referred to in some of the *Upanishads*. Since the mention of it in the *Gita*, various *Smritis* have adopted it and it is referred to in various places in the *Mahabharata*. The system as we know it in its complete form was not then in existence; there were probably fragments of an original of which no trace can be found; there was what we might call a torso or a skeleton. At any rate the *Gita* accepted it as a skeleton, put life into it, and made use of it for its philosophy and ethics. It will be useful for our purpose to give a brief sketch of the *Sankhya* system in order that we may be able to see how much of it the *Gita* has adopted and how it has used the raw material. It will also familiarize us with certain terms which will occur over and over again in the *Gita*.

A. THE SANKHYA SYSTEM

Kapila, or whoever the great seer was, who brought into being the *Sankhyan* concepts, started not with an analysis of objective experience as Darwin did, but, perhaps as a result of elaborate experiments in the laboratory of his self, arrived at the evolutionary idea with the discovery of which Darwin concluded his researches. Darwin found the planet "cycling on" from the simple beginning of "a few forms or *one*" to "endless forms most beautiful and most wonderful", and evolving through the operation of one law — struggle for life. The *Sankhya* philosopher, making provision for both matter and mind, started with two eternal principles, one conscious, unconditioned, and passive, the other unconscious but active and manifesting the operation of not one law but three; or, if we may say so, a triple law evidencing not only the struggle for life, but the stage before that, namely inertia, then the struggle for life, and lastly, 'the struggle for the life of others' or sacrifice.

The *Sankhya* philosopher, as we have said, posits the existence of two eternal principles: *prakriti* and *purusha*. The existence of *prakriti* or primordial matter or Nature is, he says, proved by the manifested universe which is its effect. The effect really exists in the cause, which necessarily is a Causeless Cause. The evolution of the manifested universe out of this unmanifest *prakriti* arises as a result of the disturbance in the equilibrium of its three constituents which are postulated as self-evident. These constituents are called *gunas*, literally meaning threads or strands which compose the string of *prakriti*, They are called *sattva, rajas and tamas,* the sources respectively of existence, of motion, and inertia, their functions being light, activity — and restraint. They are, however, not mutually contradictory, and they exist together, in fact are never separate; they slip into one another and intermingle with one another. As soon as their equilibrium is disturbed, *prakriti* begins to evolve and whatever evolves, bears an impress of these constituents, and the infinite variety of differences in the objects in the universe is due to the varying proportion of these constituents in each, and their interaction amongst themselves.

But *prakriti* cannot evolve, except under the influence of *purusha,* a principle as eternal as *prakriti* and of which the existence is posited and proved, by the *Sankhyan* philosopher by various arguments into which, we need not go. *Purusha* is the Soul that informs the *body prakriti;* unlike the *prakriti* he is inactive, he is without *gunas,* and the subject and seer of all objects possessing the *gunas,* uncaused and unproductive. But; whilst *prakriti* is one, the *purtishas* are taken to be countless, for , while the constitutive stuff is essentially one and the same in all, there are separate births and deaths, separate organs and varying functions; in different individuals. The process of evolution of the *prakriti* may be thus tabularly shown:

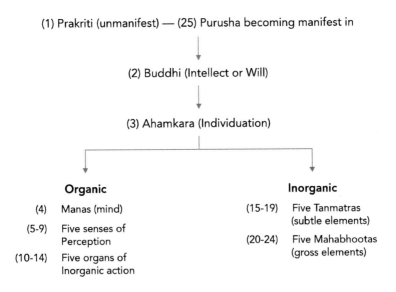

(1) Prakriti (unmanifest) — (25) Purusha becoming manifest in

(2) Buddhi (Intellect or Will)

(3) Ahamkara (Individuation)

Organic		**Inorganic**	
(4)	Manas (mind)	(15-19)	Five Tanmatras (subtle elements)
(5-9)	Five senses of Perception	(20-24)	Five Mahabhootas (gross elements)
(10-14)	Five organs of Inorganic action		

The *Sankhya* system, as we find it in *Ishvara* Chandra's *karika* has no Supreme or God, *prakriti* and *purusha* being the only two eternal principles. The presence of the inactive *purusha* is said somehow to disturb the equilibrium of the unmanifest *prakriti* which begins to evolve. The very first step in the evolution of the homogeneous *prakriti* was its determination or will *(buddhi),* however unconscious, to manifest itself; it is, therefore, regarded as its first product. The next was individuation *(ahamkar),* the product of *buddhi,* a principle whereby the *prakriti* broke up into different innumerable entities divided into two sections, organic and inorganic. Eleven elements consisting of the mind, the five senses of perception (hearing, touch, sight, taste, and smell) and the five organs of action (the hands, the feet, the tongue, and the two organs of evacuation) were evolved out of individuation, or the formation of the organic world, and five subtle elements (sound, touch, form, savour, and smell) for the formation of the inorganic world composed of the five gross elements. These three quintets really suggest one another. Each sense has a single realm— the eye, for instance, has the realm of form and no other; the ears have the realm of sound and no other, and so on—and so there could be no more than five realms (also called sense-objects) corresponding to the five senses of perception and no more than five gross elements, Ether, Wind, Fire, Water, Earth could reflect the five subtle ones.

This shows *prakriti* in its cosmic aspect. No doubt the seer who arrived at this process of evolution as evident in Nature did so from an observation of the small human physical and mental frame. This microcosm was to him the microcosm in miniature. In the individual the senses of perception provide the material to the mind which forms percepts out of it, then individuation refers them to the self and passes them on to *buddhi* or the determining' principle which forms concepts and decisions and sends them back to the mind which gets them executed by means of the five organs of action.

How *purusha* is entrapped in *prakriti* is sought to be explained somewhat in this manner. *Buddhi,* which after the evolution starts, plays an important part, almost simulating as the *purusha. Buddhi* coloured in *sattvika* character helps to release, and coloured in *tamas* and *rajas* character, helps to tighten, the bondage of *purusha.* In fact all the psychic experiences—desire, hate, likes and dislikes, pleasure, pain,—are the modifications of *buddhi* which the *purusha* takes upon himself. .When affected by the *Sattva guna, buddhi* gives rise to virtue, discrimination, and dispassion, the process of release begins, the distinction of *purusha* and *prakriti* becomes apparent to the *buddhi*, and *purusha* and *prakriti* are emancipated from each other. *Samsara* or the cycle of birth and death means suffering and the only means of ending that suffering permanently is this knowledge or discrimination. The individual or the lower self ever struggles to realize its identity with the higher self and as soon as the identity is realized, arises the discriminative knowledge consisting in the realization that 'I am not' (i.e. I am not *prakriti* but *purusha*), that 'nothing is mine', and that 'the ego exists not' (i.e. I am not the doer or experiencer). This knowledge is permanent release from the "dread machinery of sin and sorrow". (The 'lower self' and the 'higher self' is, however, not the language of *Sankhya*).

Just as there is a process of evolution, there is a similar process of dissolution. When the human organism is dissolved, the five gross elements in it mix up with the five gross elements in Nature, but the remaining eighteen, described as forming the subtle body (called *linga-sharira)*, containing the impressions (*sanskaras*) of the deeds (mental and physical) done during one birth take on a new habitation and go through the fruit of the deeds of the past birth. This migration and transmigration go on in the case of all but the freed souls, and the law of *karma* carries them through all kinds of organisms—deity, man, animal or plant, until the ultimate dissolution of the world. We shall have occasion to deal with this doctrine of *karma* and rebirth in detail later on.

This in brief is the bare skeleton of the *Sankhya* system. The difficulties of some of the conceptions are obvious. If the presence of *purusha* helps to start the process of evolution of *prakriti*, that *purusha* must be obviously as cosmic and as much one and unified as *prakriti* itself. How they co-operate is an eternal puzzle, and the conception that *prakriti* carries on its passing show in order to release *purusha*, who by reason of his association with *prakriti* is deluded in the belief that he is bound, is more baffling still. As Keith puts it: "Unconscious Nature cannot experience misery, the spirit in itself does not experience misery, and the union of the two which results in the apparent experience of misery by spirit which wrongly thinks that the misery which it brings to light in Nature is misery which it itself endures, thus creates the very misery which it is the object of the union to abolish... The epithets given to the 'subject in the *Sankhya* are applicable to the abstract conception of the subject as opposed to all its content: there can be no multiplication of this abstract conception as the *Sankhya* asserts. The existence of the numerous individuals who are conscious is totally a different thing, for their number and individuality are conditioned by the possession of a different objective content in consciousness and when this is removed, there would remain nothing at all, or at the most the abstract conception of subject, which could not be a multiple of individual spirits. Had the *Sankhyan* conception been that of a number of souls as opposed to spirits, no logical objection could be raised to the theory of multiplicity, but the sharp distinction of spirit and nature and the assertion that there is no real connection between them deprive the spirit of any possible reality." "There is," as Dr Radhakrishnan remarks, "Throughout the *Sankhya* a confusion between the *purusha* and the *jiva*. *Purusha* is the perfect spirit, not to be confused with the particular human spirit. The *purusha* is certainly in me as my very core and substance; and *the jiva*, or the individual, with all his irrational caprices and selfish aims is but a distortion of *purusha*. To say that every *jiva* is striving to realize its *purusha* means that every *jiva* is potentially divine." Again, "if anything be regarded as the presupposition of all experience, it is a universal spirit on which both the tendencies of *purusha* and *prakriti* rest, for the two, *purusha* and *prakriti*, do not stand confronting each other. In the becoming of the world, the contradiction is resolved. It shows that the two things rest on a fundamental identity. The *Sankhyan* insistence on *purusha*, when it is not confused with *jiva*, amounts to nothing more than the recognition of a pure and perfect presence not divided by the division of things, not affected by the stress and struggle of the cosmic manifestation, within it all, while superior to it all.... This Supreme personality combines within himself the peace and the bliss, the calm and the silence of *purusha* on the one hand, and the jarring multiplicity, the strife and suffering of *prakriti* on the other. The Supreme contains within itself all lives and all bodies, and each individual is nothing more than a wave of this boundless surge, a fragment of the world-soul. Only such a view can make the *Sankhya* philosophy more consistent."

B. THE GITA VIEW

1. Prakriti and Gunas

The Vedanta and the *Gita* step in to make the *Sankhya* system a consistent whole. The *Gita* supplies the head to the torso and makes the whole the basis of its edifice. All the 24 principles of the *Sankhya* system are adopted by the *Gita* in one form or other, the conception of evolution to explain the breaking up of the unmanifest into the manifest world is also accepted, the idea of *gunas* is most completely worked out, but it denies any independent existence to *prakriti* and *purusha* and cuts at the root of that dualism by making Absolute *Brahman* the prime source and cause of all that exists, an All-pervading Spirit which is the *prius* of all matter, animate and inanimate. This Absolute is thus described as having two aspects or natures—the higher and the lower, the higher consisting of the Essence that vitalizes and sustains, and the lower being the world of Nature. The higher aspect—*jiva*— is the individual self in all, and the world of Nature is nothing but the *Sankhyan prakriti* shortly summed up thus: Earth, Water, Fire, Wind and Ether (which presuppose the five subtle elements), Mind, Individuation and Intellect (which are intended to include all the ten senses of perception and organs of action), which thus make up 23, and the 24th unmanifested *prakriti* being omitted as being evidenced in its manifest form (VII. 4-5). It is this *prakriti* again which is referred to in VIII. 18 where it is simply referred to as the unmanifest from which all the manifested entities spring at the coming of the Cosmic Day, and into which they dissolve at the coming of the Cosmic Night and again come into being at the coming of the Day. But higher than this Unmanifest is the Permanent, Unchanging, Unmanifest which perishes not while all beings perish, and while the unmanifest *prakriti* changes (VIII. 19). That Permanent Unmanifest is the Imperishable or the Absolute (VIII. 20) which informs and sustains the world (XV. 17). The same *prakriti* is referred to in the thirteenth discourse. *Prakriti* is here the body, the *kshetra,* or the field, made up of the 24 principles we are now familiar with, every one of them being mentioned (XIII. 5). It is called the field, as the body and the world constitute the field of toil and turmoil from which and through which the individual has to emancipate himself and to realize his unity with the Self of all universe. It is these twain —*jiva* and *prakriti* combined

— which are said to form the womb of the whole creation—moving and unmoving (VII. 6; XIII. 26; XIV. 3-4), the Absolute as God being the Father depositing the seed in this great womb of all being (XIV. 4). He is thus the origin and the ultimate end of all (VII. 6), the seed itself of all (VII. 10). The individual self is the same as the Universal Self, only seeming different in different bodies, because he identifies himself with the various adjuncts, the body, the mental and the intellectual apparatus, and experiences the objective world. It is his attachment to these adjuncts — these *gunas* that binds him to the body and drags him from birth to death and death to birth.

2. The Gunas

The *Sankhya* doctrine of *gunas* as the constituents of *prakriti* has been worked out elaborately by the *Gita* and has been adopted by all the *Smriti* works, and it has taken such a hold of the Hindu mind that the words *sattva, rajas,* and *tamas* and their derivatives *sattvika, rajasa,* and *tamasa* are common terms of the Hindu vocabulary in every Indian language and immediately convey their ethical connotation even to an unlettered peasant. Though the word *guna* literally means "strand" and *sattva, rajas* and *tamas* in their non-technical sense mean essence, dust or foulness, and darkness respectively, the word "strand" is hardly appropriate to convey the full ethical and non-ethical content of the word *guna*. As constitutive stuff of all that exists the three *gunas* represent the three modes or modifications or moments of being — "intelligible essence, energy, and mass" to use Dr Seal's phraseology. As mental states they are the states of purity or clarity, restlessness, and torpidity. Ethically, *sattvika* state is pure, *rajasa* is alloyed, and *tamasa* is impure. The *Gita* says *sattva* binds man to his body by conscious happiness and knowledge, *rajas* by restlessness and misery, *tamas* by heedlessness, lethargy and sleep (XIV. 5-7). Knowledge, light, happiness indicate the predominance of *sattva*; greed, restlessness, yearning indicate the predominance of *rajas;* dulness, heedlessness, lethargy of *tamas* (XIV. 11-13). Those characterized by *sattva* rise upward, those by *rajas* remain of the earth earthy, those by *tamas* go down to the lowest species (XIV. 18). The terms are further applied to represent modes, aspects, characters or tendencies of men and things, of activity and temperament, *saitvika* indicating the highest state of selflessness, *rajasa* that of calculating selfishness, and *tamasa* of blind passion and fury.

Make as many permutations and combinations as possible of infinitely varying degrees of these constituents and you have an explanation of the astonishing diversity that you find in the universe. He who has seen the play and interplay of these *gunas* and who can detach himself from them, he who can isolate himself from them and realize the unity at the basis of this diversity is a seer — a *tattvaoid* who has known the truth of things, he is free, his action does not bind him, his action is no action. That is the metaphysical aspect of the doctrine of *gunas*, as *guna* also means subordinate, not principal, and hence shadow not substance. *Prakriti*, we are told again and again, is ever active and so long as one is imprisoned in the tabernacle *of prakriti,* he has to act whether he will or no. The *gunas* are not separate from *prakriti*; they are often described as "born of *prakriti*", but they are the very stuff of *prakriti,* as indeed we have them described as synonymous with *prakriti*. Man's senses, mind, intellect etc. are his *prakriti* or his *gunas.* When a man's body is fat, he says, 'I am fat' identifying himself with the body; when his feet walk or the body sleeps, he says 'I walk', 'I sleep', again identifying himself with the body. In similar way man identifies himself with the mind, the will, the intellect, and arrogates to himself the various activities of those internal organs. All these constitute *the-gunas,* or the not-Self, or we might say the lower 'self', and all activity in which man identifies himself with the instrument of the activity is thus self-fill, and all activity from which man has completely detached himself is selfless. The attachment to the fruit of action in the shape of reward or pleasure 'springs from this identification with the not-self or lower self. This identification is described as delusion, as ignorance, as the root of bondage and the man who has cut at the root of it, who has rid himself of it, is the seer or *tattoavid* (III. 28; V. 8).

The Western reader will perhaps understand the distinction between the changing *gunas* and the unchanging Self, the shadows and the substance, much better from the following memorable lines from *Julius Caesar:*

> "Between the acting of a dreadful thing
> And the first motion, all the interim is

Like a phantasma, or a hideous dream;
The *Genius* and the *mortal instruments*
Are then in council; and the state of man,
Like to a little kingdom, suffers then
The nature of an insurrection."

Shakespeare, as I have said more than once, had his grip on the fundamentals of things, and in this passage he sensed the distinction between the Genius (i.e. in the language of the *Gita,* the unchanging, imperishable *atman* or Self) and the "mortal instruments" (i.e. in the language of the *Gita,* the *gunas).* And no word could be happier than the word "instruments", which indeed all *gunas* are, in the hands of the Genius, or the Master, or the Self. The self-controlled, the self-possessed, the *tattoavid,* does have an experience of the insurrection, but he quells it by making the "instruments"—*gunas*—act according to his will.

Now this state of self-control and ultimate peace can proceed from self-realization or knowledge which is the fruit of ages of endeavour. Man is, therefore, advised to take refuge in religion and ethics. He has to work himself upwards towards *sc.ttva* dedicating all his activity and endeavour to the Giver of all good and ultimately reach beyond the three *gunas.* This state beyond is the state of true knowledge and freedom.

There is still another aspect of *prakriti* with its *gunas* which also it may be useful to indicate in this connection. There is a part of man's nature which will assert itself and no amount of coercion will avail against it. There is another part which is amenable to culture and discipline. The *Gita* distinguishes the two, but does not, excepting indirectly, indicate the scope of each. It is apparent, however, that the first is the physical and mental constitution which man brings with him at birth and which normally determines his vocation. It is with a view to man's self-development and his being able to fulfill his function as a member of the social organism that his vocation is determined according to his native aptitudes and qualities. Here, says the *Gita,* let not man wrestle with nature, but obey the law of his being, of course, casting all on Him (111.33). But there is the other part, viz. the moral part of his nature where man may not rest content until he has thoroughly cleansed himself. 'Lust, wrath and greed form the triple gateway to hell' says the *Gita*. 'Flee from that fiery hell.' (III. 34; III. 37; XVI. 21). Shakespeare, who had the heavenly gift of knowing what man's nature is, seems to make this distinction over and over again. The royal nature and material valour of King Cimbeline's sons living in captivity as barbarous rustics from their very childhood, are described as clamouring out again and again, while Hamlet tells his mother that

"Use almost can change the stamp of nature
And either curb the devil, or throw him out
With wondrous potency."

The doctrine of *gunas* as the constitutive stuff of man, at least in its ethical aspect, was not quite unknown to thinkers and philosophers in the West, though they did not visualize it in all its aspects and certainly did not work it out in any detail, except perhaps Plato. His division of the springs of human behaviour into three main sources — desire, emotion and knowledge, would seem to be a recognition of the three *gunas* in another name. And his division of men according to their powers and aptitudes and later Aristotle's modification of it, were certainly due to a recognition of the three *gunas*. Was not Bacon too faintly thinking of the triple division of man's character into *sattvika*, *rajasa* and *tamasa* when he distinguished "the three grades of ambition in mankind"? "The first" he said, "was the desire to extend their power ... which is vulgar and degenerate. The second to extend the power of their own country which has more dignity, but not less covetousness... (The third) if a man endeavours to establish and extend the power and domination over the universe, his ambition is nobler than the other two." In the same way Spinoza was using only another language for one *guna* passing out into another when he talked of man's "emotions or modifications" as "passages or translation from a lesser state of perfection to a greater". And look at Herbert Spencer's division of knowledge into three kinds: "Knowledge of the lowest kind is ununified knowledge; science is partially unified knowledge; philosophy is completely unified knowledge." — an almost direct paraphrase, of the *Gita* (XVIII, 20-22) describing the *sattvika*, *rajasa*, and *tamasa* kinds of knowledge. To come to more recent times,

Dr. Henry Drummond when he talked of "Self-ism" and "other-ism" as the two permanent tendencies of nature — "not painted on the canvas but woven through it", was he not describing the *rajas* and *sattva gunas*? Lastly, is not Prof. Mackenzie describing the three *gunas* in man's moral character when he says: "There are, in fact, we may say, three selves in every man. There is in the self that is revealed in occasional impulses which we cannot quite subdue, the 'sin' that after all dwelleth in us. On the other hand, there is the permanent character— the universe in which we habitually live. And finally there is the true or rational self in which alone we feel that we can rest with satisfaction — the 'Christ' that liveth in us and in whom we hope more and more to abide." Is not this last phrase almost an echo of that memorable verse (II. 45) in which Krishna asks Arjuna to "abide ever in *sattva*"?

3. Karma and Rebirth

Closely allied to the doctrine of *guna* is the doctrine of *karma* and rebirth which the *Gita* accepts as axiomatic and which has come in for a lot of criticism from Western thinkers. Let us see what it means and what part it plays in the Hindu view of life. We know for a fact that, although sometimes action is but 'the movement of a muscle this way or that', its consequences are infinite and untraceable beyond a certain point. If the consequences cannot thus be followed out, the roots of what apparently appears as the cause must also be too deep and hidden to trace back. For actions are not merely "things done that take the eye and have the price".

> "All instincts immature,
> All purposes unsure
> That weighed not as his work, yet swelled the man's amount;
> Thoughts hardly to be packed
> Into a narrow act,
> Fancies that broke through language and escaped
> All I could never be All men ignored in me,
> This I was. worth to God, whose wheel the pitcher shaped."

These lines from Browning's *Rabbi Ben Ezra* seem to me to bring out the content of *karma* in a striking manner. It is He, working through His law, that takes into account "all men ignore" in men. And if He is the Accountant and the Judge, His book cannot be the narrow book of a man's lifetime but the vast one of countless lifetimes. What we are, what we think, what we do is the result of what we have been through ages gone by. Locke, when he insisted that the mind at birth is a *tabula rasa* was talking from a limited experience. Bacon before him had penetrated into the truth deeper, and in his famous *Idols* he gave the world more perhaps than he knew. 'Human mind is born,' he said; composed like 'uneven mirrors' imparting 'their properties to different objects'. Those unevennesses could not but have their roots in various pre-existences. Even primitive man knew that one reaped what one sowed, but the Indian seer found out the universality of the law and made an attempt to gauge its stupendous implications.

> That which ye sow, ye reap. See yonder fields!
> The sesamum was sesamum; the corn
> Was corn. The silence and the Darkness knew!
> So is a man's fate born,
> He cometh reaper of the things he sowed.

Even in case of the sesamum we do not know how much earth and manure and water and sunshine went into the making of it. We know just the seed. Even so we do not know how much went into the making of ourselves. We have personal experience of our action affecting our lives and those of others every moment, and we also have some idea of what a share our parents' and grand-parents' characters had in our making and what share our own characters will have in the shaping of our children's character. But children sometimes manifest qualities which none of their parents or grand-parents, however remote, were ever known to have possessed. While thus heredity explains a part, it fails to explain the whole, of our make-up, and it has certainly nothing to offer in defence of the sins of die parents or grand-parents being visited on the children. The law of *karma* here steps in, supplements heredity and makes it understandable and tolerable. When a man dies, we are told, the gross elements are dissolved, dust returneth unto dust, but the self with the subtle psychic elements remains, it seeks a new home, leaving the old which is broken up (XV. 7-8). The parents provide for this unknown guest a new home with a character of its own (VI. 41-42). The guest—whom the parents fondly called their child — appropriates the home that it has deserved. Its new home, good or ill, is the result of its stock of *punya or papa* — not the "things that took the eye and had the price", but all that the man was worth to God, — in the language of the *Gita,* 'man's attachment to the *gunas'* (XIII. 21). It is through this home that he proceeds to work out his destiny. The effort lasts through a lifetime, the mortal coil is shuffled off once again, and the self with the psychic apparatus, altered, developed or deteriorated, as the case may be, goes out in search of fresh fields and pastures new.

Thus if we do not know how much went into our making, we know that every one of us had an inevitable past with which we have to count. That serves to make us humble, warns us against being fretful and against judging our fellow-men. But the law of *karma* should not be mistaken for fatality or retributive justice. It is wrong to interpret it to mean that our enjoyments are a reward of a past life of virtue and our sufferings that of a past life of vice. Our enjoyments may well be the result of an inclination to a life of pleasure that we brought with us and failed to curb; and the readiness to go through suffering with joy, for the good of humanity, in a Buddha or a Jesus or a St. Francis, may be the rich harvest of nearly perfected past life. In these instances the sufferings, we will be told, were self-invited. Well, even in instances in which they seem to be imposed by nature, we may not make the mistake to think that they are the result of a life of vice. It is puerile to think that what we call 'pleasure' is the echo of virtue, and 'pain' the echo of vice. They are nature's ways of bringing into play the forces of evolution. The godly Ramakrishna Paramahamsa suffered from a fatal cancer and the Christ-like Henry Drummond who had never had an illness in his life had an excruciating disease of the bones which proved fatal. In both cases, who could say what the suffering was the result of? But it was clear to all that in both cases the suffering came in order that the world may have examples of perfected lives from which one might learn how to endure one's ailments. In both cases the doctors were amazed at the patient's reluctance to talk about their illness.

No, the law of *karma* is not one to be trifled with, it is one to which we may bow with benefit, but not dare to dissect. Let us remember that neither action nor consequence may be judged by its outward form. The exquisitely sensitive balance to weigh them is in His hands, not ours. The law teaches us not to judge but to understand, not to ignore human suffering but to rush out to alleviate it, for it makes the whole world kin.

That leads us to its counterpart, the doctrine of rebirth. They are the obverse and the reverse of the same coin. If we came with something, we also pass away with something. We know that careers of the highest value abruptly come to an end, and often enough children with extraordinary gifts and attainments are born. Neither is there an abrupt end in the one case, nor a fortuitous beginning in the other. Death is but 'a sleep and a forgetting' and the individual self with the new birth wakes up in other physical environments to continue the old unfinished race towards the goal. This, being born again and again, is not "the Indian philosopher's bugbear", as Monier Williams called it; neither is it, as he thought, an escape from the quest of Truth. The doctrine was a direct product of the Indian seer's successful quest of Truth. It was a corollary of the discovery of the immortality of the soul and the indestructibility of matter. Man being ever-born endeavours to be one with God the never-born, and while each birth is a sad reminder of the race yet to run, it is also a fresh opportunity to finish it. Each rebirth is a fresh school of discipline, a fresh prison through which to work out one's release.

Does man then pass through various wombs according to his conduct here? Do those of foul conduct "enter foul wombs, either that of a dog, or a swine, or an outscaste" as the *Chhandogya Upanishad* says? One does not know. The *Gita* simply echoes the prevailing belief of the times. It of course changes the *Upanishad* phraseology and refers to three kinds of birth—birth in spotless worlds, birth among men attached to work, and in gross species; or "going upward", "remaining midway , "going downward" (XIV. 15; XIV. 18). The reference, the ancient commentators say, is to the highest type of creation — the deities, the middle type — man, and the lowest type — animals, worms, plants. The *Gita* does mention 'heaven' about half a dozen times (II. 2; II. 32; II. 37; II. 43; IX. 20; IX. 21) and 'hell' four times (I. 42; I. 44; XVI. 16; XVI. 21); but it is difficult to say whether the author meant by the terms unearthly perpetual abodes of happiness and misery, as the popular judicial notion of the *karma* theory would have it. The *Mahabharata*, of which *Gita* is but a part, thus defines *svarga* and *naraka* (heaven and hell): "Heaven, they say, is light and hell is darkness." *(Shantiparva).* The *Tattvakaumudi* (9th century A.D.) quotes a definition of *svarga* (heaven) which has no reference to a perpetual abode, but which means 'unalloyed happiness'. Hell would thus mean 'unalloyed misery'. Dr Radhakrishnan quotes a verse from the *Vishnu Parana* (belonging to the same or perhaps an earlier date) which would mean by 'heaven' pleasant mental state and by 'hell' the reverse, and identifies one with virtue and the other with vice. It would, therefore, be doing no violence to the spirit of the *Gita,* if we said that walking with God is 'heaven', walking away from God is 'hell'. The *Gita* also refers to the two paths of soul after death — that of the gods and that of the manes (VIII. 24-25), but nearly sums them up as the paths of light and of darkness, i.e. of knowledge and ignorance. There is mention often enough of *devas* (gods) and other heavenly beings. Whilst these have reference to the traditional belief in unearthly beings, let us remember that the ancient etymologist Yaska (5th century B. C.) derives the word from that which gives, shines or illumines.

However, all these terms need not detain us, inasmuch as they belong to the surface of the *Gita* and do not touch the central theme. Perhaps these references to traditional belief only serve to bring the central picture into prominent relief. Even the theory of *karma* and rebirth is an explanation and a hypothesis and need not affect the central message which does not hang on it. Whether a man believes or not in the theory, he has to work out his salvation or self-realization through the law of self-sacrifice. It may be remembered that the human birth is regarded by the Hindu as a piece of evolutionary good fortune which should be turned to the best and noblest account, and one may conceive even an orthodox Hindu completely associating himself with the Sufi who out — Darwined Darwin several centuries ago:

> I died as mineral and became a plant,
> I died as plant and rose to animal.
> I died as animal and I was man.

Why should I fear? When was I less by dying?
Yet once more I shall die as man, to soar
With angels blest; but even from angelhood
I must pass on : all except God doth perish.
When I have sacrificed my angel soul,
I shall become what no mind e'er conceived,
Oh let me not exist! For non-existence
Proclaims in organ tones, 'To Him we shall return.'

That would seem to bring out the *Gita* ideal to perfection, though of course the *Gita* says in no uncertain terms that those who give themselves to lust and anger and greed — the triple gateway to hell — go to perdition. Indeed the language of the sixteenth discourse is not dissimilar to the terrible text: "He that is unjust, let him be unjust still: and he that is filthy, let him be filthy still: and he that is righteous, let him be righteous still: and he that is holy, let him be holy still." But the idea is clear and unmistakable. The self which has narrowed itself and imprisoned itself 'like unto a frog in a waterless well' has to expand itself into the ocean of the Universal Self, it has to go on age after age shedding its countless trappings and extinguish them into the Eternal Radiance of Knowledge, Light and Bliss — *Brahmanirvana*.

4. The Individual, World and Reality

That brings us again to where we began. Man, as we have seen, is born in the body and in the environment that the sum of his character-impressions (*sanskaras* or *karma*) have earned for him. The physical world, with man as apparently the principal actor in it, has its beginning in the Absolute. How the Absolute translated itself into the universe we do not know, we cannot know; but it is a beginningless process. At every world period, says Krishna, speaking as the Creator, I send forth the world of beings, and at the end of such a period they come back to my *prakriti*. Man—physical man—as part of the world finds himself subject to this apparently endless process, but his position in the universe is unique. He observes, thinks, reflects, finds himself captive, and struggles against the captivity. He finds himself witness of ceaseless change of the elements about him and around him. His reflection tells him that he is the subject of an objective world not only inside him—composed of his body, senses, intellect etc. — but also of the objective world that surrounds him. While both these change and apparently perish, there is an abiding something in him which certainly does not change. And if it does not change in spite of ceaseless change, how can it perish in spite of the destruction that seizes both the outside and the inside world? The world of change and the world of mortality give him intimations of an eternality and immortality. There is a secret something in him which makes the finite, imperfect, mortal in him to hanker after the Infinite, Perfect and Immortal; and he does not take long to arrive at the truth that the Infinite and the Immortal Self that informs him informs and pervades also the universe. Bound up as he is with the world of sense, he has fleeting glimpses of this oneness with the Universal Self, but those glimpses are few and far between. Unless he can completely isolate himself from all that differentiates and separates, he cannot abide in this unity.

What differentiates is the sum of adjuncts that condition the Unconditioned. As the late Mr. Kirtikar said, quoting Heraclitus, "Our senses"— internal and external both — "are liars," and further quoting the French astronomer-seer Flammarion illustrated how the senses are liars: "We see the sun rise above the horizon; it is beneath us. We touch what we think is a solid body; there is no such thing (as a solid body). We hear harmonious sounds; but the air has only brought us silently undulations that are silent themselves. We admire the effects of light and of the colours that bring vividly before our eyes the splendid scenes of Nature; but, in fact, there is no light, there are no colours. It is the movement of opaque ether striking on our optic nerve which gives us the impression of light and colour. We burn our foot in the fire: it is not the foot that pains us; it is in our brain only that the feeling of being burned resides. We speak of heat and cold; there is neither heat nor cold in the universe, only motion. Thus, our senses mislead us as to the reality of objects around us." And what is true of the outer senses *is truer still of the inner senses. The more complex and subtle the inner organs the more confusing the experiences thereof.

These lights, these colours, these experiences of heat and cold are the *gunas*. *Guna*, as we have noted before, etymologically means 'subordinate', the "mortal instruments". The senses show us the 'subordinate' part of things, and hide from us the primary part, show us the unreal and hide the Real. As Fichte strikingly put it, "our seeing itself hides the object we see; our eye itself impedes our eye." The reality at the back, the substance of which the diversity is but the shadow, is seen not with the eye of flesh, but with the eye of the spirit. "It is the disciplined, and the self-controlled *yogis* who see Hint seated in self; with the eye of the spirit; those without self-control do not see Him, in spite of all endeavour." (XV. 11).

It is in this sense that the *Gita* uses the much-discussed term *maya*, the mystery which deludes or cheats one of the Reality. *Maya* is not an illusion, or a mirage, but a veil or an obstacle that hides the Real, the thick strata, physical and mental, which overlay the Divine in us, the clouds that obscure the Sun in us, the golden lid that covers the face of Truth. The *gunas* or *prakriti* within us and without us are *maya* which dazzles us and blinds us and leads us astray. The bondage, the separateness, the diversity is caused by this *maya*. The world of name and form strikes on our senses, the various ornaments of gold, for instance, appear to us as so many different ornaments, the multitudinous waves appear to us as so many waves, but we do not see the gold and the unchanging sea, we do not see the Nameless and the Formless of which we see numerous forms. The *Brahman* or the Absolute is the Real substrata behind the world of name and form, which has existence only in it and through it; the "divine life appears broken up," as Fichte said, "in a multiplicity of things as the one light in the prism is broken up into a number of colour rays." The prism is the gross medium of our fleshly senses. It is because of the prism that the one looks many, and it is because of the prism of *maya* that the free self sees itself bound. "Life like a dome of many-coloured glass stains the white radiance of eternity." If the world is but a reflection of *Brahman*, the individual self is but a spark of the Universal effulgence. Indeed both are one, but for the limiting conditions. We have both the embodied self which finds itself united to body after body, and the Imperishable, Eternal and the Unborn identified in the *Gita* (II. 13; II18-25; XIII. 2,13-20; XV. 7, 11), for, as a *Mahabharata* verse says : "*Atman* associated with the *gunas* of the *prakriti* is called *Kshetrajna* (knower of the field). Released from this association *Atman* is *Paramatman*, the Supreme Self." They seem separate, but they are essentially one, otherwise no identity or union would be possible, and we know that identity is an actual fact of mystical experience in all ages and climes. All mystical endeavour lies in getting rid of the bondage of *maya*. It is such a fatally delusive thing. "Of all the deceptions with which *maya* the mighty misleads the embodied self," said the venerable Dr Besant, "of all the obstacles and difficulties that *maya* puts in the way of Self-realization, that is worst of all hypocrisies, of all delusions, which makes a man declare, with lips impure, with life unpurified, being the slave, the tool of *maya,* identifying himself with *maya :* 'I *mayavi* shell am *Brahman*.'"

We have seen how Vedanta (and the *Gita)* bridges the unbridgeable gulf set up between *prakriti* and *purusha*, spirit and matter in the *Sankhya* system, by making both dependent on the Supreme, by making them reflections (one inferior and the other superior) of the Supreme. Let us see how this Supreme is presented in the *Gita.* One may "say that we have It presented in as many aspects as the limited, no matter how spiritual, vision of man can conceive It. While It is Unmanifest, Supreme, Exhaustless and Imperishable, It displays itself in the garment of the ever-changing phenomena and so appears to partake of their character. It transcends all and yet it pervades and permeates all. Everything is strung on it like gems on a thread (VII. 7), and yet It is above and beyond all modifications (VII. 13, VII. 24, VIII. 22, X. 22). As immanent It seems to possess the attributes of all It fills, and as transcendent It is free from any of the attributes that man can think of or human language can devise. "It is neither Being, nor Not-Being. It appears to possess the functions of the senses and yet is devoid of the senses; without all beings and yet within; not moving, yet moving; far and yet so near; undivided, yet seeming to subsist divided in all beings" (XIII. 12-16) — a description which brings together several texts of the *Isha, Katha,* and *Mundaka Upanishads.* The Supreme is really neither exclusively transcendent nor exclusively immanent. It is idle to imprison the Inconceivable in finite concepts. But that should not mean that It is an abstraction or a negation. It is altogether too big and too vast to be confined in concepts, It baffles complete or anything like adequate description. As Prof. James put it in his picturesque American way, "It is super-lucent, super-splendent, super-essential, super-sublime, super-everything that can be named."

And because It is not a negation but something above positive and negative, It does not exhaust Itself whilst It sustains and pervades all. It is the exhaustless source of all. Even when It becomes manifest and conditioned, It does not cease to be absolute and unconditioned. In a mathematical simile which would have gladdened the heart of Spinoza, the *Upanishad* says: "*That* is infinite, *this* is infinite. From *that* infinite *this* infinite issues. If you take *this* infinite from *that* infinite, the remainder is still infinite." Here clearly *this* infinite is the universe *that* Infinite is *Brahman*. That is why the *Gita* says, though the universe rests in Him, He is not in it. All the modifications of the three *gunas* are due to Him, but He is not in th^m, they do not condition or taint Him. Whilst all reflect Him, all cannot contain Him. "With but a particle of Myself I stand upholding this universe" (X. 42). Whilst He or *Vasudeva* is all, everything is not *Vasudeva* V Hegel, in his *Philosophy of Religion,* seems to have had the Seventh and the Tenth Discourses of the *Gita* in mind when he wrote: "If you say God is all that is here, this paper etc. you have indeed committed yourselves to the pantheism with which philosophy is reproached; that is, the whole is understood as equivalent to all individual things. It has never entered into man's mind that everything is God, that is to say that God is all things in their individual and contingent existence. . . When Brahma says, 'In the metal I am the brightness of its shining, among the rivers I am the Ganges, I am the life of all that lives', he thereby suppresses the individual. He does not say, 'I am the metal the rivers, the individual things of various kinds as such, nor in the fashion of their immediate existence.' The brightness is not the metal itself, but is the universal, the substantial, elevated above any individual form...What is expressed here is no longer pantheism; the idea expressed is rather that of the essence of things." Spinoza who was accused of a similar pantheism also repudiated the charge: "I take a totally different view of God and Nature from that which the later Christians usually entertain, for I hold that God is the immanent and not the extraneous cause of all things. I say all is God; all lives and moves in God. . . It is, however, a complete mistake on the part of those who say that my purpose is to say that God and Nature, under which last term they understand a certain mass of corporal matter, are one and the same. I had no such intention." The *Gita* does not believe in an extraneous God. One phrase in that sublime rhapsody of prayer and praise — the Eleventh Discourse — sums up the thing beautifully: "Thou holdest all, and, therefore, thou art all" (XI. 40). He is all, because all cannot exist independently of Him. We do find Arjuna identifying the Sun and the Moon and the Wind and Fire with the Universal Form of Krishna, but all these are described as such because He holds all, or better still because as the Lord said, "whatever exists having any kind of richness, beauty, might, know thou that every such thing issues from a fragment of My splendour" (X. 41). In moments of vision it is possible for even ordinary mortals to see the face of God in the ugliest and evil-looking things, whilst the reborn soul of an Eckhart "is as an eye which having gazed into the Sun thence forward sees the Sun in everything." But that is far from cosmotheism. The seer, "with an eye made quiet by the power of harmony," "sees into the life of things."

But what of the personal God who is the source of all religious emotion? That leads us really to the two viewpoints from which the *Gita* has treated the question. For the philosophical attitude, God as the Absolute is enough. The philosophic mystic—*jnanayogi* and the meditative mystic — *dhyanayogi* will reflect and meditate on the Supreme, but what about the erring mortal and the contrite aspirant? Through the *Gita* we find a clear line drawn between the transcendental and the empirical view of looking at things. The self, *sub specie aeternitatis* is free and actionless, 'seated in the citadel of the nine gates', serene and blissful; but the empirical self which struggles to be one with the Universal Self is active, has agency, identifies himself with the outward trappings and has a load of *karma* to throw off. It is to this straggler that the *Gita* is addressed. Whilst the philosophical attitude is there for him who can rise or has arisen to the heights of philosophy, the struggling soul wants something to lean upon, something to throw his cares upon. Even he shall have a vision of the Reality, says the *Gita*, and the way for him is either to dedicate all his actions to God or to offer heart-felt devotion to God. A personal God becomes a fundamental necessity in this case. Man is the image of God, and as the *Bhagawata Parana* puts it, just as the reflection in a mirror will show only those ornaments which the object reflected possesses and none else, even so man superimposes all kinds of perfections on God in order that they may be reflected in him, His image. But he always finds himself far away from the ideal and hence casts himself on His exhaustless grace. — In His strength does, he hope to be strong, in His purity does he hope to be pure. There is no self-delusion here, no fundamental contradiction.

Contradiction there could only be, if one believed in *Brahman* as a mere metaphysical concept, or a "stream of tendency" as Mathew Arnold called it and hence said that "there was not even a low degree of probability that God is a person who thinks and loves." But *Brahman* as super-conceptual and super-everything includes a personal God. "The difference between the Supreme as spirit and the Supreme as person is one of stand-point and not of essence, between God as He is and God as He seems to be," says Dr Radhakrishnan. "When we consider the abstract and impersonal aspect of the Supreme we call it the Absolute; when we consider the Supreme as self-aware and self-blissful being, we get God. The real is beyond all conceptions of personality and impersonality. We call it the Absolute to show our sense of the inadequacy of all terms and definitions. We call it God to show that it is the basis of all that exists and the goal of all. Personality is a symbol and if we ignore its symbolic character it is likely to shut us from the truth. Even those who regard personality as the ultimate category of the universe recognize that God is vast and mysterious, mighty and ultimate." The *Gita,* whilst it mainly addresses itself, to the empirical self, the aspirant, has room for all temperaments and moods, provided they do not lose sight of the might and vastness and the absoluteness of the God that they would confine in a concept or symbol. It is those who would close their eyes to the higher aspect that the *Gita* calls deluded (VII. 25 and IX. 10), and yet in a noble pragmatism recognizes all temperaments and vouchsafes them fruit according to the purity of their conception (VII. 23; IX. 25). "In my Father's House are many mansions," and there is room in them for all.

5. Avatara

I have talked in the foregoing section of the fundamental necessity, in certain cases, for positing a personal God and have shown that such an assumption involves no violence to truth. A belief, identical in origin, is the belief in *avatara* or the Lord's descent on earth in human form. In its essence the theory of *avatara* is neither strange nor peculiar to India. Almost all religions have this conception in one shape or other, though the Hindu conception has some distinctive peculiarities. Its origin, everywhere, would seem to lie in man's realization of his own powerlessness and looking to something superhuman to intervene with its unique power and infinite mercy, in all situations which baffle man's mortal resources. The Jews believed in the Messiah or the Messenger. The Christians have their son of God, whom one of the Gospels describes as identical with God: "I and my Father are one." In the *Koran* there is indeed no idolatry or anthropolatry, and the Prophet declares over and over again that he is but "a plain warner" and "a mortal messenger"; but his equally emphatic insistence that he was revealing what was inspired in him by God — "I do but follow and declare what is inspired in me" — lead the bulk of his followers to attribute to the Prophet something very much like divinity and not far removed from an *avatara*. The Jain's conception of their Arhat and the Buddhists' of the Buddha are also similar. But broadly one may say that, while in other cases God's spirit is said to descend into a chosen human being, the Hindus believe that God descends as man, when, Right declines and wrong prevails, in order to re-establish Right. Though the word-*avatara* means descent, and generally, it is the descent of God on earth that is at the back of our minds when we talk of an *avatara*, the belief in an *avatar a* would seem to have several aspects. Thus belief in an *avatara,* may be belief in God incarnating as man and identifying this incarnation with a human being of extraordinary mental and spiritual dimensions striking man's mind with amazement at the qualities which make him a saviour and deliverer. That attitude is the imaginative attitude. But the same belief rationalized becomes a belief not in God embodied as man, but either in God working out the cosmic purpose through the universal law or in man ascending to the estate of God by wholly divesting himself of all his earthliness and completely spiritualizing himself, or sacrificing himself in God. Having the spark of the divine, we are all incarnations of God; but it is not usual to consider every living being an 'incarnation' for the simple reason that almost all of us reveal the human or the mortal part of us more predominantly than the immortal and the 'incarnate' part of us. Arguing thus we might say that the ultimate reach of human endeavour is the realization that the aspirant himself^ as indeed everything around him, is an incarnation of the Divine. The mere belief in the Incarnation, which, as I have said, springs from die imaginative attitude, can scarcely carry one very far, and may indeed be a delusion and a snare, unless it becomes rationalized into a belief in "a perpetual cosmic and personal process", to adopt Miss Underbill's phrase. As she has so beautifully put it, "It is an everlasting bringing forth, in the universe and also in the individual ascending soul, of the divine and perfect life, the pure character of God, of which the one historical life dramatized the essential constituents. Hence the soul, like the physical embryo, resumes in its upward progress the spiritual life — history of the race. 'The one secret, the greatest of all,' says Patmore, 'is the doctrine of the Incarnation, regarded not as an historical event which occurred two thousand years ago, but as an event which is renewed in the body of everyone who is in the way to the fulfillment of his original destiny.'"

We have both these aspects of the belief in *avatara* in the *Mahabharaia*, though in the *Puranas* it is the exclusively imaginative aspect that predominates. It is difficult to trace the belief in *avatara* in the *Vedas* and the *Upanishadsy* though two *Vedic* texts are cited as containing the belief in the germ: "The Lord of the beings travels in the wombs. Though unborn, He is born in many ways" (*Vajasaneya Taj. Samhita* 31.19); and "this same God is in every quarter. He was born before and is born again. He was before and will be born again." *(I.c.* 32.4) This is the rationalist aspect of the *avatara* theory. In the *Mahabharata* we have both the imaginative and the rationalistic conceptions running, so to say, a close race. Thus whilst Krishna, the warrior and the statesman is represented as the Incarnation in many places, we have also the cosmic aspect emphasized in other places. In a striking passage in the *Drona Parva* Krishna declares: "I am four-formed, ever ready to protect the worlds. One of the forms practises penance on earth; the second keeps watch over the actions of erring humanity; the third resorting to the world of men is engaged in activity; and the fourth is plunged in the slumber of a thousand years."

I feel strongly persuaded that though in the *Gita* we have Krishna referred to as the human incarnation and addressed sometimes by Arjuna as 'the slayer of foes', it is the rationalistic conception that is presented, and it is that fact which, with other things, goes to make the *Gita* the crown and culmination of the *Mahabharata*.

Thus after declaring that for the good of mankind He is born again and again, Lord Krishna says: "He who knows the secret of this divine birth and work of Mine comes to Me" (IV. 9). By 'divine birth and work' here is not meant the activities attributed to Him as warrior and slayer of foes, or as the Divine Cowherd, but the perpetual cosmic process of the victory of Right over wrong of which to know and understand the secret and which to live is to fulfill one's destiny, to experience the process of *avatara* going through at every moment of our life. In another place Lord Krishna says in effect: "Be thou unslumbering in the performance of thy duty, even as I am unslumbering" (III. 23). In a third place (IX. 9) there is again a reference to the Lord's activities. There they are patently cosmic— the creation and the dissolution of the worlds; and in the Eleventh Discourse we have a vision not of a personal in-carnation but of the Divine Energy engaged in cataclysmic dissolution. It is idle to pretend that the activities referred to in all these contexts are those described in the *Mahabharata* or in the *Bhagwata Pur ana*. "Thou knowest not what is the way of the spirit, nor how the bones to grow in the womb of her that is with child : even so thou knowest not the works of God that maketh all," said the Jewish prophet. The author of the *Bhagawata Parana* has woven into matchless poetry the divine play of Krishna, as he had felt and seen Him, but even he has left a warning which is true for all time: 'Not even in thought should one who is not *Ishwqra* (God) attempt to do these things. Should he do it, he is sure to perish, as one who would attempt to drink poison in imitation of Shiva. For those who have 'noughted' the self there is no benefit in behaving well, nor harm in behaving ill; how then does good or ill — matter to Him who is the Lord of all beings on earth and in heaven?" Herein — is contained in a nutshell the meaning and purpose of the *avatara,* whatever one may believe or imagine to be the activities of the *avatara.* To paraphrase: ' 'Be first an *Iskoara* — God — (who is defined as having the power of doing, undoing, and transforming anything on earth and in heaven); achieve His supreme detachment, and then if there is any 'self5 or 'will' left in you, you are welcome to will and do whatever good or ill you may," That seems to me to be the meaning also of (III. 18) and of that difficult *shloka* (XVIII. 17) which we shall have occasion to consider later on. The utmost self-purification, through action without attachment to fruit, and without thought of self, is what the *avatara* in the *Gita* teaches to us in every *shloka* that the author has put into His mouth. 'Be thou perfect even as thy Father in Heaven is perfect. Be thou holy even as I am holy,' said Christ. 'Be thou unslumbering in the performance of the duty, even as I am: Look on all alike, even as I do, and in Me shalt thou rest,' says Lord Krishna. Complete 'noughting' of self, supreme detachment and perfection are the tests that the *avatara* in the *Gita* lays down for whomsoever we would associate with the name of *avatara*, and by that test only can the activities we attribute to an incarnation be judged. Those are the only tests whereby we can measure the extent to which we might say God has descended in our own individual life. There can be no other tests. And in laying down these tests, and in presenting the perfection that a human being has to reach in the most unmistakable terms, the *Gita* stands out as unique in our literature and the crowning glory of the *Mahabharata.* As that fine verse in the *Gita Mangalacharanam* says, '*Gita* is the *bharata-pankaja*—the lotus sprung out of the mud of the *Bharata* (or the *Bharata* war) and the Krishna of the *Gita* or the Incarnation is the spodess, untainted embodiment of the highest aspiration of man.'

Whether we worship a personal but inconcrete God, or a personal and concrete God, we do so in order to be like unto Him. 'It is all right to be born in church,' Swami Vivekanand used to say, 'but not to die in it,' and the devotee Narsinha Mehta, practically unlettered, who spent the bulk of his life singing the praises of the Incarnation as he had conceived Him to be, delighting himself and intoxicating himself with the worship of that Krishna, ultimately outgrew that stage and towards the end of his days broke forth in songs of matchless vision: "How am I to worship Thee, O Lord of infinite mercy ? When Thou pervadest every particle of the creation, how may I limit Thee in an image? I see Thy eternal light burning without any oil or wick. Formless it is indeed to be seen without eyes, and enjoyed with the senses of the spirit."

6. The End and the Means

The foregoing should be sufficient to show that the theme of the *Gita* is to indicate the end of man's existence on earth and the means for the attainment of it. The end is for man to realize completely what he .is, what the world about him is, and to experience that what sustains him and pervades him and what sustains and pervades the world about him is the one — the Truth or the Reality. As soon as man can completely spiritualize himself he will have a vision of this Reality as also of his oneness with It. "As soon as man abolishes himself," said Fichte,: "purely, entirely, to the very root,

God alone remains and is all in all; man can produce no God for himself, but he can do away with his self as the great negation and then he passes into God." That is *brakma-niroana* in the language of the *Gita*. "He will see Me, enter into Me", "He will be one *brahman*", "He will become one with My nature", "He will attain *brahma-mrvana*" are some of the expressions used by the *Gita*. These are interpreted by various schools of commentators in various ways.

> 'Enough if in our hearts we know
> There's such a place as Yarrow.'

Let us not be drawn into those whirlpools. Fichte's phrase, 'He passes into God' is real enough for us mortals who have ages to cover before we can have a glimpse of that state. Let us concentrate on the means, the goal will reveal itself, as it may in due season. Let us remember that we have to prepare for a rebirth. We have to wear off loads of *karma* by means of action, we have to be free from the trammels of the body through the body itself. As the *Bhagawata Purana* beautifully says: "This is the understanding of those who understand, and the wisdom of the wise that, with the unreal and the mortal (body), man attains to Me the Real Immortal." We have to sublimate the *gunas* to be *nirguna*, to cease to dance to the tune of *prakriti,* but to make her dance to the tune of Self, if dance she must. In short, every one of the 'senses of the flesh' has to be turned into a 'sense of the spirit'. Every one of them has to be intimately related to the Self which alone gives them light and life, until, in the language of a famous text, 'all the senses, the whole not-Self, become Self, even as iron when every atom of it is in contact with fire, becomes like fire.'

The *Gita* sums up this means in one word — *yoga*, of which the varying aspects we shall see in the course of the analysis which follows. This ancient word is pressed by the *Gita* into service to mean the entire gamut of human endeavour to storm the gates of Heaven. It is derived from the verb *yuj* (tr. and intr.) which has numerous meanings: to join, to attach, to yoke; to direct, to concentrate one's attention on; to use, to apply, to employ. In the *Yoga Sutras* it is used to mean discipline or control. It thus means the yoking of all the powers of the body and the mind and soul to God; it means the discipline of the intellect, the mind, the emotions, the will, which such a yoking presupposes; it means a poise of the soul which enables one to look at life in all its aspects and evenly. The *yogin* is therefore one who reflects all these attributes in his life, who, in the midst of raging storm and blinding spray, will keep his vision of the Sim undisturbed, who will look difficulties and death in the face, who "goes with the same mind to the shambles and the scaffold," and "whose mind is so serene that thunder rocks him to sleep."

If we may call this many-faceted word *yoga* mysticism, the *yogin* will be a mystic. In the terms of work, the philosophic mystic will be a *Jnanayogi*, the active mystic will be a *Karmayogi*; in the terms of devotion, the *Jnanayogi* will be a *Dhyanayogi* (meditative mystic), and the *Karma-yogi* will be a *Bhaktiyogi*, worshipper mystic. We shall have both these dichotomies, but we shall also see them coincide in the end.

V. INTERPRETATIVE ANALYSIS
THE DELUSION (DISCOURSES 1 AND 2)

The *Gita* opens with a vivid description of men and things on the eve of the great battle of Kurukshetra. Earlier chapters in the *Mahabharata* show how all methods of persuasion and compromise have been tried and failed. , Krishna has on one hand pleaded unsuccessfully with the aggressors, the Kauravas, and they in their turn have unsuccessfully appealed to the magnanimity of the Pandavas. They admitted that they had wronged the Pandavas but argued that the latter could afford to ignore the wrong, seeing that that war was sure to involve the ruin of the .whole house of Kurus, that nothing but sin would accrue out of the carnage, and that their fair name would be tarnished. This unctuous appeal coming from those who on their own admission were the aggressors failed to make any impression on the Pandavas and the challenge was accepted. The dialogue between Arjuna and Krishna does not begin before these negotiations nor even at the close of them, but *after* the seal of approval had been set to the declaration of war by all, including of course Arjuna, the renowned Bowman, hero of many a battle in days gone by. His charioteer is no less than Krishna himself who has come at his express invitation. The war-lords on both sides are in their chariots, even the conch-shells have been sounded and the fatal arrows are about to fly. It is at this eleventh hour that an anguish seizes the soul of Arjuna, his heart sinks within him at the sight of the venerable preceptors, sires and grandsires, sons and grandsons, gathered for fratricidal carnage. He conjures up a vision of the terrible ravages of war, physical, moral and spiritual, puts aside his bow and arrow and sits down in utter distraction. His streaming eyes fail to soften Krishna who characterizes his attitude as one of impotent feeble-heartedness and unworthy of an *Arya*. But Arjuna repeats in the manner of one raving with grief: "No good do I see coming out of slaying my own kinsmen. Nor do we know which is better for us, whether that we conquer them, or that they conquer us; standing in front of us are Dhritarashtra's men, having killed whom we should have no desire to live." He is torn as much with doubt as with despair, and in the manner of a humble disciple appeals to Krishna for light and guidance (I. 1-47; II. 1-10).

I have already referred to some of the tragic situations in Shakespeare's dramas. Though in the passage quoted from *King John,* Lady Blanch's situation is different from Arjuna whose difficulty is more moral and spiritual than hers, the inertia in both cases is the result of a stupendous obsession with the sense of 'mine' or 'one's own' and 'other's'. Arjuna's situation is more tragic in that his obsession has very much a semblance of altruism. There is no doubt in Arjuna's mind that the opponents are all "proclaimed felons". Had they been "others", i.e. not kinsmen, his mind would not for a moment have suffered "the nature of an insurrection", as did that of Brutus. Brutus' inner spirit revolted against "the acting of a dreadful thing", the like of which he had not done before. For Arjuna the deed as such was not dreadful — as a *Kshatriya* he had done it over and over again. But it was made dreadful by the thought of the victims being *his* kinsmen.

There is yet another circumstance to be noted. The phantasms before Arjuna's mind were not of his creation. As I have already pointed out, some of the earlier chapters in the Epic tell us that the old king had tried in various ways to dissuade the Pandavas from the fight — the arguments used by him being the *very same* as we find Arjuna using in the First and Second Discourses. Indeed, Arjuna repeats the very language used by the messenger of Dhritarashtra, who was no other than Sanjaya who narrates now to the blind king the dialogue between Krishna and Arjuna! That is why Krishna simply brushes the arguments aside, calling them "vain words of wisdom" (II. 11). It was after all a superficial ebullition of compassion occasioned by the dark suggestion of Dhritarashtra, and not a revulsion springing from the depths of spiritual certitude. It was all right to recount the dreadful results of fratricidal warfare, but was it not a parade of wisdom? The fighting spirit was part of his innermost being, and no one knew this better than Krishna — his counsellor, the charioteer who was not only in charge of his war-chariot but who had in his hands the reins of Arjuna's inner being. That is why we find at the end of the *Gita* Krishna summing up the whole argument in these prophetically peremptory words: "If obsessed by the sense of 'I' thou thinkest 'I will not fight', vain is thy obsession; thy very nature will compel thee." (XVIII. 59).

It is this distinction between the Self and the not-Self which Krishna first brings home to Arjuna in the very language of the *Upanishads*. The specious arguments of Dhritarashtra have affected Arjuna's mind because he has identified the not-Self with the Self, the perishing with the Imperishable, the seeming and the seen which is *not,* apart from the Eternal Unseen whichever *Is.* 'The imperishable Self that inhabits the impermanent bodies pervades the universe. Him no weapon can wound, no fire can burn, no water can wet, no wind can dry. Thou art that permanent imperishable Self and not the ever-changing, ever-perishing vestment of the Self called the body, O Arjuna. It is because — one identifies the perishable with the Imperishable that the delusion of 'mine' and 'thine' is caused. For when thou sayest that thou wilt be the cause of the destruction of thy kinsmen, and of thy venerable preceptors, thou art forgetting that the Dweller in those bodies called Arjuna and Duryodhana, Bhishma and Drona is the same and imperishable, as in you and me, unaffected by heat and cold, pleasure and pain. It is thy attachment to the body and those feelings of kinship that spring from it, that makes thee lament the death and destruction of things which are doomed to perish' (II. 12-30).

The argument does not still Arjuna's doubts, but checks the ebullition, makes him throw off the "unprevailing woe" and compels him furiously to think why he has thus gone off the rails. He had in the past fought many a battle, but he had not paused to think *whom* he was killing, no sense of 'sin' had obsessed him, he 'had fought because he had felt that it was part of his duty, part of his day's work, perhaps because thought of heroism and glory or an overpowering rage had prompted him on those occasions/Indeed Krishna puts his finger on Arjuna's weak spot when he reminds Arjuna of the duty of a *Kshatriya*, a duty to which he was born, the fulfilling of, and not the running away from, which led to heaven and glory, (II. 31-37). Krishna knew his Arjuna better than Arjuna knew himself. The 'old Adam' was still sleeping in Arjuna's breast, whilst he was rolling out those swelling words of wisdom, and Arjuna realizes the situation in a flash. Well might he have asked: 'If the Self is imperishable, if the Self does not kill, does not act, why should I then engage in this violent undertaking at all?' But he does not interrupt the flow of Krishna's argument. The sense of reality has been quickened in him. He might even have asked: 'Dost thou indeed want me to fight as I did of old, prompted by thought of pride and glory and heroism, and to suppress the promptings of a better and a finer self?' Even that question is stilled. For as soon as Krishna feels that Arjuna's manliness has been roused, he touches the higher key in his nature and advances a loftier argument: 'Count equal loss and gain, success and failure, and gird up thy loins to do thy duty. No sin will touch thee.' That leads up to the teaching of the Art of Life—*yoga*. The wisdom (*Sankhya*) has been expounded, now follows the Art (II. 38, 39). Sin is born of ignorance and so long as man acts from ignorance, he goes on forging fresh chains of bondage. Thou hast done so in the past; I want thee to cease to do so from now. Attachment is of the essence of ignorance; cut off attachment and thou wilt cut off ignorance. In the past thou wert wont to fight with a sense of 'If, thou wert wont to attach thyself to the fruit—glory and reward and other interest perhaps. Today the attachment arises from a different obsession, but it is attachment and ignorance none the less; cast it off. Only action is thy concern and not the fruit. Forget all thought of fruit and fight. This forgetting of the fruit, this detachment from the sense of '1% this equanimity in success and failure is *yoga*. Indeed in that indifference to fruit lies the secret of success. *Yoga* is skill in action. Herein there is no loss of effort, no going back; even a slight performance is credited to man's account. The beaten track is the one prescribed by the *Vedic* ritual, the one which puts in men's minds hopes of various rewards. That is the way of the world, which is eternally moved by the three *gunas*. The minds of men tossed about by wordly desires have no moorings. Trust thou not such as speak to thee of heaven and similar rewards. For "when they speak great swelling words of vanity, they allure through the lusts of the flesh, . . those that were clean escaped from them who live in error." Only when one steers clear of the path of success and gain, heaven and happiness in a future life, can one hitch oneself to the star of freedom—freedom from the cycle of birth and death. Be thou not conformed to the world, for the world is nothing but tribulation. Free from the pairs of opposites, free from the care of success or failure, hitch thyself to the Self. For one who has a discriminative knowledge of the Self will conform to the Self and not to the world. As little use will such an one have of the *Vedic* ritual as men have of a well when surrounded by an all-spreading flood of water. This path of ritual rivets one's thoughts to merit and sin, but the path of *yoga* cuts clear through merit and sin alike and leads to the heaven where all ills, alike of the flesh and the spirit, are unknown. Cross thou this slough of delusion (II. 40-53J.

Arjuna too had probably heard of *yoga* before, but he now finds it presented to him in a new light. If *yoga* means the forgetting of all fruit, all attachment, then it means detaching oneself from the lower self and iden-tification with the supreme Self. One has to disjoin oneself from the impermanent to join oneself to the Permanent. But so long as the Self is encased in the impermanent tabernacle, one cannot disjoin oneself from it, except by purifying it, spiritualizing it, by making the not-Self work in tune with the Self. *Yoga* is thus both means and end.

Were there indeed men who had achieved this *yoga*? Arjuna would like to know, and Krishna now describes the state of that *yogin*.

The *yogin* whose understanding is Secure from all attachment to objects of senses, is free from fear and wrath and resentment, free alike from likes and dislikes, pleasure and pain. The most important step towards the haven of security is to rein in the senses, which if not kept in control carry off even the wisest to the abyss. Physical starving of the senses works but a temporary purpose; it is only when the intellect realizes its moorings in the Highest and prevents the mind from wandering that one can feel secure. But is that not a puzzling circle indeed? It is to realize the Highest that one is asked to go through the endeavour and he is told to realize the Highest before the earthly craving and yearning can be extinct! It looks a puzzle, but is not one when one remembers that the realization is in embryo in every one, and as soon as the process of self-purification starts, the full realization to come casts, so to say, a helpful flash of light on the path (II. 54-61).

With unerring psychological insight the *Gita* indicates now that ladder of doom of which the first step is brooding on sense-objects, the second is attachment to them, the third is hankering after them, the fourth, resentment over unfulfilled hankerings, the fifth, heedlessness which all resentment brings, the sixth, self-forgetfulness, the seventh, destruction of all discernment which takes one finally down to the abyss. It is not that one should close one's eyes and stuff one's ears, but that one should close and stuff them to the wrong things and open them to the right ones. The *yogin* closes his eyes to the things that worldly men pursue, and keeps wide awake to the things to which the latter are blind. Wordsworth has talked of the "blessed mood" in which "the heavy and the weary weight of all this intelligible world is lightened,"

—that serene and blessed mood
In which the affections gently lead us on,
Until the breath of this corporeal frame
And even the motion of our human blood,
Almost suspended, we are laid asleep
In body, and become a living soul;
While with an eye made quiet by the power
Of harmony and the deep power of joy
We see into the life of things.

With the *yogin* of secure understanding it is not a transient mood however, but a perpetual state of blessedness and serenity, which is the result of an ever-wakeful discipline of the soul.

And like the ocean, day by day receiving
Floods from all lands, which never overflows;
Its boundary line not leaping and not leaving,
Fed by the rivers, but unswelled by those;
So is the perfect one!

To his soul's ocean
The world of sense pours streams of witchery
They leave him, as they find, without commotion
Taking their tribute, but remaining sea.

Having stopped all brooding on the objects of the senses, the *yogin* broods on the Highest, and rises towards Him ultimately resting in Him — *brakmi sthiti*. It is not a sudden conversion, but a result of incessant brooding on the Supreme. The endeavour dissolves in the achievement and what once was a conscious endeavour becomes as natural as the process of breathing (II. 62-72).

Look at this description of a Western mystic where we find the means and the end thus mixing up: "True rest in God [*brahmi sthiti* (72)] is as unchanging as God Himself. It stills all passion, restrains the imagination, steadies the mind, controls all wandering: it endures alike in the time of tribulation and in the time of wealth, in temptation and trial, as well as when the world shines brightly on us."

KARMAYOGA (DISCOURSES 3 AND 4)

That takes us to the third discourse. Since realization thus changes the whole man, and makes him like unto God Himself, resting in God, why not cling on to realization? At any rate, one cannot expect to wade through slaughter to that Throne of God. The secret to wade through what was inevitable slaughter with one's limbs unstained has been already told, but Arjuna forgets the means in the dazzling vision of the end. To give up the fight and sit silent musing on the Self seemed apparently easy enough to him, but it really was not so. Krishna, as we have said, knew his Arjuna better than Arjuna knew himself. Who knows, if he physically withdrew, he might still mentally brood over the progress of the war and ultimately decide to plunge, or if he did not actually do so, his mind might be still deep dyed in blood. And mind ties the knot of *karma* tighter than the body. The body may be inactive, but if the mind continually runs after things from which the senses have been held back one deceives himself and deceives the world. Freedom from the bond of action is the *summum bonum*, indeed, but inertia is not freedom. There are two attitudes of life

— the attitude of *Jnanayoga* (philosophical mysticism) and that of *Karmayoga* (active mysticism), but there is no such thing as an attitude of inertia. The attitude of *jnana* where there was complete Self-realization, where action and inaction were one, is a consummation devoutly to be wished, but it is not a state to be preferred to some other state. It is a state where there is no room for preferences. So long as preferences arise and are to be thought of, there is but one course and that is *Karmayoga*. Between inertia and action, action is any day better. Inactive life is a contradiction in terms. *Prakriti,* with its *gunas,* knows no inactivity and leaves no one in peace. Therefore action is inevitable (III. 1-8).

If that is the case, does it mean that one has to be always bound down to the apron-strings of *prakriti* and consequently to the cycle of birth and death? All work, indeed, binds, says Krishna, save that done for sacrifice. For sacrifice is the law of life, the law of all creation. God whispered into the ear of man the message of sacrifice when He created him and said to him, 'by sacrifice shall ye grow and fructify.' Indeed, as the *Vedas* put it, He sacrificed Himself in order that the world may be created. In sacrifice all creation starts, by sacrifice it is sustained, sacrifice is at once the cause and the consequence. He who does anything but for sacrifice, breaks the law, sins, eats but sin, accumulates sin. For selfishness is sin, selflessness is freedom from it. And indeed those who have shed all thought of 'self', who have ceased to dance to the varying tunes of their mind, intellect and senses derive all their delight from Self, all their solace from Self, all their satisfaction from Self. For such there is nothing obligatory to do, no law is imposed on them, for they have no 'self to serve; then a life of sacrifice or oneness with the world is the fulfillment of the Law. That blissful state of active inactivity or inactive activity is attainable only by incessant performance of detached action which alone leads on to the Supreme (III. 9-19). So did king Janaka of old achieve his salvation. His very life-breath must have been sacrifice and service of mankind, or else how could he placidly say when his capital was burning: "Even if Mithila turn to ashes, nothing that is mine is destroyed" ? And yet no one misunderstood him. While the name of Nero is a by-word for diabolical heardessness, Janaka's name is held in reverence until today and the words in which he uttered his detachment are still remembered. He had achieved a state when every thought on his part meant the service of mankind and he might have retired to live a life of meditative calm, but he ruled his kingdom instead. There had been others too like him. They lived and worked not for themselves but for the world—

> Souls heroic and good
> Helpers and friends of mankind.

God Himself is ever at work, silent and slumberless, lest the worlds should come to an end. The enlightened, too, should work away if only to set an example to the unenlightened. The secret of 'free' action is detachment, the knowledge that it is the *gunas* that act, and not the Self. But the deluded attribute to the Self what belongs to the not-Self and arrogate to themselves the responsibility and claim the reward for action. To wean these from their attachment and their error, the enlightened should set an example of detached, selfless action, rather than confuse their minds with the enunciation of a principle of renunciation of action which might well lead them astray. They would sink into inertia which would be worse than the selfful activity in which they are immersed (III. 20-29).

But even for those who have not achieved the wisdom of isolating the Self from all activity, and rendering unto not-Self the things that belong to not-Self, there is a way of freedom. Let them cast off all action on God, working as His bondslaves, taking what He gives, expecting naught. That is a saving rule of life (111-30-32).

Men whose faith is blasted ignore the rule, so strong sometime is the force of nature. But that does not mean that man is born the slave of his nature. There is a part in one's make-up which predisposes him to a particular kind of activity and vocation. He is born to it and may not with impunity do any violence to that part of his nature. But there is another part which is entirely under man's control, viz. his moral nature. Willing obedience, in a spirit of selflessness, to that part of one's nature which is not in his hands, and control of that part which is controllable is the law of man's being—*svadharma*, if one were to free oneself. Doing aught else was not his law, but other's law, not his work, but other's work.

But one is often drawn into things which are contrary to the law of one's being, often drawn into sin. Why? Lust and Wrath, the twin brood of the Devil, strive to subvert the law, and they do so because they make man's senses, mind and reason their home, if man be not wakeful. They are the enemy of man, as Krishna has already taught in the second discourse. He now gives the same teaching in a different psychological setting. The senses, the mind and the intellect—they are the seat of the enemy, each subtler and more difficult to control than its predecessor. But the subtlest is He the Dweller in the innermost. Let man obey His law and reject the allurements of the rest, subduing each, one by one (III. 33-43).

This again is no puzzle, for the very faintest vision of the Sun of Self is enough to put one on the path of self-control and with increasing self-control the vision grows brighter and brighter. Let the aspirant only hold fast to the master-key—let him do all for His sake and leave the rest to Him. 'Thou enjoinest continence,' said St. Augustine, addressing his prayer to God, 'give me what thou enjoinest and enjoin what Thou wilt.'

The exposition of *Karmayoga* is continued in the fourth discourse. We were told in the third discourse that God whispered 'sacrifice into the ear of man when He created him.' We are now told that this law of sacrifice Krishna taught to Vivasvat (Sun) and he to his son and so on, which means to say that God taught it to the first human being who has passed it on from generation to generation. The very first man who put himself in relation with the universe about him, that is, realized a unity, no matter how partial, with his environment, acted according to the law, and handed it down to posterity. Is there anything strange in this? The Truth has been revealed over and over again and will go on being revealed until the end of time. We hear it said that there is nothing new under the sun. Well, there need be nothing new, for the Sun of Truth, exhaustless in his manifestations, ever presents aspects and visions new. Each seer presents the aspect appropriately to his environment, but it is an aspect of the same Truth nevertheless. Whatever the Muslims may think, was the law of surrender to Allah that their Prophet revealed anything different from the law the *Gita* or the Bible teaches? "A man is right and invincible," said Carlyle, "when he joins himself to the great deep law of the world, in spite of all profit and loss calculations. This is the soul of Islam and is properly the soul of Christianity. Islam means in its way denial of self, annihilation of self. This is yet the highest wisdom revealed to our earth." "The very thing which is now called the Christian religion existed among the ancients, and never failed from the beginning of the human race to the coming of Christ in the flesh," said St. Augustine. Long before Islam and Christianity the same law of surrender or love or sacrifice, whatever you may call it, was delivered by the *Gita*; but it was really delivered by God to man ever since his birth on this earth. "This law of sacrifice or sefless action or *yoga* I taught in ages gone before us," says Krishna to Arjuna; "thou seemest to marvel at it: Well, I tell thee that thou wast born often before; yea, even I the Unborn and Exhausdess Lord of the worlds also had many births ere this. In this marvel not. Understand the secret of My coming and of My work and cleanse thyself in the fiery ordeal of knowledge and come to Me. The ancients knew the secret and worked in the light of it. Do thou, too, likewise. I suffer myself to be born again and again whenever I find that Right declines and Wrong prevails. The *yoga* I taught dwindled away with the passage of time and so I have to declare it once again. I also engage Myself in establishing the fourfold order of the human community according to their *guna* and *karma*. But nothing that I do touches Me" (IV. 1-15).

That perhaps was, for Arjuna, a further phase of the revelation. His counsellor and charioteer was God Himself descended to the state of man in order that man may ascend to the state of God. 'The incarnation was a tear of the divine compassion,' says a Christian mystic. It was not for His sake but for man's sake that God became man. It is rarely that man has a vision of such, though it is these gods become men that sustain the earth. The author of the *Gita* had evidently the vision and so makes us see Him through His dialogue with Arjuna.

> It shall be
> A face like my face that receive thee; a Manlike to me,
> Thou shalt love and be loved for ever; a Hand like this hand
> Shall throw open the gates of new life to thee,
> See the Christ stand.
>
> (Browning—*Saul*)

So Arjuna saw the Lord stand before him as Krishna in order "to throw open the gates of new life to him." He realizes more clearly than ever before that it is not Krishna his friend and kinsman and charioteer but God Himself who is unfolding to him the mystery of *yoga*, teaching him what he was to do.

And again the Lord harks back to the doctrine in a different language. The law of *yoga* and sacrifice is now presented as the law of action in inaction and inaction in action. Man must go to the root from which action or inaction springs. All that springs from lust and passion is clearly binding action of the grossest type — *vikarma* — binding one in the coil of a snake; so is action with an eye to reward, binding one perhaps with a silver chain; running away from one's duty is equally binding, the chain may be of silver or of iron; what does not bind is action or refraining from action in obedience to the Law, in obedience to Him. That man is not the agent, but He the Law-giver is the agent, that man is but the instrument in His hands, that the reward is not for him to seek but for Him to give, is true knowledge. That Knowledge makes ashes of all action, nay of all *karma*, i.e. potential action. Sacrifice thus not only prevents but cures all bondage (IV. 16-23).

The *Koran* says the same thing in not very different language : "Whosoever surrendereth his purpose to Allah while doing good, he verily hath grasped the firm handhold" (31.22). Good deeds annul ill deeds" (11.114).

But there are sacrifices and sacrifices. Sacrifices performed in order to enter the gates of paradise were common enough. "To what purpose is the multitude of your sacrifices to Me?. . . Bring no more vain oblations. Wash you, make you clean, put away the evil of your doings. Learn to do well." These were the words of the Lord as they were heard by the Jewish prophet. St. Paul paraphrased them: "Present your bodies a living sacrifice, holy, acceptable unto God." The author of the *Gita* reveals the word of the Lord on sacrifice somewhat to this effect: "Make every act of thine a sacrifice unto the Lord; sacrifice even the thought that what is so offered is a sacrifice. All is sacrifice that takes you near the Lord. Thus the discipline of the senses, of the emotions and the will, of the vital airs, the pursuit of holy knowledge, all this is sacrifice. Whatever leads to the knowledge of the Supreme is 'knowledge-sacrifice' which is the best of sacrifices. Sacrifice taught in the books of ritual — material sacrifice—is not of much account, for it does not release, it binds. Knowledge is release, and no action is of any worth unless it fulfils itself in knowledge" (IV. 24-33).

We have seen how Lord Krishna again and again harks back to the end — knowledge — even in the midst of the discourse over the means. So here too we have the true content of knowledge presented to us. True knowledge is that with the eye of which one sees each and every being in the universe in one's self and then in God. True spiritual knowledge makes one rest 'in the vision of consubstantiality of the Self in man and God. The *Upanishad (Mundaka)* had taught that all sacrifices based on various kinds of ritual were "unreliable boats"5 and that man should leave them and resort to the properly qualified *guru*, learn the Truth from him and make that his sheet anchor. The *Gita* succinctly sums up that long section of the *Mundaka*, declares knowledge to be the sure boat to take even the most abandoned sinner across the ocean of sin, and describes the ways and means to find that knowledge — loving homage and service and repeated questioning and inquiry of a Master of Knowledge. But it adds that this purifying knowledge which makes ashes of all sins may be won by perfecting oneself with *yoga* — selfless action in faith and surrender and self-control. One need not necessarily sit down at the feet of a *guru* to learn it. Arjuna must rend his doubt with the initial knowledge of Self, and cast off the bondage of action by dedicating all action to God. "Equipped with knowledge, betake thyself to *yoga* and arise" (IV. 33-43).

JNANAYOGA AND KARMAYOGA COMPARED (DISCOURSE 5)

Again Arjuna is pictured to us as puzzled, for again we have the end and the means extolled in the same breath with perhaps an added emphasis on the purifying virtue of knowledge. 'Which of the two then may be better? Renunciation of action or performance of action, exclusive pursuit of knowledge (*Sankhya*) or practice of action (*yoga*)?' True knowledge is the end, sure enough. May it not be that an exclusive pursuit of knowledge may be a better way than much preoccupation with the noise and bustle of the world ? It is to remain unworldly that seekers after God retire from the world and occupy themselves completely with trying to realize the mysteries of Self and God. Why then *Karmayoga?*

Both, says the Lord, are good; both lead to the same goal; but *Karmay-oga* is better, if only because *Jnanayoga* is well nigh impossible without *Karmayoga, sannyasa* well nigh impossible without yoga. It is quite likely that he who takes a sudden leap into philosophic mysticism may come to grief, whereas he who goes through the necessary discipline of active mysticism, doing the daily duties in a spirit of selflessness, remaining in the world and yet not of it, naturally steps into the state of the Self-absorbed mystic.

When one comes to think of it, there is but a faint line of demarcation between the perfected *Karmayogi* and *Jnanayogi*. In fact one may doubt for a moment whether a particular verse in this discourse is meant to refer to one rather than to the other. Thus, verse 7 describes the active mystic: 'The *yogin* who has cleansed himself, who has gained mastery over his mind and the senses, and whose Self has become one with the Universal Self and all creation, though always in action, is not smeared by it.' Why should not this apply to the philosophic mystic? His action indeed may be of a different character, but act he will. Both will go — through what are usually voluntary movements of all the internal and external organs as though they were all involuntary (V. 8-9). Again the philosophic mystic will sit secure in 'the city of nine gates' (body), master of himself, resting serene, doing nothing nor getting anything done (V. 13) This all may equally apply to the active mystic whose action will be inaction as it will be dedicated to God. The difference then will be a difference of attitude or emphasis: The philosophic mystic will sit secure in the wisdom that *he* is doing nothing, that it is the *gunas* that act and not the Self; the active mystic will rejoice in the knowledge that it is God who acts, that it is God who is the agent, and his limbs but instruments worked by Him. Take verses 14 and 15. The life of the *Karmayogi* and *Jnanayogi* will reflect the truth of the verses, in a seemingly different way. The Self does not act, creates no agency, takes not the sin or merit of any one upon Himself. That will be the conviction of the *Jnanayogi*. The *Karmayogi* will feel and act in the conviction that he is under the rule of a law which is God's law—the Law which "doth preserve the stars from wrong".

But whereas a merely philosophical position may well be a delusion and a snare, the religious position of a *Karmayogi* is sure to lead to the *real* philosophical position. A mere assertion of the metaphysical truth, that

Self does not act, may drag one into the depths of hypocrisy and worse; but he who holds his will at the disposal of God will ultimately reach the knowledge that his will and God's will are one, that he or his Self wills and acts not at all.

When in a state of complete immersion in the Absolute, Kabir sings that all outward acts of his — seeing, eating, drinking, etc.—are all so many acts of piety and dedication, he says so because for him there was no 'other' God. Here we have the vision of the seer described in verses 8-9. But who will say that that state of self-absorption was reached automatically? It was a result of an unbroken life of self-purification (V. 11-12).

Therein lies the essence of the discourse. The true *sannyasi* will no doubt rest in serene equipoise, free from the delusion of ignorance which the Sun of knowledge has dispelled, his body and mind and intellect rivetted on the Highest whose vision he has had. He will look with an equal eye on learned *brahmana* and a cow, on a dog and a dog-eater, resting in unity and perfection which is *brahman* (10-19), finding peace within, bliss within, light within (24). But how is the state to be achieved? Not without *Karmayoga*, which" is a condition precedent. The highest intellectual effort will not put one in that condition. Intuition in some rare cases may do it, but intuition is nothing more than a result of ages of endeavour. Thus *brahma-nirvana* (absorption in *brahman)* is said to be ever in front of the *yogin* whose sins are extinguished, whose doubts are dispelled, who is absorbed in the good of all creation, and who can withstand the flood-tides of the passions of lust and wrath (V. 25, 22-23). The description itself presupposes an intense state of selfless, God-dedicated activity — *Karmayoga*. To take another instance. The *jnani* or the philosophic mystic looks on the savant and the fool, the dog and the dog-eater with an equal eye. How will he do so? The *Bhagawata Parana*, parts of which are like a luminous commentary on the *Gita*, lays down the conditions: "The feeling that God is in every one — the saint and the sinner, the *brahmana* and the untouchable, has to be assiduously cultivated, and then only will the feeling of disgust vanish. A step to the cultivation of that feeling is to prostrate oneself on the ground in front of even the most loathsome, regardless of one's self-consciousness, prestige and of one's own sense of shame and of physical differences. This should be done unless and until one actually sees Him in every creature." St. Francis cured himself of his feeling of disgust for the lepers by adopting practically a similar course.

That is why the Lord put the truth of the matter in one word at the very opening of the discourse: "*Sannyasa* is well-nigh impossible to achieve without *yoga*." But we have thus far had *yoga* presented to us in terms of action. We shall now have it presented in terms of devotion. Here too we have two divisions exactly corresponding to the philosophic and the active mysticism, namely, meditative and devotional—*Dhyanayoga* and *Bhakti-yoga*. In the last analysis there are only two attitudes towards Reality —the philosophic and the religious, and in the ultimate analysis even these two dissolve into one, as we shall see. But for the sake of clearness we have these dichotomies given us. The *Jnanayogi,* as we have seen, has his eye fixed on the Absolute, takes his cue from it, and turns all action into inaction; the *Karmayogi* takes his cue from a God willing to take upon Himself the burden of all the actions he casts on Him in self-surrender. In the terms of prayer the former becomes *Dhyanayogi*, the mystic contemplating and meditating on the impersonal Absolute, and the latter becomes *Bhak-tiyogi,* the devotee-mystic basking in the glow and warmth of His presence and His praise and His grace. We have these two fresh aspects introduced to us towards the close of the fifth discourse— meditative mysticism in V. 27-28 and devotional in V. 29. The discourses that follow deal with these two. Roughly it may be said that *Dhyanayoga* is the subject of discourses 6 to 8, and *Bhaktiyoga* that of discourses 9 to 11, both being compared in the 12th.

DHYANAYOGA (DISCOURSES 6 TO 8)

We have again (VI. 1-4) a slightly varied phraseology for the philosophic and the active mystic. The one has scaled the heights of *yoga*, the other has to scale them. He who would achieve those heights and enjoy tranquillity in toil, active repose, or "an attentive and recollected inaction", to use Amiel's phrase, must remember that it can only be the result of strenuous self-endeavour. By the Self does one sink or swim, for the Self is self's friend and the Self is self's foe. It is he who has thus conquered himself and mastered the art of conforming himself to the Self, that will be able to look with an equal eye upon friend and foe, happiness and misery, respect and disrespect, a clod of earth and gold. This mention of strenuous endeavour is necessary to introduce the method of meditative mysticism— *Dhyanay-oga* (VI. 5-9). Verses 10-17 define in brief the spiritual qualifications of one who elects to tread this path, and the necessary physical environments which facilitate the path of one determined to retire in the sanctum of Self. External purity and *brahmacharya,* continence of the body, thought and mind, are the *sine qua non* before one thinks of choosing this path. And yet one may not violently mortify oneself. Let him give *prakriti* its moderate yet necessary toll of food and drink, rest and sleep. This *yoga* is a toilsome process and hence necessarily means patience and freedom from extremes. Thus equipped he should sit secure in contemplation of the Self, secure from all the winds and storms that blow, even as the steady flame of a taper in a windless spot. In spite of this effort the mind with its inveterate habit of wandering will do so. Slowly and gradually, with tireless effort, it has to be reined in, with understanding secured by will, and chained to the Self. Then all disturbing thought shall cease. The result when attained will be something ineffable which will preclude all desire for other gains and other joys. It will be a *yoga* or union with Supreme Bliss, meaning an extinction of union with all that is not-Self, an annulment of union with all ills. It will be the absolute bliss of an everlasting contact with *brahman.* These rare souls will not, like the stoics, "seem to bear, rather than rejoice"; theirs will be a rejoicing which knoweth no surfeit or satiety (VI. 18-28).

But this *yoga* must show itself in life. Lord Krishna gives the criterion which equates the philosophic and the religious vision. Such an one will see the Universal Self in all beings, and all beings in that Self—deriving their existence and their sustenance from the Self. And since that Self is the same as Lord Himself, he will see the Lord in all, and all in the Lord. As a commentator quoting from the *Mahabharata* says, from out of the vision of the *yogin* who has attained self-realization, God flashes forth before him even as the lightning flashes forth from out of a rain-cloud. Such an one will naturally, in the vastness of his love, embrace all beings as part and parcel of himself. He will, so to say, be unique alike in his detachment and tenderness. From such an one God will never vanish, such an one will never vanish from God. It is a tremendous assurance. God will not fail him but He gives the added assurance that He knows that he will not fail God. Of such an one Lord Krishna says that however such an one may live and move he will live and move in Him. As Plotinus put it: "He becomes established in quiet and solitary union, not at all deviating from his own essence, not revolving about himself, but becoming entirely stable, becoming as it were stability itself. Neither is he then excited by anything beautiful, for he runs above the beautiful, he passes beyond even the choir of the virtues. (VI. 29-32).

But, says Arjuna, this *yoga* of equality with the whole creation is no easy matter. The mind is such a forward, fickle thing that one may sooner chain the wind than rein in this mind. How then is one to rest stably in that equality or union? 'Just so,' says Lord Krishna, 'but tireless effort and dispassion can overpower even the unruly mind. Indeed those two are the essentials. *Yoga* should not be thought of by one who has not stilled his passion; but for one who has done it, it is not difficult of achievement by the proper method.'

'But if the aspirant fail in his effort, he will be neither here nor there. Neither will he be on the path of the Vedic ritual which he has abandoned, nor on the path of *brahman* which he has lost.'

'No effort is lost,' Lord Krishna reassures him. 'A man who has chosen the path and is on it never comes to grief, here or there. Man grows by countless lives into oneness with *brahman*. What he has done in one life is a step, however, inadequate, towards the goal. After a period of discarnate existence he is reborn in a family suited to help him further forward towards the goal, even from the point where he left it in the previous existence. No, there is no cause for despair. The very fact that he has chosen this path will not let him look back with longing on the path of the Vedic ritual' (VI. 33-44).

He is, however, in for an effort carried on from life to life; about that there should be no mistake. Such a *yogin* is better than a. mere practiser of austerities, who simply tortures the flesh; he is better than one revelling in learning; he is certainly better than one wedded to the Vedic ritual (VI. 45-46). But let it be remembered that among all *yogins*, 'he excels who, ever attached to Me, worships Me in faith' (IV. 47). In this last verse peers out Lord Krishna's preference for *Bhaktiyoga*, which we will find demonstrated with argument in the twelfth discourse.

The seventh discourse, part of which we have summarized in the introductory background to this analysis, deals with the nature of the world and the Reality which a meditative mystic will realize. But hardly one in a thousand strains after the perfect vision and hardly one succeeds from among those who thus strive. This vision is the vision of the Absolute in Its two aspects, the higher being the vitalizing thread in all life, the lower being the physical world. The Absolute thus pervades the animate and inanimate creation, sustaining all, holding it all even as a thread sustains the gems in a necklace, immanent through and through. All that exists, 'where-through runs the warp and woof of the three *gunas*, exists through the Supreme, but rather than take all that as a symbol and expression of the Divine the deluded ones fix their eyes on the form and forget the substance. The world is a delusive mystery indeed, it hides what it ought to reveal, but we have to see the Unseen through the veil of the Seen. "The whole temporal world," said Henry Drummond, "is a vast transparency through which the Eternal shines." But only the blessed ones, the good doers — not the evildoers— have this vision, can penetrate the veil, having made the Lord their refuge. Of these devotees there are four types; he who, as a reward of devotion, seeks relief from distress; he who seeks knowledge; he who seeks material gain, and he who seeks the Lord. This last — *the jnani* — is the best, for he has no other end to serve, no other goal to think of, no other haven to hide himself in. He is ;the Lord's very self. It is as a result of effort which must have continued through several births that this *jnani* thus happens to win the vision and to see that *Vasudeva* is all (VII. 1-19).

There are, says Lord Krishna, others who have other ends to serve and who, therefore, in pursuit of those ends, seek other gods. He does not disturb their faith, on the contrary he makes them secure in their faith and dispenses them what they seek. But limited is their fruit, for they would limit Him, the Exhaustless, the Supreme, and would not look beyond their little gods. Such is the delusive mystery of the Lord that it precludes the vision of the Unborn and the Immutable. Man is born with a heritage of likes and dislikes which draw his mind and his senses to outward objects, never allowing him to look inward. Only those whose sins have come to an end are freed from that sorry heritage and resort to Him in steadfast faith. They indeed know the whole *brahman,* including *adhyatma,*

karma, adhibhuta, adhidaiva, and *adhiyajna.* They also have a vision of the
Lord at the time of death (VII. 20-30).

What, Arjuna wonders, is this *brahman* which includes so many
puzzling terms. It is nothing but the several stages in which the Absolute
transforms Itself into the individual and the individual comes back into
the Absolute. *Brahman* thus translates Itself into the unmanifest *prakrili*
(termed here *adhyatma), prakriti* starts evolving (which is termed *karma* or
action), as a result we have the perishable creation (termed *adhibhuta*), the
Absolute limited in each created being is *adhidaiva,* and each gifted with
and purified by the power of sacrifice *(adhiyajna)* expands again into the
original *brahman.* The whole mystery, bereft of its technical garb, is really
nothing more or less than the mystery of the law of sacrifice which we have
learnt in the Third Discourse. The Supreme Being sacrifices Itself to be the
individual and the individual has to sacrifice himself to reach the original
source (VIII. 1-4).

There is a secret of shuffling off one's mortal coil with a vision of this
brahman. One has to rivet his thoughts on Him when passing away and he
goes nowhere else but to Him. This thought of Him at the hour of death
is no fortuitous circumstance, but the culmination of a life-long habit.
'Whatever therefore thou doest—whether thou art fighting the outward
powers of darkness or the inward ones —do it at all times with the thought
of Me,' says Lord Krishna. With an exclusive devotion one must concentrate one's powers of meditation on the Supreme Being (VIII. 5-8). Here
follows a description of the Supreme and the way in which the Supreme is
to be meditated upon. OM is the symbol of that imperishable Absolute,
OM which is at once the means and the end, as the *Katha Upanishad* text
on which the *Gita* text is based declares. This and similar other *Upanishad*
texts crystallize the spiritual and psychical experience of the seers who
intuitively found the symbol and used it as an open sesame for their
spiritual goal. As the *Prashna Upanishad* has it : "As a snake is relieved of
its skin, even so verily he (who meditates on the Supreme with the symbol
OM) is freed from sin… He beholds the Being that dwells in the body and
which is higher than the highest living complex… With the syllable OM
in truth as a support, the knower reaches that which is peaceful, imaging,
immortal, fearless Supreme" (VIII. 9-15).

The verses that follow describe the fleeting show, in order to rivet man's mind on the Unfleeting. The worlds are ceaselessly perishing and reappearing, all bound in the unending chain of *karma* — even those who do good deeds (for rewards). These go to the several worlds they aspire after to reap their rewards, but even those who reach the world of Brahma must be born again, for all including Brahma himself are caught in the cycle! At the beginning of each period of a thousand *yugas* — or at the beginning of each day of Brahma — the beings come into manifest existence from the unmanifest state, and at the coming of Brahma's night — of a thousand *yugas* they return to the unmanifest state. The same multitude of beings as are dissolved come to birth again at the coming of each Brahma's day and go through their cycle of existences until the coming of Brahma's night. The unceasing process goes on, whether the beings will or no (VIII. 16-19). The same idea is repeated in IX. 7-10 where the Brahma's Day is called *kalpa*, the unmanifest is referred to as 'My *prakriti*' and is said to bring forth the beings "under My control."

The description strongly reminds one of the vivid stanzas in Thomson's *City of Dreadful Night:*

This little life is all we must endure,

The grave's most holy peace is ever sure.

We fall asleep and never wake at all.

We finish thus; and all our wretched race

Shall finish with its cycle and give place

To other beings with their own time-doom.

Infinite aeons ere our kind began;

Infinite aeons after the last man

Has joined the mammoth in earth's tomb and womb

All substance lives and struggle evermore

Through countless shapes continually at war

By countless actions interknit:

If one is born a certain day on earth

All times and forces tended to that birth;

Not all the world could change or hinder it.

I find no hint throughout the universe
Of good or ill, of blessing or of curse,
I find alone necessity supreme;
With infinite mystery, abysmal, dark
Unlighted ever by the faintest spark
For us the flitting shadows of wisdom.

It is a powerful description of the inexorable law of *karma*. Only we do not "give place to other things". We ourselves take "those countless shapes", for infinite aeons indeed the show will go on, but the peace is not to be found in the "grave's most holy peace", for we fall asleep to wake up once more. The great poet contradicts himself when he says that we live and struggle evermore "by countless actions interknit", and yet says that it is all an abysmal and a dark mystery "unlighted ever by the faintest spark". We could not be interknit by countless actions, unless there was unity at the basis of this diversity, unless the whole thing was governed not by a blind necessity, but by a law which is the expression of God. The peace is not to be sought in the peace of the grave, but in the bosom of the Lord. The *Gita* verses that follow complete the thought, lest we should run away with an impression not unlike Thomson's grim vision. For, says the Lord: 'This manifest and unmanifest is not the final word. Higher than that unmanifest is *brahman* Supreme, abiding, imperishable whilst all beings perish. It is the Supreme Being, in whom all beings are and which is in all. It is the highest haven, where having reached there is no coming back. Unwavering devotion to that Being is the only way to reach It, but it also is a way which never fails (VIII. 19-22).

A day of a thousand *yugas* must hearten one, rather than dismay, for we have to work through life after life for ages, whilst our spirit strives to be one with Universal Spirit, through instruments and vestments that dissolve and decay, leaving him ever free for a fresh struggle. And after all, is not the whole picture such as to make one not only patient but feel as humble as a grain of dust? The great physicist Planck says: "Reason tells us that both the individual man and mankind as a whole, together with the entire world which we apprehend through our senses^ is no more than a tiny fragment in the vastness of Nature, whose laws are in no way affected by any human brain. On the contrary they existed long before there, was any life on earth, and will continue to exist long after the last physicist has perished."

One of those laws is the law of sacrifice, as the seers have found it. The *yogin* has to live that law, has to annihilate self to become one with the Universal Self. Him who does this the traditional paths—known as the paths of the gods and the manes — will not touch. He will know the secret of the paths and live by the path of light, and living thus he will travel beyond the minor rewards promised by the *Vedas* and reach the ultimate goal (VIII. 23-28).

BHAKHYOGA (DISCOURSES 9-11)

We have had an idea of *Dhyanayoga* and the *Dhyanayogi*, the mystic who would devote his mind and soul to a contemplation of the impersonal Absolute. It is, as we have seen, a path of strenuous endeavour. We have now described to us the path of *bhakti*—devotion to a Personal God. *Bhaktiyoga* is described as the supreme mystery, the king of sciences, purifying and of sovereign virtue, capable of direct comprehension, and easier to practise than the path we have had described. The basis of this *Bhaktiyoga* is the knowledge of the Lod as He is, and a discriminative knowledge of Him in His manifestations. Only men of faith take to this path, scoffers go and revolve through the cycle of birth and death over and over again (IX. 1-3).

This background of knowledge is now presented to us in three discourses in various ways. Lord Krishna as the Imperishable Unmanifest becomes manifest as the world which rests in Him, but He as the Unmanifest is not in it, because He transcends it. He sustains the beings and runs through them as the string in the gems. He is their ground, not they His ground. Again He contains all, nothing can contain Him fully. All beings live and move in Him without affecting Him, as does the wind in ether without affecting it (IX. 4-6).

We have a description of how the Lord creates all and is in all, and is thus all—sacrifice and the oblation, the herb and the mantra, fire and the offering; Father, Mother, Creator, Friend, the Goal and the Abode, the Source and the Dissolution, Death and Deathlessness, Giver and the Withholder, and the Acceptor of all sacrifices (IX. 16-19; IX. 24).

Again He the Unborn and Unbegun is the birth of and beginning of all, even the gods, the source of all the various modifications of the mind, the supreme *brahman,* the everlasting Being, the primal Lord. "All that and more thou art," says Arjuna. "Thy amazing and unique power is recognized by even the high and the mighty gods and the *rishis.* But oh *yogin* (Master of that power)! May I not know these various manifestations, so that I may be constantly reminded of Thee by them?" (X. 1-8; 12-18). That gives Lord Krishna another occasion to describe just a few of his various manifestations. He, the beginning, the middle and the end of all, is all that the eye and the mind and the imagination of man holds as the highest and the noblest and the best, in all the species of creation, real or imaginary, in all classes of existence, real or imaginary, in heaven as on earth, in the universe and in the mind of man. He is the essence of all that infinity of delights for the eye and the ear and the understanding of man that exist in Nature. He is the seed of all. Anything that is possessed of richness and the beauty and majesty arises out of a fragment of His glory. Just by a part of Him is all held (X. 12-42).

> Truly
> Earth's crammed with heaven
> And every common bush afire with God.

'We are complete in Him who is the head of every principle and potency,' said St. Paul.

And yet again Arjuna would have the Master reveal Himself still more. A vision would indeed be a more real revelation than hearing. For to see is to believe. He wonders Jf. he might not have that vision of Him. The master grants his desire. The world in front of him is not changed; his vision is transformed and made divine, and so he begins to see things he had never before seen. The Lord was there unchanged. It is not He who is transfigured, it is Arjuna who is transfigured. With this divine vision he is made to see all eternity in a moment, in narrow room Nature's whole wealth', the universe in one focus, the multifarious and myriad forms concentrated in One, as one. Sanjaya, the narrator who had stood aside all this while, steps in to lend colour and charm to the divine drama. He does so because the vision seems to bewilder him no less, and he for a moment breaks the narrative and exclaims his own wonder. How is he to give an idea of the vision to the blind king? If one could conjure up a vision of the blended splendours of a thousand suns, then perhaps something like a glimpse of that glorious vision might be given. With this he narrates in Arjuna's words the awesome majesty of that vision. For, when Arjuna's eye— even the divine eye — cannot contain the vision, his tongue breaks out in speech, and when the speech fails, the eye leaps in to rest on the vision. The Universal, Infinite, All-pervading, almighty form alternately amazes and terrifies him. The serene and the awesome aspects both are there, the Moon that soothes is one of the eyes of the Lord, the Sun that dazzles is the other eye. The Sun that gives life and warmth is there, but the Sun that scorches and burns is also there. A myriad forms are worshipping Him, and myriad forms are being devoured in His volcanic flame. And now the great war-lords are seen rushing to their doom in that divine conflagration like so many moths in a flame.

Can the Lord be terror incarnate? The eye would for a while let the tongue express its terror. 'Not only Terror incarnate, am I,' is the answer. 'I am the very Doom. I have incarnated Myself for this very purpose. The warlords, the prospect of whose death dismayed and made thee break out in a lament, are already devoured by Me. Be thou but an instrument.'

The first flashlight thrown on Arjuna's mind was in the second discourse with a revelation of Imperishable Self. The second comes now. *'Not thou,* but *I* am the Agent. If thou couldst not understand it up to now, see it with thine own eyes. Cast thou thy acts on Me and fight.'

The conviction now comes in letters of living fire and makes him break out in praise and prayer. The Birthless, the Ageless, the Being and Not-Being, the Finite and the Infinite, all the elements and what not! All and yet more in Him. He is in front and in the rear, above and below, and everywhere. Where was one to bow to Him? We must extol Him first, Him last, Him midst, and without end. In breathless adoration Arjuna utters his worshipful prayer to Him who is all, for He holds all. In unpardonable blindness he had limited Him in the form of a friend and a comrade, jested with Him and even slighted Him. Would he forgive him all that, as a father forgives his son, a friend his friend, and a lover the loved one? His thanksgiving knows no bounds, as indeed his exultation also; but so has terror too seized him. 'Wear thou again,' he prays, 'Thy form benign, and be again as Thou wast' (XI. 1-47).

What a rich vision for the *bhakta!* He may see the Lord as Creator and 'Parent of Good as in discourse 9; he may see Him as Preserver and Sustainer of all, reflected in His various manifestations which through their borrowed glory declare the parent glory, as in discourse 10; and he may see Him as the Destroyer, as in discourse 11. Indeed, if he be an Arjuna, "he may be permitted to behold the ecstatic vision of the universal form of the Lord. But whether he happens to be vouchsafed that vision or not, if he will but walk with eyes open, he will see Him shining

> In all things, in all natures, in the stars
> Of azure heaven, the unenduring clouds,
> In flower and tree, in every pebbly stone
> That paves the brooks, the stationary rocks,
> The moving waters, and the invisible air,

and utter in humble adoration,

> We, who from the breast
> Of the frail earth, permitted to behold
> The faint reflections only of Thy face
> Are yet exalted, and in soul adore!

Singing incessantly His glory, bound in steadfast devotion to Him, the *bhaktas* worship Him (XI. 14). They leave all and follow Him, because He is their all; they need not take any thought for their all, as He takes the burden of providing all that Himself (IX. 22). Their thoughts and their lives absorbed in Him, speaking and talking only of Him, they rest content exulting in His praise. Them the Lord blesses with the power to act rightly, as also with the vision of knowledge which dispels for all time their ignorance (X. 9-11). The Lord makes the dumb speak and the halt cross the mountain. Indeed, as we have it in another scripture the Lord has said: "I will guide thee with Aline eye."

But the *bhakta* must fulfil certain condition. He must not lose his hold of the Reality. Whilst he may worship god of his choice, let him not limit God in that form, let him not forget that his god is but the symbol of the Great Lord of Beings (IX. 11; IX. 23-24), let him not by a narrow vision be vain of hope and vain of work and vain of knowledge (IX. 12). "They that worship Him must worship Him in spirit and truth." Let him know that he who worships God will go to God and he who worships stone will go to stone (IX. 25). But once the *bhakta* has hold on the Reality and steadfast faith, God expects very little of him. In one word, let him do whatever he has to do—be it working, eating, sacrificing, going through any vow or penance—let him do it as an offering to Him, let him do it to His glory. For there is nothing, however trifling, offered in earnest devotion, that the Lord does not love to accept. Shabari, the pariah woman, who tasted her wild fruit, lest it be bitter, before she offered it to the Lord, and her devotion which compelled the Lord to eat the tasted fruit with extra zest, are as much remembered as the Lord Himself. A *bhakta* in such self-effacing devotion combines both *sanyasa* and *yoga* and wins to the Lord. The Lord favours none, disfavours none, but belongs to them who belongs to Him. And thus the most confirmed sinner, having resolved to die to sin and live to Him may earn the epithet of a saint.

For, although he may have wasted his substance in riotous living, he returns to be as one of the Father's hired servants. "He was dead and is alive again, he was lost and is found." Therefore, he is accepted right royally even as a saint.

'Rest assured, oh Arjuna, My *bhakta* perishes not.' The highest goal reached through *bhakti* is not the monopoly of caste or creed, race or sex, rank or station. The unlettered woman, and the petty shopkeeper, and the labourer going through "the narrow avenue of daily toil for daily bread", nay even those who are hated and despised as of foul birth, may through *bhakti* storm the gates of Heaven. Only let them dedicate their worship, their sacrifice, their mind and all their attachment to Him (IX. 26-34). Vedas are of no avail, neither austerities, nor costly gifts, nor sacrifices. Only exclusive and unwavering devotion can avail to secure a knowledge of Him. "He who does My work, who makes Me his goal, who is My devotee, who has cast off all attachment and shed all ill-will comes to Me" (XI. 53-55).

To do His will, to live in Him—that is all the *bhakta* knows. St. Paul summed up *bhakti*, the *bhakti* that was his life and meat, in a word : 'For me to live is Christ.'

Dhyanayoga and Bhaktiyoga (Discourse 12)

Lord Krishna sums up the teaching about the two forms of devotion in reply to Arjuna's question as to which of the two was the better *yogin*—he who meditated on the impersonal Lord and he who worshipped Krishna as his all. Lord Krishna's preference for the worship of the Personal is based on the same reasoning as his preference for *karmayoga* to *jnanayoga* in discourse 5. The fruit of both *dhyanayoga* and *bhaktiyoga* is the same, as we saw the fruit of *karmayoga* and *jnanayoga* was also declared to be the same. Both the meditative mystic and the *bhakta* come to the Lord. But as in discourse 5, whilst path of the *dhyanayogi* is one of hard and toilsome endeavour, that of the *bhaktiyogi* is comparatively easier. The devotee of the Absolute has to rid himself to such an extent that he sees Self everywhere and absorbs himself in the welfare of all. But inasmuch as he contemplates on the Absolute, he has nothing but his own spiritual and moral resources to draw upon. Unless the process of catharsis has reached to perfection, his effort may well be endless. But the *bhakta* with an exclusive, unwavering devotion throws himself on his Lord with all his weaknesses and imperfections, and the Lord pulls him out ere long even from the lowest depths (XII. 1-7). Perhaps the contemplative devotion to the Absolute is best achieved as a result of devotion to a personal God. Otherwise there is no difference. In the Father's many mansions there is room just as much for an iconoclast and meditative mystic like Kabir, as for Tukaram who sang: 'Be Thou formless for those who want Thee to be so, but for me take Thou on a form, O Lord! I have fallen in love with Thy name'; as much for a philosophic mystic like Akha as for Narasinha Mehta who wanted no release from birth and death but craved to be born again and again, in order to be lost in the ecstatic worship of Nandkumar (Krishna); as much for a Self-absorbed mystic like Eckhart who exclaimed: 'I ask to be rid of God, i.e. that God by His grace would bring me into the essence, that essence which is above God and above distinction,' as for St. Francis of Assisi whom the sight of the crucifix sent into trances; as much for Catherine of Siena who saw Him as 'Acceptor of Sacrifices', as for Mirabai who saw naught else in the world but Giridhar Gopala (Krishna) her beloved Lord; as much for Chaitanya whom the name of Krishna was enough, to melt into ecstacies as for Ramkrishna Paramahansa whom a vision of Kali, the Mother, sent into the same rapturous trances.

Names and forms and symbols do not matter, provided the hold on the Reality is unshaken. It is gross intolerance to label the worship of a personal God as "crass idolatry". There is no idolatry so gross as the slavery to the letter and slavery to the lusts of the flesh. The true devotee never loses sight of the Reality. *Vasudeva* Kirtikar quotes a beautiful *abhanga* of Tukaram. The poet-saint sings:

> "I made an earthen image of Shiva
> But the earth is not Shiva;
> My worship reaches Shiva,
> The earth remains the earth it was.
> I made a stone image of Vishnu
> But the stone is not Vishnu;
> My worship reaches Vishnu,
> The stone remains the stone it was.
> I made a pewter image of Amba,
> But the pewter is not Amba;
> Amba receives my worship,
> Though the pewter that pewter remains.
> Even so are saints worshipped,
> The worship reaches the Lord,
> The saint is but His servant
> An instrument, a conduit pipe."

Easy stages in the path of *bhaktiyoga* are now suggested. Concentration on work for the Lord; if even that is impossible, renunciation of the fruit of all action. This last is so simple and so convenient that from mere mechanical performance one rises to perfected renunciation: the mere practice leads on to a knowledge of its essence, this knowledge makes one concentrate one's energies on it and thence springs the perfected renunciation of fruit which brings everlasting peace (XII. 8-12).

The last eight verses contain the quintessence of *bhakti* and is a summing up of all the four discourses 9-12. *Bhakti* is no mere emotional rapture but the very perfection of humility and service of all that lives, the extinction of all 'otherness' and ill-will, and contentment in willing surrender, freedom from all depression and elation and from all unquiet care—a life in which the *bhakta* feels at ease with the world and the world feels at ease with him, where his whole joy is to do His will. And verily the man who fulfils all His will, declares the Lord, 'is the *bhakta* after Mine own heart*. That is the essence of *bhakti,* the very core of *dharma.* Dearest to the Lord are they whose life is an expression of this *bhakti,* whether they are worshippers of the Personal or the contemplative devotees of the Impersonal (XII. 13-20).

THE WORLD AND THE REALITY (DISCOURSES 13-15)

Purusha and Prakriti and Knowledge

We have already summarized discourses 13 and 14 in the introductory portion preceding this analysis and, hence, need touch on the contents but briefly. The thirteenth discourse puts together the scattered threads of the teaching about the world and the Reality found throughout the other discourses. We have the field of man's activity and the Knower of the Field described in the first six verses, we have them described again by their commonly accepted names as *prakriti* and *purusha*, with the *Purushottama* that pervades and transcends both. Wedged in between these two sets of description is a paradoxical description of the Supreme Spirit, seated in the heart of every being as the Knower of the Field. As Unmanifest It has all the negative attributes—if one may indeed call them attributes — of the Unmanifest — above all the supreme attribute of being without an attribute; and as manifested in the world It seems to possess all the attributes of the manifested world (XIII. 12-17). A knowledge of this Reality is what has been up to now held up before Arjuna as the end and the *summum bonum,* the goal which leads to immortality, but lest there should be any illusion about it that it was something like an intellectual process, the *Gita* gives an elaborate definition of knowledge, which in the very nature of things includes the means to the end. For knowledge to which one may claim to have leaped without having used or practised the means must be a travesty, and the means employed with the conscious end of unification with the Lord presupposes knowledge. Since it means final deliverance, the definition starts with deliverance from the little ills that the reason and the mind of man is heir-to. At the top of the means is freedom from pride, which is likely to survive the extinction of all other ills like passion and attachment. 'Pride is a sin of the temper,' Henry Drummond used to say, 'and is often found with the purest moral character.' It is thus a dead weight and hence the man who aspires after true knowledge must begin by "pouring contempt on all his pride." The rest of the virtues are of course there — homage to the teachers, external and internal purity, inoffensiveness, uprightness, detachment from ties that bind one to the world, inclination to solitude and a perception of the true meaning of spiritual knowledge. It includes, too, an exclusive and "unfornicating" devotion to the Lord (to use an expression of St. Augustine, which is a literal translation of the *Gita* word *avyabhicharini bhakti)* for "the soul doth commit fornications when she turns from Thee." Perhaps the Prophet of Islam expressed it in simple beauty when he said, "And whoever hopeth for the meeting with his Lord, let him do righteous work, and *make none sharer* of the worship due unto his Lord." (7-11).

Towards the end of the discourse is a recapitulation of the whole teaching: (i) The four methods of knowledge of the Self are mentioned —*jnanayoga* and *karmayoga* (discourses 3-5), *dhyanayoga* and *bhakti-yoga* (discourses 9-12) (XIII. 24-25) ; (ii) the creation of the world through the connection of *Purusha* and *Prakriti* (XIII. 26) ; (iii) a short definition of true knowledge and true vision—seeing the Supreme dwelling alike in all things, not perishing when they perish (XIII. 27-28), and seeing that it is the not-Self *(Prakriti)* that acts, not the Self, and thus' sitting content and unconcerned (XIII. 29); (iv) all diversity is based on unity and proceeds from it; (v) the nature, of the Supreme — informing every fibre of our being and untouched by it, like the ether pervading all space, untouched by it; illuminating every pore of our being as the Sun the universe; (vi) discriminate knowledge of *Purusha* and *Prakriti* and a perception of the secret of the release of the one from the other leads to the Supreme (XIII. 34).

Often enough even in the humdrum affairs of the world we catch a glimpse of this unity in diversity. Does not the happening of an earthquake (physical certainly, moral and political often enough) stir millions to a sudden realization of unity in diversity? And yet we soon return to the narrower vision and believe that diversity is all. The ether fills all space, the sun illumines every nook and cranny of the universe. We see it and yet we do not. "We have this treasure in earthen vessels, that the excellency of the power may be of God, and not of ourselves," but we cling on to earth, as though it was all and ours.

The Gunas

The constituents of *Prakriti* are, as we have already seen, exhaustively dealt with in discourse 14. We need not go over the ground already covered. One or two points not touched before may be noted here. We are bound by the *gunas,* but we have to get free from them through them, use a thorn to get rid of a thorn. The ultimate truth is the knowledge that all action, all the world is the result of the interplay of these *gunas* and that untouched and above them is He (XIV. 19). One has to transcend them to taste of immortality. The characteristics of this spiritualized *yogin* who has transcended the *gunas* are described. They are, as one can easily understand, practically the same as those of the *yogin* of secure understanding (II. 54-72), of the *dhyanayogin* (VI. 7-9; VI. 29-32), or of the *bhakta* (XII. 12-20), for the life of perfected vision always presents the same face. The *gunatita* — the spiritualized man — is neither worried when the three *gunas* are in action, nor misses them when they have ceased to act. Though in the body, he will not identify himself with any of the internal or external organs. The body, so long as it is there, will exact its toll of conscious existence, activity and sleep, the *gunatita* will pay the toll unmoved and undisturbed by them. He will thus be naturally indifferent of pleasure and pain, respect or disrespect. He will look with an equal eye on friend and foe, he will have no castles to build in the air but do what comes to his lot. The secret to reach this state is exclusive and "unfornicating" devotion to the Lord. Such an one passes beyond the *gunas* and becomes one with *Brahman* for the Lord is the image of *Brahman*, eternal law and endless bliss.

The goal is to transcend the three *gunas*, but it is not reached unless we strive to reach upward from *tamas* to *sattva*. In the seventeenth and eighteenth discourse we shall see that all *sattvika* activity is selfless activity, all *rajasa* activity is selfish, and all *tamasa* activity is ignorant and blind. Every aspirant has to reach from inertia or blindness to supreme luminous selflessness. But there is a stage beyond even that. The *Gita* simply indicates it but later commentators have explained it in detail. Thus the *Bhagavata Purana* does not rest content with defining *sattvika, rajasa* and *tamasa* knowledge, happiness, and doer, as the *Gita* has done (XVIII. 19-21; XVIII. 37-39; XVIII. 26-28), but defines the fourth variety transcending the three, viz. *nirguna* knowledge, *nirguna* happiness, and *nirguna* doer — *nirguna* variety being defined as "proceeding from the Lord". Shankaracharya, with his characteristic scientific precision, defines not the three but four *gunas,* in his *Vioekachudamani* calling the third and fourth *mishra saliva* (mixed *sattva*) and *oishuddha sattva* (pure *sattva)* respectively. The characteristics of *rajas* and *tamas* are practically the same as in the *Gita,* but those of mixed *sattva* are said to be conscious performance of virtues, conscious faith and devotion etc., whereas those of pure *sattva* are serenity, light, bliss, self-realization etc. The idea is briefly this: The three *gunas* are said to adhere together and so long as *sattva* is alloyed with *rajas* and *tamas,* no matter however minutely, *sattva* is not pure; it is pure when it has shed the alloy. The purest water in its natural state is not as pure as distilled water. Even so, as long as man is not completely spiritualized his *sattva* will have a tinge of 'self' but even that 'self' will be shed when he becomes God-man. The *gunatita* of the *Gita* is the God-man, the man for whom life in tune with the Self has become as natural as the function of breathing or circulation of blood.

ASHVATTHA AND PURUSHOTTAMA (DISCOURSE 15)

The fifteenth discourse is a restatement in different language of the truth about the world and Reality. The world is described as the *ashvattha* tree sprung from the heaven above as its root, and, therefore, ageless and changeless in its essence, the expanse of its branches coming down, and showing as the manifest world. Too often we lose sight of the Root and think of the worldly roots which are below, going up into branches which again throw down in the earth rootlets in the shape of actions which shoot up again to bear their consequences. The tree is sustained on the sap of the *gunas,* its offshoots are the sense-objects. We do not discern its beginning, basis or end. It is attachment that sustains it and through attachment man remains tied down to it. The wise hew it down with the sure axe of detachment. "Every tree that my Father hath not planted must be rooted out." Even thus can man seize hold of the Imperishable Root — the Abiding, the Imperishable Abode, whence there is no returning, which is all light, not needing a sun and moon to illuminate it. Only those who have shed all self-sense, delusion and selfish desires, who are hitched on to the Supreme, and free from the pairs reach that imperishable haven (XV. 1-6).

The process of how the cycle of birth and death goes on is now described — i.e. how the tree is planted and kept alive, how a part of the lord embodies himself as *jiva* (individual soul) and passes from birth to death and death to birth, taking the psychic apparatus of the mind and the senses of perception from everybody he leaves. It is in association with this apparatus that he experiences the sense objects, stays in and departs from the body. Him, the Supreme who is untouched by the *gunas,* only the *yogins* who have cleansed themselves see with the eye of the spirit, not the intellectual vision, which is, after all, the eye of the flesh (XV. 7-11).

The immanence of Him seated in the heart of all is again described (XV. 12-15), and *Purushottama* is held up as the supreme object of worship, called *Purushottama* (the Highest Being) inasmuch as He transcends the two beings or aspects of the world — the perishable manifest and the comparatively imperishable manifest. Transcending both He yet informs and sustains all. He who worships Him in all His forms is the man who has known all. The knowledge is the fulfillment of man's mission on earth. The supremely mysterious doctrine of which the exposition was begun in discourse 9 really finishes here, for though the description of the path of *bhakti* was concluded in the twelfth, its basis and background are concluded with this discourse.

INDIVIDUAL ETHICS (DISCOURSES 16 AND 17)

We have had throughout the previous discourses constant references to a pair of characters — enlightened and unenlightened (III. 25-26; IV. 40-41), the disciplined and the undisciplined (V. 12; XV. 11), the man of faith and the man without faith (III. 31-32; 40-41), the good-doer and the evil-doer (VII. 15-16), and so on. The author now classifies them broadly into the good and the bad, men of God and men of the devil. In doing so the *Gita* is using the language of the *Upanishads*. George Sand has somewhere divided mankind into two classes — the healthy and the unhealthy, and Coleridge says that as there is much beast and some devil in man, there is some angel and some God in him. Though broadly we may make the divisions, there are no water-tight compartments of the kind. We sometimes run towards God, harkening to the God within us, and often enough to the devil. The stably good are the rarest on earth, and yet if one were to ask them, they would say they were far away from God. Let no one, therefore, misunderstand these labels and misapply them. We may only say that when particular characteristics pre-dominate us we are of God, and when the opposite ones do so we are of the devil.

Naked we came out of our mother's womb and naked we must return to the womb of Mother Earth. But this is a partial truth. As we have seen in last discourse, we do not come quite naked, we come with something— the impress of our actions, our character, our *karma* — and we return with something, if we do. The *Gita* says that this heritage that we bring with us is either godly or ungodly, the godly helping to deliver us from .the bondage of flesh, the ungodly tightening the bondage. Fearelssness is declared to be at the top of the godly heritage of virtues, and with reason. Fear presupposes otherness, and a vision of God cures one of the otherness and hence of fear. It is thus at the root of all virtues. Then follow the cardinal virtues — truth and unoffensiveness, purity and self-restraint, and a grip of the end and the means—*jnana* and yoga, and a number of other virtues like charity, compassion, spiritedness, long-suffering, etc. The opposite of these constitute the ungodly heritage — hypocrisy, snobbery, cruelty and the like. But the *Gita* goes on to describe at length the characteristics of ungodly men. Lust and lawlessness may be said to be the law of their life, anything they do is with a view to secure those ends, for they do not accept any reign of law on earth and recognize no lawgiver. There is no godly sorrow that enlightens or enlivens their lives, they carry through life a load of ungodly sorrows which drag them down to their doom. Such people, says the Lord, He casts (or do they not cast themselves?) unto devilish wombs, the jaws of hell, for indeed they live in hell, there being no hell on earth but the one with the triple door of lust and wrath and greed (XVI. 1-21).

It is not that the path of the godly involves no struggle. He must not forget that the virtues and vices are die manifestations of the three *gunas* which coexist. They may have a preponderance, in their nature, of *sattva,* but *rajas* and *tamas* are there — dormant yet ready to awake if *sattva* relaxes its vigilance. Sleeplessly, therefore, has the godly soul to keep watch against those heralds of hell, and fight them "by the armour of righteousness on the right hand and the left" or "with the whole armour of God." (XVI. 22).

The Lord now sums up the whole teaching: 'Make *shastra* thy sole guide of conduct for he who forsakes the *shastra* comes to grief' (XVI. 23-24). This *Shastra* (science) is none other than the *yogashastra* taught in the *Gita,* the science of selflessness or detachment, considered in terms of devotion, worshipping the One Lord of all beings.

'But,' asks Arjuna in the opening verse of the seventeenth discourse, 'this *shastra* that thou hast expounded may not be understood by all, may not be acceptable to all. Would it do if they shaped their conduct according to their faith or belief in the scripture? Thou hast also before mentioned people worshipping gods, hosts, manes and other beings (IX.25). They must be doing so according to their belief in the scripture. How wouldst thou characterize their attitude—*sattvika, rajasa, or tamasa ?'* (XVII. 1).

Lord Krishna's reply covers the rest of the discourse. It all depends, He says, on the character of their belief in scripture, for like other qualities of the mind, this belief is of three kinds — *sattviki, rajasi* and *tamasi.* Man is made of the stuff of his belief, and his Object of worship will be determined by the character of his belief. Those of *sattviki* belief will worship gods, those of *rajasi* belief will worship *yakskas* and *rakshasas,* and those of *tamasi* belief will worship the spirits of the dead and ghosts. Even in their penance or austerities their belief is bound to be reflected.

Those who practise austerities not according to the science of selflessness, but out of selfishness will do so with hypocrisy and pride, passion
and desire, and torture their flesh and Me the Dweller in it. Their belief
is devilish indeed (XVII. 2-6). Their belief will even be reflected in the
kinds of food they eat (XVII. 8-10).

Indeed the three virtues in which the whole ethical conduct of man
may be summed up — sacrifice, austerity, charity — the three purifying
agents as they are called (XVIII. 5) — even these virtues can become vices
if divorced from the rule of selflessness or detachment. The belief in the
scriptures will help little. The scriptures lay down well enough that truth,
harmlessness, continence shall be practised, that sacrifice shall be offered,
that charity shall be given. But it depends on the spirit in which man
practises these scriptural injunctions. The science of selflessness declares
the spirit in which action should be done, if it is not to bind, but to free
one. Thus the *sattuika* sacrifice will be the true sacrifice — performed
Without an eye to reward and as a matter of duty, the *rajasa* one will be a
matter of show and hypocrisy, and the *tamasa* will be miscalled 'sacrifice';
for even the belief in the scripture will not play any part there, because no
scripture lays down a sacrifice in which some giving is not involved.
Austerity of the body, of the word, of the mind is indeed a sum up of
purity of conduct, humility, continence, inoffensiveness; speech which
gives no offence, truthful, sweet and helpful; serenity of mind, silence and
purity of the inner self. Now the practice of these virtues, if *sattvika*, is a
power for good. But if it were *rajasa* it would become self-serving, and if
tamasa a monstrous engine of oppression. The same is the case about charity which if done in a *sattvika* spirit would not let the left hand know what
the right hand doeth; if done in a *rajasa* spirit, would be done in expectation of return and with a flourish of trumpets; and if done in a *tamasa*
spirit, would be a wasteful and demoralizing excess (XVII. 11-22).

All works of austerity, sacrifice, and charity to be of liberating power
should, therefore, be done in a spirit of perfect dedication. *OM TAT
SAT* has been the dedicatory formula from ancient times and the worshipper and the sacrificer offering his worship and sacrifice in the name of *OM
TAT SAT*—the triple symbol of *Brahman*, would dedicate them to the
Absolute — the All-pervading, the Unconditioned, the True, the Beautiful and the Good. This is no theological formula — it simply expresses

the rules of selflessness and dedication. Let all work be dedicated to Him — however one may think of Him and by whatever name one may call Him. And dedicated work is good, all undedicated work, divorced from selflessness and scripture is bad, availing neither here nor hereafter (XVII. 23-28).

DELUSION DESTROYED (DISCOURSE 18)

The eighteenth discourse recapitulates the teaching of the *Gita,* We have had *tyaga* (abandonment) and *sannyasa* (renunciation) mentioned over and over again. In answer to Arjuna's question Lord Krishna explains the distinction that is ordinarily made between the two and shows that it is really a distinction without a difference when one considers the essence of both.

The ordinary belief, of course, means by *sannyasa* the renunciation of all action springing from desire, and since according to those who hold that belief there is no action but springs from desire, all action must be abandoned as tainted at its source and, therefore, binding. There are some who would make an exception in favour of the three purifying principles of sacrifice, austerity and charity. Lord Krishna's considered opinion is that what determines the nature of all action is not its outward expression, but the spirit in which it is done, the taint attaches not to the action as such but to the selflessness and attachment at the back of it. From that point of view, says the Law, even abandonment of action may be tainted and questionable if it is selfish, since like all other things abandonment too is of three kinds — *sattuika, rajasa* and *tamasa.* Therefore, even austerity, sacrifice and charity, if they are to be the purifying agents that they are known to be, have to be pursued without desire for fruit and without attachment (as we have already seen in the seventeenth discourse). Then there are obligatory acts that one has to perform as a member of the social organism, and they may not be abandoned. To abandon them out of a deluded sense of one's being above those humdrum tasks, is blind — *tamasa* — abandonment indeed. To abandon them because they are troublesome or arduous is sheer selfishness — *rajasa* abandonment. The ideal abandonment is the abandonment of fruit and of the attachment in respect of all action that comes to one's lot. That indeed is pure *tyaga* and pure *sannyasa,* call it what one will. As for *sannyasa* — renunciation of *all* action it is a physical impossibility so long as one bears the body: it is only the fruit and attachment that can be the objects of abandonment, and those must be abandoned by all aspiring to be free from the cycle of birth and death. Those who do not abandon the desire for fruit cannot escape the reward — good, bad, or mixed in the shape of rebirth in the different species (XVIII. 1-12).

The *Gita* next describes the necessary factors in all action — the body, the agent, various instruments, various processes, and the unseen element working to bring about the completed act. These factors show an interdependence of all Nature, show how "all substance lives by countless actions interknit". It is futile, therefore, for man to take the burden of agency on oneself. From another point of view, when there are these various factors at work—which briefly described are nothing but *gunas* — the unconditioned *Atman* cannot be the agent. The wise man who has woven this truth into his life and has thus annihilated all 'self' will not be held responsible for anything he does, yea even though he annihilated all the worlds (XVIII. 13-17).

Now follows a description of the three *gunas* as they are reflected in all the things of life to show how they determine their character, and make it pure, alloyed, or impure as the case may be. Thus these three kinds of agent, act, perception, understanding, will, happiness, are described, in order that man may never bend his energies zestfully and without thought of success or failure (XVIII. 26) to rise from the impure to the pure, from selfishness to selflessness, from darkness to light.

'From the unreal lead me to the Real,
From darkness lead me to Light,
From death lead me to Deathlessness.'

Let him blazon on the tablet of his mind three things: pure act or pure abandonment is the performance of what comes to one's lot, without attachment, without like or dislike, without thought of reward; pure perception is the vision of unity in all diversity; pure happiness is the straining for eternal bliss through arduous, even apparently painful endeavour (XVIII. 18-40).

These *gunas* are thus woven into every fibre of man's being; no one is free from them not even the gods (40). The four-fold division of the social organism is also based on what gifts and what special aptitudes one can bring to bear for the service of the organism. A *Brahman's* function or work presupposes and must evidence the qualities of serenity, self-denial, long-suffering, spiritual knowledge; a *Kshatriya's* work, the qualities of valour, spiritedness, magnanimity; a *Vaishya's* work will be the production of wealth from land, cows and commerce; and a *Shudra's* work is to help the rest by bodily labour (XVIII. 41-44).

Each one doing his allotted task in the proper spirit is sure to win his salvation. Only it should be done in His name, and as an offering of service to Him. Disinterested work for Him, i.e. for all God's creatures is true worship. Under the circumstances there is no occasion for choice, for choice may involve one in interestedness. One's own duty, though uninviting, is better than that of other's which, though seemingly easier of performance, may ultimately prove a snare and a delusion. A man's birth on earth is a result of bondage to one's *karma* and, therefore, involves this inherent imperfection, all actions done by the body would be inherently imperfect in some respect or other. But the alchemy of detachment will turn all imperfection into perfection. Let man go through life in a complete spirit of detachment, and his detachment will win him the supreme perfection of non-binding action (45-49).

The author now proceeds to show how the man who has achieved this secret of converting all binding action into non-binding action ultimately rests in the final stage of knowledge. We find ultimately all the *yogas* coalescing here. This selfless work purifies his understanding, his whole self will have been brought under the control of his will, he will cast off likes and dislikes for objects of sense, and equipped with perfect discipline and dispassion he will be intent on meditation. He will thus cast off everything that presupposes a sense of 'I' or 'mine' and thus fit himself for being one with all Nature. Having become one with all Nature, he will be at peace with himself, will regard all creation alike, and will be suffused with the purest devotion to the Lord, will know him in all his greatness, discover Him truly and enter Him (XVIII. 50-55). Compare these verses with this passage from the mystic Ruysbroeck and note how in his description all mysticisms coalesce : "He goes towards God by inward love, in eternal work, and he goes in God by his fruitive inclination in eternal rest. And he dwells in God, and yet he goes out towards created things in a spirit of love towards all things, in the virtues and in works of righteousness. And this is the most exalted summit of the inner life."

The whole doctrine is now summed up and Arjuna finally exhorted to awake to a sense of his duty: 'Throw thyself on Me and do everything that comes to thee at every time, as at My instance, to My glory. Thus shalt thou by My grace attain to the supreme goal, by My grace cross over every obstacle. But if thou wilt not listen to. Me, fancying that thou canst escape thy duty, rest assured, thy nature will assert itself and will compel thee. What thou wilt not do at My bidding thou shalt do at the bidding of thy nature and so perish. The Lord is seated in the heart of every being. It is open to them to listen to His bidding, and put themselves in His hands; but if they will not, then the Lord will let them be whirled round as on a machine, and dance to the tune of their *prakriti*. In Him therefore seek refuge, His grace shall lead thee to lasting peace' (XVIII. 56-62).

"That Lord," Krishna again reassures Arjuna, "am I. I have revealed to thee, My beloved, the supreme mystery. Consider it fully and act as thou wilt. Dedicate thy thought, thy worship, thy sacrifice, thy homage to Me and I solemnly promise that thou shalt come to Me. Disturb not thyself by conflicting duties. Seek refuge in Me. I will deliver thee from sin. Sorrow rot" (XVIII. 63-66).

The Lord finally warns Arjuna not to waste the doctrine on those who have no qualifications to take it in—no self-restraint, no devotion, no inclination to listen. Narration of the doctrine, conveyed in the dialogue, by worthy persons to worthy persons, will endue them with true devotion. A devout study of it will be a kind of 'knowledge sacrifice' offered to God, a devout listening will earn the listeners brighter worlds of birth (XVIII. 67-71).

'Has thy ignorant delusion now been destroyed?' asks the Lord at the end. The final flash-light revealing Krishna's knowledge of Arjuna's true make-up has clinched the matter and Arjuna exclaims with the serenity of certitude and the conviction of religious faith that his doubts have been resolved, that he has recovered his knowledge of the true Self and that he would do His bidding (XVIII. 72-73).

With that Sanjaya's story ends, but the ecstatic vision haunts him, the accents of the divine discourse reverberate in his memory. Fain would he love to linger on the memory of it all. But rather than make the blind king sadder thereby he concludes: 'What more shall I say? Where the Lord of *yoga* expounds the doctrine and where there is one most fitted to carry it out, there is bound to be eternal right and hence sure victory.'

That, one takes it, made the blind king resigned to the inevitable. Perhaps he saw that therein lay the good of all.

VI. A FEW QUESTIONS

I have discussed a few points which were necessary to an understanding of the analysis that followed. I propose now to discuss a few questions that arise from the teaching and are often raised.

THE FOUR VARNAS AND SVADHARMA

Quite an amount of ignorant criticism is levelled at the doctrine of the performance of *svadharma* (one's duty or function) taught in the *Gita* and the reason for it is the much-abused *varna* system. This is no place for making out a case for or against the so-called 'caste-system'. It is necessary here to make a few points clear and to point out the bearing of the system on the *Gita* doctrine. Much of the criticism is directed against a thing which is just a shadow of what existed ages ago. There was a system which existed in ages gone by, which served the then existing social organism magnificently, which was elastic and hence made it possible for a number of different groups of the same race and several races to live together in amity and peace. What we see today is its travesty, a fossil formed out of the incrustations of customs and practices of several centuries. Let not one judge the original from the ghost of it, and say that the author of the *Gita* sought to clothe a loathsome thing with divine sanction. The system of *varnas* we find described is certainly no rigid one. The division is no division into water-tight compartments. If the *Gita* can be said to admit a division, that division is, as we have seen, into two classes — *daiva* (divine) and *asura* (devilish) — and that too would hardly appear, on examination, to be a permanent division, inasmuch as there is an eternal war going on between the divine and the devilish in us, no matter to what class or caste *we belong. It is therefore difficult for man to characterize or label brother man. If he cannot label himself correctly, much less can he label anyone else. Let us note then the main features of that elastic system: (i) The division was entirely vocational, in order that each might serve the best interests of the organism. If men devoted themselves to tasks for which their character and aptitude best fitted them, they would be able to give of their best to the community. — The criterion was not what one needed but what one could give to the community; (ii) The division had regard to the requirements of the *then* existing society and these were broadly divided into (a) intellectual and spiritual, (b) defence, (c) production of wealth by (1) intelligent economy and by (2) labour. Each requirement was assigned to be fulfilled by a class possessing the particular gifts necessary for its fulfillment. The evident inequality of individual attainments was recognized, but the possession of gifts added to one's responsibility rather than improved one's rank. Thus to possess naught was. one of the characteristics of a *Brahmana* whose wealth was that of spirituality and self-denial, while the production of wealth for the community was necessary for a *Vaishya*, to provide body labour was the privilege of a *Shudra*. (iii) Purity or virtue was the monopoly of none. Salvation was through the proper selfless performance of one's task. The *Bhagawata Purana* describes what have been rather loosely described as functions *(karmani)* in the *Gita* as the natural characteristics — *(prakritayah)* — of the various classes and then says, the ethical rule of life is the same for all, viz. inoffensiveness, truth, non-thieving, freedom from wrath and greed, desire to do good to mankind. Hence salvation was more difficult for those who had greater tasks to perform and easier for those entrusted with humbler functions. For these were not cumbered with much knowledge. Whilst it was easy, for instance, for a butcher or for a scavenger to carry on his forefather's profession with equanimity and detachment and as a sacrifice offered to God, it was quite likely for a learned *Brahmana* to darken counsel with much learning and even "with devotion's visage and pious action sugar o'er the devil himself." Among the Indian saints we have fewer from among the *Brahmanas* than from the non-*Brahmanas*. Among the saints of revered memory, Sena was a barber, Sajana was a butcher, Gora a potter, Raidas a cobbler, Chokhamela an untouchable, Tukarama a *kunbi,* and so on.

None disclaimed his profession but worked his salvation through a detached prayerful performance of it. (iv) The functions were hereditary because heredity is a law of nature, but there were no exclusive divisions, as we know from several cases of intermixture of functions and *varnas* in the *Mahabharata.* (v) The organism is shattered to pieces today and there are no defined classes that can answer to the description of the old *varnas,* but the rule to respect the law of nature may stand even today and all societies which are to any extent well-ordered would on examination be found to be based on a vocational division of some kind.

'What then is one to do when performance of one's *dharma* is considered to be the highest morality, and *dharma* is to be determined by the shattered caste system?' is a Critic's poser. The answer is that *dharma* or one's duty or the task to which one is born is no wooden phrase. It means the task to which one is born in the particular time or place we have in view.

> New occasions teach new duties,
> Time makes ancient good uncouth;

and whilst one's allotted task may have been fighting 2500 years ago, today it may be to carry on a bloodless war to end all wars; whilst it may have been a duty to kill a foe then, today it may beyone's duty to lay down one's life in defending a sacred principle or individual or national honour. 'One's allotted task' has its natural meaning and it should not be more difficult for any one in India to find it out than it is for anyone in the West. This is how a modern author on Ethics expresses the moral law: "Thou shalt labour within thy particular province, with all thy heart and with all thy soul and with all thy strength and with all thy mind." That is too what Carlyle meant when he said: "Know what thou canst work at, and work at it like a Hercules." The *Gita* makes the moral law clearer than any other ethical system in the world by adding to the above somewhat to this effect : 'Work like a Hercules indeed, but offer thy work at the feet of the Lord as your humble flower of worship, without the thought of reward. A selfish performance even of the best thing would render it worse than void.' For, according to the *Gita,* doing one's duty is not the highest morality as our critic would assert; doing one's duty in complete detachment and selflessness is the highest morality. Provided the work taken up is not morally forbidden, the sole criterion to determine its moral value is detachment, selflessness. Selflessness is the sole content of right.

'But why, then, this insistence on *svadharma* and *paradharma?*' the critic rejoins. 'The *Gita* has no answer to give but this, viz. doing of other's duty is dangerous.' Why does the critic want a better answer? The reason lies in the experience of the seer that when one runs after a duty which is not his he runs into a pit. Duties, like things, come to those who prayerfully wait not to those who run after them. As Cardinal Newman sweetly said:

> "So works the All-wise! Our services dividing
> *Not as we ask:*
> For the world's profit, by our gifts deciding
> Our *duty-task."*

KNOWLEDGE A TALISMAN?

Throughout the *Upanishads*, says Hume, "metaphysical knowledge" is held up as a "magic talisman" and in distinguishing the Socratic doctrine of the identity of knowledge and virtue from the *Upanishadic* doctrine, he says that in the *Upanishads*, "the possession of metaphysical knowledge actually cancels all past sins and even permits the knower unblushingly to continue in 'what seems to be much evil' with perfect impunity, although such acts are heinous crimes and are disastrous in their effect for others who lack that kind of knowledge," Later on he saves himself from this extreme position by a number of qualifications which the *Upanishads* themselves, compel him to make, but finally reverts-to the charge that "moral distinctions do not obtain for the man who has metaphysical knowledge." This is not the place to examine this extraordinary-statement made by such an eminent, scholar and apparently a votary of the, *Upanishads*. But mention of it has become necessary inasmuch as he has made the same charge against the *Gita*. The *Gita*, according to him, adopts the *Upanishadic* position as stated by him, and under, the authority of the *Katha Upanishod* 1. 2. 19 (repeated in *Gita* II. 19) that "This one slays not nor is slain", "the divine incarnation quells the scruples of Arjuna over, the murdering of his enemies."

The first thing to see is whether *the Gita* adopts the position that "'metaphysical knowledge" permits the perpetration of crimes? Without examining the statement in any detail that that is the position of the *Upanishads, just* one or two things may be mentioned. The doctrine that knowledge is not only virtue but that it leads to salvation and nothing else does it, may be traced to the famous Vedic text which declares: 'What will he do with, a knowledge of the text, who has not known That?' That Vedic text to my 'mind emphasizes the distinction between dry learning and metaphysical knowledge which suffuses every pore of one's being, that furnace-fire that turns, the whole iron into fire. This distinction was never lost sight of in the *Upanishads.* The trouble is due to the unfortunate English word 'knowledge' which has not the content of *jnana* which far from meaning mere metaphysical knowledge means a new vision, a new life, a rebirth., The Greek, word *gnosis* as used by the Gnostics has that full content and means a full unification with the Universal Self, or as Prof. Nicholson points out a complete "realization of the, fact that the appearance of 'otherness' beside Oneness is a false and deluding dream. Gnosis lays the spectre which haunts unenlightened men all their lives, which rises like a wall of utter darkness between them and God." The" *Upanishads* make the meaning *of jnana* clear beyond any misunderstanding. But let us content ourselves with the *Gita.* If there is anything about which all the commentators' of the *Gita* are agreed — for the simple reason that there is no room for misunderstanding — it is the content arid the conditions of *jnana.* Is it possible to have more comprehensive definition of *jnana* than we have in XIII. 7-11 already noticed in detail in the foregoing analysis (Pp. 88-89)? It sums up elaborately the moral life that leads up to the vision, not temporary, but permanent of the Dweller in 'the inner-most. It is the transformed life of the seer which is the subject of those nineteen verses in the second discourse (II. 54-72) and we have the substance of it repeated at ^very stage. The third discourse is concluded with the statement that the spiritual enemy of man has to' be killed by taking hold of the highest (III. 43). The fourth defines knowledge over again, not by an assurance' of impunity to one who has knowledge, but by declaring the unique purifying power of knowledge(IV. 38) which is no knowledge unless it makes one see the whole creation in one's Self and in God (IV. 35). The fifth is a paean of praise of the transformed life where the whole mind and heart and soul of man are cleansed by all impurity and made a worthy dwelling for the perpetual abode of the Deity (V.17). The sixth repeats the comprehensiveness of the transformed vision in words unforgettable (VI. 29-32). But need we go on? We should then have to summarize the whole *Gita* over again. And the conditions of real knowledge are writ large on every page of the *Gita* [II. 54-72; XIL 13-20; XlV. 22-26; XV. 5; XV. 11; XVI (whole); XVIII. 51-55 etc.]. Not With the eye of the flesh shall one see Him, but with the eye of the spirit is the burden of every verse dealing *with jnana.* It is possible for one to wrench verses from their context, as Hume has wrenched texts from the *Upanishads,* and say that *jnana* is presented as the panacea for all ills. We can quote a string of such verse - IV.9, IV. 14; IV. 32; V. 29; IX. l; X. 3; XIII. 18; XIII. 23; XIV. 1; XIV. 19 and many more — but will anyone have the hardihood to maintain *that jnana* in these verses has a narrower content than the *jnana* referred to in the whole contexts we cited a little while ago? No, not even an enemy of *Gita* can misunderstand the content of knowledge. Whoever will misunderstand the famous verse in which St. John declared: "Whosoever abideth in Him sinneth not"? For it is apparent to the meanest understanding that he who abideth in Him cannot bear to breathe anywhere else. *Jnana* is knowledge of Him in truth, and entering Him and abiding in Him (XI. 54; XVIII. 55). It is no intellectual or metaphysical jugglery, but a refinement of the whole soul by taking it through the fiery furnace of self-discipline. Metaphysical knowledge is necessary, but it is the beginning and not the end. "Life is different," says Dr. Radhakrishnan, "from the moment of insight. The vision of the One is the beginning of the process of conversion. The soul has seen, the mind must consent, and the heart approve. The new experience must control our whole being, the word recognized as true must become flesh." The statement that sin does not touch a man of knowledge or that knowledge turns all sin to cinders means in one case that sin dare not approach a seer, and in the other that sins, or more accurately past *karma*, will cease to take effect like parched seeds which do not sprout. It is in this sense that the *Maitri Upanishad* in a beautiful image says:

'As to a mountain that's enflamed
Deer and birds do not resort—
So with *Brahman* knowers, faults
Do never any shelter find.

Are there not then *any* verses in the *Gita* which have an anlinomian odour? There are two — perhaps three — which may be cited, viz. VI. 31, XIII. 23 and XVIII. 17. But in the first the condition mentioned would leave no room for any suspicion that by knowledge anything less than the transformed vision is meant. For what else can be meant by, 'he who, anchored in Unity, worships Me abiding in all things'? The second must be read in the light of the whole teaching of the *Gita*. The third, i.e. XVIII. 17 would appear to have semblance of antinomianism and a parallel verse or two (even more extravagantly worded) may be cited from the *Upanishads*. But let us see what is antinomianism and then find out if the verse in question can bear to be labelled as antinomian. Pascal who exposed the casuistry of the Jesuits of his days in his "Letters to a Provincial" thus quoted the Jesuit Father's defence of homicide : "The Father proceeded: In so far as it is in our power we turn away from forbidden things; but when we are unable to prevent the action, we at least try to purify the intention, and so correct the vice of the means by the purity of the end. That is how our Fathers have been able to permit acts of violence which are committed in defence of honour: It is only necessary to turn away one's intention from the desire of vengeance which is criminal and to restrict it to the desire of defending one's honour which is a lawful desire." Are the positions taken in *Gita* XVIII. 17 and in this quotation from Pascal the same? There is between the two positions all the difference that there is between GOD and DOG though the letters in both the words are the same. He who has rid himself of all sense of 'I' will have no left 'I' to put up any defence for anything he does. The very anxiety to defend himself will recoil on him and make a mockery of all his claim to freedom from egotism and to pure intent. The words in the *Gita* are not put in the mouth of Arjuna, but of Lord Krishna who is giving Arjuna glimpses of perfect knowledge every now and then in varying language, and asking Arjuna to fight not for himself but for His sake and in His name. As Gandhiji has said in his note on XVIII. 17 the verse describes the condition of God or a God-man—a *gunatita*. It is God alone who can slaughter all the worlds, not man.

We come now to the second charge of Hume which is already partly answered. We shall rest content with showing that the little statement that under the authority of metaphysical teaching "the divine incarnation quells the scruples of. Arjuna over the murdering of his enemies contains three misstatements. I shall briefly attempt to show this. (1) The metaphysical truth does, not quell Arjuna's doubt. If it did, the *Gita* should have been finished at verse II. 19. But it is the beginning of the argument which ends in the eighteenth discourse. The metaphysical truth is mentioned to assure him that, his lament was misdirected. Nowhere in the *Gita* is Arjuna represented as having grasped-knowledge — metaphysical or spiritual; he is assured and he is convinced,: that if he left all conflict of duties and followed Him, and did, not what; he had reasoned out as belonging to his self, but as God bade him to do, he would incur no sin, and that sort of dedicated performance of one's duty led to true knowledge. (2) Arjuna had no scruples over fighting his enemies; any scruples that he had were over I having to slaughter his kinsmen. (3) Arjuna lived in an age when war was not taboo— even we are yet far off from that golden age — and he had not the slightest suspicion that killing one's enemies in war was "murder". The first argument — the statement of the metaphysical truth — makes him pause and think. The second where the climax is reached convinces him that he has to be but an instrument. Vengeance was not his, but God's who said: 'Vengeance is Mine, I have already repaid' (XI. 33). The third and the last argument is that however much he might delude himself, his nature was sure to assert itself. That dispels all delusion and doubt. He sees clearly that Krishna knew his Arjuna better than Arjuna himself. He knew how "the elements mixed in him."

But, it may be said, any man may call himself an instrument in the hands of God and perpetrate all kinds of excesses. Such an one has yet to arise and be believed in by the world! The exhortation to fight without the feverish delusion of ignorance (III. 30), and to become an instrument in His hands (XI. 33) was addressed to Arjuna who had cleansed himself of all desire for sovereignty, enjoyment and life (1.32). Apparently, at any rate, he had no interest left in fighting and that is why he, was worthy enough to be urged to fight without the thought of reward of the sense of 'I'. The divine sermon would have been lost on a Duryodhana or a Kama or even a Bhima, who could not have fought without the thought of 'I', without the thought of success or failure, without hatred or vengeance.

It is one in millions that God thus chooses to do His will, whilst the rest go oil from life to life, struggling to find but what is. God's will. Arjuna was that rare one whom God had chosen to, make him know His will and to do it. And after all is said and done, it is God who is represented as justifying Arjuna's conduct, not Arjuna.

Let hot Christian friends run away with the thought that the teaching, however one explains it away, is bound to mislead people. There is indeed the fear of the *Gita* being used in defence of murder, but the world has luckily its rough arid ready standard to judge the man who makes the claim to murder in God's name. There is indeed Hitler today who, boiling with rage and burning with hate which he does not conceal, vows vengeance against the whole Jewish race arid declares: "By fighting against the Jews I am doing the Lord's work." The world does not believe that he is doing God's work, nor would it do so if a follower of the *Gita* made such a claim. Besides, die Hindu has. from ancient times had handed down to him the glorious example of the seer Dadhichi who laid down his life and offered his bones to be made into a thunderbolt to fight miscreants, of king Shibi who risked his life in order that the life of a dove may be saved, of Prahlad and Sudhanva who went through untold ordeals for His sake — not one Christ but many Christs if I may permit myself to say so. However, the test; after all, is not the claim advanced by the doer of the deed, but how the world judges him.

KARMA AND FREE-WILL

We have already discussed the doctrine of *karma* and rebirth. Whilst one critic says that the author of the *Gita* contradict himself by asserting the doctrine of *karma* in one breath and the doctrine of grace in the other (IX. 27-28; XVIII. 56, 58, 66), another critic says that there is no freedom of will in the *Gita* and man is but an automaton— 'a being spun round on a machine' (XVIII. 59), asked to be no more than an instrument (XI. 33).

The first criticism betrays ignorance of the doctrine of *karma*, and may be disposed of in a paragraph. The doctrine of *karma* or the moral law contains and comprehends the doctrine of grace. The same law that tells us that we shall reap as we shall sow, also tells us that if we throw ourselves on God in a broken and contrite spirit our contrition will by His grace result in rebirth. Mercy and grace form but another phase of God's justice, in fact mercy is ever hidden in His justice if we can but see it. The critic's objection arises solely from the orthodox Christian's belief in grace coming from somewhere outside man. But, as Principal Gaird says, "that to which we thus surrender ourselves is in reality our truer self", — God who is in the heart of man.

The criticism about the absence of free-will must be dealt with in some detail, though that too involves the orthodox Christian assumption we have just mentioned. Man's *prakriti*, the make-up with which he is born is, as we have seen, the result of the past and has to be reckoned with. There is no short-cut to the goal, it must be through the handicaps and hurdles that are a necessary condition of the race. But He who has determined the race and the conditions has also endowed man with the capacity to cope with them. A man born dumb and blind cannot obviously speak and see, but a Hellen Keller born dumb and blind can do better than speak and see — infinitely better than millions who speak and see but who really don't speak and see. 'By thyself shall thou free thyself, for Self is the friend of self and Self is self's foe' (VI. 5-6).

The material is given to us, we can use that and no other, but we have freedom in the manner of using it. Dr Radhakrishnan employs a happy simile: "Life is like a game of bridge. The cards in the game are given to us. We do not select them. They are traced to past *karma*, but we are free to make any call as we think fit and lead any suit. Only we are limited by the rules of the game. We are more free when we start the game than later on, when the game has developed and our choice becomes — restricted. But till the very end there is always a choice. A good player will see possibilities which a bad one does not. The more skilled a player the more alternatives does he perceive. A good hand may be cut to pieces by unskilful play and bad play need not be attributed to the frowns of fortune. Even though we may not like the way in which the cards are shuffled we like the game and we want to play." I would just add one word: the cards seem to be given to us, though really they are chosen by us, or rather they belong to us, for the law of *karma* works not from outside but in us and through us.

It depends on how one defines free-will. If it is a will free of all law, man has no such will, or plenty of it to go to the devil with. The fact is that our freedom is commensurate with our freedom from all that we falsely identify with Self. Even the most unfortunate of us is endowed with the consciousness of Self, and his conduct will be free to the extent that he is conscious of that Divine in him. "To thine own Self be true, and it shall follow as the night the day thou canst not then be false to any man," said Shakespeare in his immortal language. We have to be true to our Self, and "the truth shall make us free."

God is not outside us. He is in the heart of us all and we perpetually revolve round Him. The unfortunate part is that most of us forget that we revolve round Him and feel that we revolve round some other centre, the centre of our narrow selves. The centre is within us, but we have made an orbit with a centre outside us. When we are under that delusion we fare no better than automatons, but when we live and move and have our being in Self, we can share the exultation of the Sufi who said:

"I fare as one by whose majestic will
The world revolves, floods rise, rivers flow,
Stars in their courses move."

He can sing thus because his will coincides with the Divine will. When Mathew Arnold sings:

We, in some unknown Power's employ
Move on a rigorous line;
Can neither, when" we will, enjoy
Nor when we will, resign;

he expresses one phase of the truth. We cannot enjoy and we cannot resign, because we want to do, so when we should not. The Power knows better, and will .not let us do what we should not. If we will but understand the Power we will not fret against the captivity but will sing with Newman:

So long Thy power hath blest me, sure it still
Will lead me on.

There is no freedom and no peace except in conforming our will to
His will. When the *Gita* asks us to be mere instruments in His hand, it is
not any outside master that we are asked to obey but the Master who is in
us. We have the freedom of surrendering ourselves' to the Worthiest of
Masters, but we delight in pandering to unworthy ones. We pine for an
unrestricted, undetermined free-will, which is but a will-o-the wisp,
forgetting that

Our wills are ours, we know not how
Our wills are ours to make them Thine.

Seated in the heart of all He does see beings 'whirled, mounted on a
machine', says the *Gita* (XVIII. 61) but we are also told: 'Go, and seek ye
shelter' in Him, and by His grace not only shall you cease to be whirled,
but rest in the Abode of Everlasting Peace. (XVIII. 62).

VII. SOME CONTROVERSIES

I fear I shall be charged with having tarried unnecessarily long over questions and controversies raised by Western critics, and with having ignored
those which have raged here. In the nature of the case, I could, not ignore
the former, for the readers of die book are likely to be familiar more with
them than the latter. As regards these latter, it may be worthwhile noticing
a few broad aspects here, Only so far as they have a bearing, on the teaching of the *Gita*. We need not go into the philosophical: controversies of an
earlier age which have little practical value today, but it is necessary to refer
to the points at issue between Shankaracharya and Lokamanya Tilak. The
Lokamanya entirely accepts the philosophical position of the great Acha-
rya, but finds fault with him for placing an excessive emphasis on *jnana*
and for having subtly but, in his opinion, unsuccessfully,, argued away the
necessity for action on the part of the man who has attained *jnana*. Now,
though it is obvious that Shankaracharya over and over again attacks
action as the root of bondage, it is Vedic ritualism that is the target of his
attack and not all action as such, and he recognizes in so many words,

often enough, that a *jnani's* activities, whatever they may be, will be all for the good of the world. The Lokamanya naturally impatient' of the *soi-disant jnanis* of the present day, revelling in intellectual jugglery and shunning all action, unjustly ; attributes this philosophical lotus-eating to Shankaracharya's insistence on a man of knowledge refraining from action. The man of knowledge that Shankaracharya has in mind is the perfected man of self-realization and' not the one who is the target of the Lokamanya's attack, and the activity, Shankaracharya taboos, is not *all* activity, but all self-ful activity, all activity that binds. Shankaracharya's own life of strenuous activity is an eloquent testimony to this. The two giants are thus at cross purposes and the whole controversy in the ultimate analysis would seem to be an unnecessary one. There is perhaps a difference between their conceptions of the perfected man or man-God, but it is after all a question of difference in temperaments due to the different ages in which they livid. But in Spite of this difference I cannot conceive them differing as to the ultimate ideal that the *Gita* sets up before us.

Another controversy pertains to the efficacy of selfless action. The followers of Shankaracharya contend that even selfless action cannot lead to Freedom, it leads to self-purification only, and knowledge alone can lead to Freedom. The followers of the Tilak school contend, on the other hand, that selfless action leads directly to Freedom. Now this controversy is equally futile, inasmuch as one school has in mind the intermediate steps leading up to the final goal, the other thinks only of the final goal and omits the intermediate steps. An earnest aspirant will throw all the energies in the pursuit of the goal, absorbed in the means and not even thinking of the goal. And what after all is self-purification in the highest sense, but just the last step to, if not almost the same thing as, Knowledge and Freedom? The *Gita* asks us over and over again to be anchored in perfect purity. Let us see what it is. Eckhart has defined it in language which it is impossible to improve upon. 'What is purity?' he asks, and answers: 'It is that a man should have turned himself away from all creatures and have set his heart so entirely on the Pure Good that no creature is to him a comfort, that he has no desire for aught creaturely, save so far as he may apprehend there in the Pure Good which is God. And as little as the bright eye can endure aught foreign in it, so little can the pure soul bear anything in it, any stain on it, that comes between it and God.'

The highest purity is thus abiding in God, oneness with God. When this is realized, it is the same thing whether you say that selfless action leads to self-purification or that selfless action leads to self-realization or Freedom.

VIII. CONCLUSION

I shall now conclude with a summary of the teaching of the *Gita* which stands out untouched by the dust and din of controversies. The *Gita* gives us a glimpse of Mt. Kailasa where Shiva dwells, keeps it ever before our vision even whilst we are trudging towards it, still leagues away in point of space and ages away in point of time, and declares in no uncertain terms that we have to scale the heights leading up to that highest peak where dwells the Lord of the Worlds, that we have not only to reach the peak but to realize that that really is our home whence we had fallen away and that the Lord occupying that pinnacled throne is none but the Lord in us—in a word that *Jiva* is *Shiva,* i.e. that the individual Self is the Universal Self. The *Gita* also every now and then gives us a glimpse of the souls who have scaled the heights and achieved the vision, who are "made One with Nature" — *brahmabhutah* (V. 24; XIV. 26; XVIII. 54); who like God Himself are seated 'as though indifferent, unattached to all they do' (IX. 9; XIV. 23); who work out the law of their being slumberless, even as the heavens themselves, who

> "Though so noble, share in the world's toil
> And though so tasked, keep free from dust and soil;"

who have so died to sin that "all battle of virtues" has ceased in them and who, therefore, however they live and move, live and move and have their being in Him (VI. 32). Some of these may not seem to work in our sense of the term, but their seeming inactivity will be the highest form of activity, as indeed their activity will be the purest form of repose. Their heart will throb with the heart of humanity, and their life will be lived in consonance with the great law.

> That does preserve the stars from wrong
> And the most ancient heavens through whom are fresh and
>   strong.

Shall we presume to legislate for them? Even the *Gita* does not.

That is the ideal that we have to achieve and the *Gita* says in one word, 'if you would be one with God acquit yourselves like men.' Only by working out our destinies as men can we work up to Godhood and there is no other way. There is work that binds and work that frees. The moving finger writes and moves on inexorably, but it can cancer all it has written, if only one will surrender the finger to Him. As it is, the work that man is born and wedded to until his dying day is a leaden chain of bondage,7 but you, can, says the *Gita*, transmute it into a golden ladder leading to Freedom, if only you will use the sovereign alchemy of selflessness, detachment, self-sacrifice, 'knowledge,' says the *Gita*, 'makes ashes of all action, as the fire of the fuel.' ?; But even as all fuel contains the fire within; all detached action contains" the purifying and! freedom-giving knowledge within. That is the' law bf dedicated activity or self-sacrifice and we must fulfill the Law, if we' would reach the state that — is beyond all law and legislation; "He who sacrifices himself, seeing the Self in all creation, and all creation in the Self, attains *svarajya*— (salvation)," — says the *Manusmriti* and that sums tip the; royal road of the *Gita*. That is the essential teaching of the *Gita*, and as such it has a universal appeal; All else that lends a local colour to the *Gita* is but a-setting incidental to the time and place in which, and, the person through — whom, it took, shape. All, the rest of the things —*karma*, and rebirth, and *varna* and even the belief in the Incarnation — are more or less, like scaffolding to the edifice, unessentials after all. They, do not touch the; universal law, which has been practised in all ages and in all climes by those who, whether they believed or not in these unessentials, lived and moved in conformity with the essential law. To recount such a succession of names is, in the language of Prof. James, "to feel encouraged and washed in better air. The lives of the illustrious founders of the different faiths apart, what were the lives of those souls but lives of utter self-spending, self-effacement, self-dedication? – the lives of Job and Harishchandra; of Janaka and Marcus Aurelius, and Jalaluddin Rumi; of Plotinus and Epictetus; of St. Paul, St. Augustine and St. Ignatius; of Vidyaranya, of Shankaracharya and Eckhart; of St. Francis and St. Catherine of Siena, Sister Julian and St. John of the Gross; of Chaitanya, Kabir, and Tulsidas; of Jnaneshvar, Ramdas and Tukaram; of Mirabai and Andal; of Akho and Narasinha Mehta; of Spinoza and Lessing and Savonarola; of Pascal and Fenelon; of Bunyan,, Wesley and Fox; of Howard and Pasteur and Madame Curie; of Father Damien and Cardinal Newman y of Lincoln and General, Gordon —not I to mention the names, of the living, or of those of our own times.

The reader will not fail to notice that I have included in these names those of Lincoln, who directed one of the fiercest, civil wars in history; and of Gordon Whose hands may be said to be dripping, with blood for the best part of his life, and of Pasteur much of whose work for humanity depended on his experiments involving vivisection In doing so, I am not oblivious of Gandhiji's view that perfect renunciation or *yoga* is impossible without perfect observance of truth and non-violence, I have included these names because I cannot forget that if it can be said with truth of any, one that he waged a war "with malice towards none, with charity for all, with firmness in the right as God gives us to see the right", it can be said of Lincoln, the whole whose life was one of spotless self-dedication and whose every private or public individual action revealed a devotion; to truth and non-violence; because in the transparent record of Gordon's life one can read the truth of his statement that he was a chisel which cuts the wood; the carpenter directs it. If I lose the edge, He must sharpen me; if He puts me aside and takes another, it is His own good will;" because Pasteur's life was a pure flame of passionate service of humanity, even as the late M. Curie's was. "What would you say," someone might ask, "of Hitler who declares that by fighting against the Jews I am doing: the Lord's work'?" Let us Remember that he also makes no secret of the fact that he is prompted by nothing better than an implacable hatred of the Jews. Anyway, it is not for me to judge. History will judge him and many, others in their proper time. That detachment is the only thing that can put life into action, is recognized by all. Even Asquith eulogizing Llyod George's devoted co-operation congratulated him on his "devotion, your (his) unselfishness, your (his) powers of resource, what is after all the best of all things, your (his) self-forgetfulness. These are the rare things that make the drudgery and squalor of politics, with its constant revelation of the large part played by petty and personal motives, endurable and gives to its drabness a lightening streak of nobility." But the automatic test of the purity and nobility of even that detachment is the dedication for an ideal, viz, service of God as embodied in the good of humanity. The *yogin* that the *Gita* regards as the ideal man is he "whose sins are wiped out, whose doubts are resolved, who has mastered himself and who is engrossed in the welfare of all beings" (V. 25).

Judged by this supreme test the names I have mentioned were, if not *yogins*, on the sure path of *Yoga*. Whilst some of them were pure mystics of devotion, some were men and women of action who were also mystics. *The Gita's* unmistakable partiality for the man of action who is a mystic is to be seen in its repeated exhortation; "Be thou therefore a *yogin*" (VI. 46; VIII. 27 etc.); "Therefore at all times remember Me and fight on" (VIII. 7). "Whosoever would come after Me, let him renounce himself and take up his cross daily and follow Me," said Christ in a perfectly identical spirit. "The mystic who is also a man of action, and man of action because he is a mystic, wields a tremendous power," says Dean Inge. "He is like an invulnerable knight, fighting in magic armour." Wherever we may be placed, fight is the lot of each one of us; each one has to fight, as Arjuna was asked to do and as all these *yogins* fought, against the powers and principalities of darkness, within ourselves and without. The victory lies in fighting with the "magic armour" on; "Therefore, at all times remember Me and fight" (VIII. 7).

The *yogins* of all ages fought with the magic armour on, in a spirit of complete self-surrender, not in the interests of their narrow selves but in the interests of the Self of all mankind, and by so doing they left humanity purer, holier, nobler, stronger. They are the salt of the earth. They were called upon to play their parts on a vast stage; ours may be an infinitely narrower one, but the Master of the stage is the same. The area in which they moved was very large; ours may be very small, but the centre, round which we have to perform the divine dance, is the same. Each one of us has to sacrifice ourselves — our petty and narrow and circum-scribing selves — in order to be one with the Self. We have to burn ourselves out with a heart and a will and a cheer each in his or her own sphere : our wicks may be ever so flimsy, our oil ever so poor, our flame ever so feeble, just enough to light our narrow paths, but ultimately our dim lights will blend right enough with the Universal Flame. All sacrifice, no matter how small or great, provided it is pure, reaches Him, ranks the same with Him, there is no last nor first.

Note on the Translation

I have tried to adhere as closely as possible to Gandhiji's translation of the text, but he is in no way responsible for the translation of numerous many-faceted and protean words like/ for instance, *buddhi*, which in any Indian vernacular may be used in the original form in any context and yet may not be misunderstood whereas in English an equivalent word as near as possible to the sense intended in each contest would be absolutely essential.

The Western reader will perhaps forgive my insistence on retaining in their original some of the strictly technical words. I have discussed them all in their several bearings in 'My Submission' and attempted to make them fairly familiar by suggesting various synonyms. These are: *Atman, Brahman, prakriti, guna, sattva, rajas, tamas,* (and their adjectives *sattvika, rajasa, tamas a), yoga, yogin.*

Then there are words like *jnana, yajna, bhakta, bhakti, tap as* which indeed have English equivalents but which mean very much more than their usual English equivalents. I have given these words in brackets along with their English equivalents, in order thereby to rivet attention of the reader on the fact that the original word is one carrying a deeper meaning. Where these words occur frequently in one context, the Sanskrit word is supplied just in the first instance.

The English vocabulary will be all the richer for these words, and as the text itself usually affords a full definition of them wherever they are treated at length, they do not put any strain on the memory of the reader.

Where, however, a protean word like *yoga*, for instance, is used in any sense other than the technical, I have given the appropriate English equivalent.

Krishna and Arjuna have numerous mames and epithets. Some of these words are substantives whilst some are descriptive and attributive. The old commentators have not only traced even the substantival names to their supposed components, but have tried to make out that every name or epithet was chosen by the author to suit the context in which it occurs. Some of these attempted derivations are fanciful and the attempt to justify the choice in each context is often forced. It is obvious that in some cases at any rate the author had to consider the exigencies of the metre. The reader need not tax himself over the meanings of these words. For ready reference I collect here the various names (with their meanings wherever they are obvious and non-controversial) of Krishna and Arjuna:

Krishna	Arjuna
1. Achyuta (Unfailing)	1. Kaunteya (Son of Kunti)
2. Keshava	2. Pandava (Son of Pandu)
3. Govinda	3. Partha (Son of Pritha or Kunti)
4. Janardana	4. Bharata (Descendent of Bharata)
5. Madhusudana (Slayer of Madhu)	5. Gudakesha
6. Arisudana (Slayer of foes)	6. Dhananjaya
7. Keshinisudana (Slayer of Keshin)	7. Kurunandana (Scion of Kurus)
8. Madhava	8. Kurushreshtha (Best of Kurus)
9. Purushottama (Supreme Being)	9. Kurusattama („)
10. Vasudeva (Son of Vasu-deva, All-pervading)	10. Bharatarshabha (Best of Bharatas)
11. Vishnu (All-pervading)	11. Bharatashreshtha („)
12. Hari	12. Bharatasattama („)
13. Varshneya (Descendent of Vrishni)	13. Parantapa (Tormentor of foes)
14. Yadava (" " Yadu)	

All these I have retained in the original, but the numerous attributive or descriptive titles I have translated. One exception I have deliberately made. In the 11th discourse I have retained even the obviously descriptive titles in the original (giving their meanings in the notes), not to break the rhythm (even in prose) of that most musical of all discourses. Mahabahu (strong-armed one), frequently used by Krishna in addressing Arjuna, and once or twice by Arjuna in addressing Krishna, I have retained in its Sanskrit form.

In some cases — I hope very few — words have been added in brackets to complete or improve the English structure of the sentences.

Asaktiyoga

The Message of the Gita

[It was at Kosani in Almora on 24th June, 1929, i.e., after two years' waiting, that I finished the introduction to my translation of the *Gita*. The whole was then published in due course. It has been translated in Hindi, Bengali and Marathi. There has been an insistent demand for an English translation. I finished the translation of the introduction at the Yeravda prison. Since my discharge it has lain with friends and now I give it to the reader. Those, who take no interest in the Book of Life, will forgive the trespass on these columns. To those who are interested in the poem and treat it as their guide in life, my humble attempt might prove of some help.

—M.K. Gandhi]

I

1. Just as, acted upon by the affection of co-workers like Swami Anand and others, I wrote *My Experiments with Truth*, so has it been regarding my rendering of the *Gita*. "We shall be able to appreciate your meaning of the message of the *Gita*, only when we are able to study a translation of the whole text by yourself, with the addition of such notes as you may deem necessary. I do not think it is just on your part to deduce *ahimsa* etc. from stray verses," thus spoke Swami Anand to me during the non-cooperation days. I felt the force of his remarks. I,

therefore, told him that I would adopt his suggestion when I got the time. Shortly afterwards I was imprisoned. During my incarceration I was able to study the *Gita* more fully. I went reverently through the Gujarati translation of the Lokamanya's great work. He had kindly presented me with the Marathi original and the translations in Gujarati and Hindi, and had asked me, if I could not tackle the original, at least to go through the Gujarati translation. I had not been able to follow the advice outside the prison walls. But when I was imprisoned I read the Gujarati translation. This reading whetted my appetite for more and I glanced through several works on the *Gita*.

2. My first acquaintance with the *Gita* began in 1888-89 with the verse translation by Sir Edwin Arnold known as the *Song Celestial*. On reading it, I felt a keen desire to read a Gujarati translation. And I read as many translations as I could lay hold of. But all such reading can give me no passport for presenting my own translation. Then again my knowledge of Sanskrit is limited, my knowledge of Gujarati too is in no way scholarly. How could I then dare present the public with my translation?

3. It has been my endeavor, as also that of some companions, to reduce to practice the teaching of the *Gita* as I have understood it. The *Gita* has become for us a spiritual reference book. I am aware that we ever fail to act in perfect accord with the teaching. The failure is not due to want of effort, but is in spite of it. Even though the failures we seem to see rays of hope. The accompanying rendering contains the meaning of the *Gita* message which this little band is trying to enforce in its daily conduct.

4. Again this rendering is designed for women, the commercial class, the so-called *Shudras* and the like who have little or no literary equipment, who have neither the time nor the desire to read the *Gita* in the original and yet who stand in need of its support. In spite of my Gujarati being unscholarly, I must own to having the desire to leave to the Gujaratis, through the mother tongue, whatever knowledge I may possess. I do indeed wish that at a time when literary output of a questionable character is pouring upon the Gujaratis, they should have before them a rendering the majority can understand of a book that is

regarded as unrivalled for its spiritual merit and so withstand the over-whelming flood of unclean literature.

5. This desire does not mean any disrespect to the other renderings. They have their own place. But I am not aware of the claim made by the translators of enforcing their meaning of the *Gita* in their own lives. At the back of my reading there is the claim of an endeavour to enforce the meaning in my own conduct for an unbroken period of forty years. For this reason I do indeed harbour the wish that all Guja-rati men or women wishing to shape their conduct according to their faith, should digest and derive strength from the translation here presented.

6. My co-workers, too, have worked at this translation. My knowledge of Sanskrit being very limited, I should not have full confidence in my literal translation. To that extent, therefore, the translation has passed before the eyes of Vinoba, Kaka Kalelkar, Mahadev Desai and Kishor-lal Mashruwala.

II

7. Now about the message of the *Gita*.

8. Even in 1888-89, when I first became acquainted with the *Gita*, I felt that it was not a historical work, but that, under the guise of physical warfare, it described the duel that perpetually went on in the hearts mankind, and that physical warfare was brought in merely to make the description of the internal duel more alluring. This preliminary intuition became more confirmed on a closer study of religion and the *Gita*. A study of the *Mahabharata* gave it added confirmation. I do not regard the *Mahabharata* as a historical work in the accepted sense. The *Adiparva* contains powerful evidence in support of my opinion. By ascribing to the chief actors superhuman or subhuman origins, the great *Vyasa* made short work the history of kings and their peoples. The persons therein described may be historical, but the author of the *Mahabharata* has used them merely to drive home his religious theme.

9. The author of the *Mahabharata* has not established the necessity of physical warfare; on the contrary he has proved its futility. He has

made the victors shed tears of sorrow and repentance, and has left them nothing but a legacy of miseries.

10. In this great work the *Gita* is the crown. Its second chapter, instead of teaching the rules of physical warfare, tells us how a perfected man is to be known. In the characteristics of the perfected man of the *Gita*, I do not see any to correspond to physical warfare. Its whole design is inconsistent with the rules of conduct governing the relations between warring parties.

11. Krishna of the *Gita* is perfection and right knowledge personified; but the picture is imaginary. That does not mean that Krishna, the adored of his people, never lived. But perfection is imagined. The idea of a perfect incarnation is an after growth.

12. In Hinduism, incarnation is ascribed to one who has performed some extraordinary service of mankind. All embodied life is in reality an incarnation of God, but it is not usual to consider every living being an incarnation. Future generations pay this homage to one who, in his own generation, has been extraordinarily religious in his conduct. I can see nothing wrong in this procedure; it takes nothing from God's greatness, and there is no violence done to Truth. There is an Urdu saying which means, "Adam is not God but he is a spark of the Divine." And therefore he who is the most religiously behaved has most of the divine spark in him. It is in accordance with this train of thought that Krishna enjoys, in Hinduism, the status of the most perfect incarnation.

13. This belief in incarnation is a testimony of man's lofty spiritual ambition. Man is not at peace with himself till he has become like unto God. The endeavour to reach this state is the supreme, the only ambition worth having. And this is self-realization. This self-realization is the subject of the *Gita*, as it is of all scriptures. But its author surely did not write it to establish that doctrine. The object of the *Gita* appears to me to be that of showing the most excellent way to attain self-realization. That which is to be found, more or less clearly, spread out here and there in Hindu religious books, has been brought out in the clearest possible language in the *Gita* even at the risk of repetition.

14. *That matchless remedy is renunciation of fruits of action.*

15. This is the centre round which the *Gita* is woven. This renunciation is the central sun, round which devotion, knowledge and the rest revolve like planets. The body has been likened to a prison. There must be action where there is body. Not one embodied being is exempted from labour. And yet all religions proclaim that it is possible for man, by treating the body as the temple of God, to attain freedom. Every action is tainted, be it ever so trivial. How can the body be made the temple of God? In other words how can one be free from action, i.e. from the taint of sin? The *Gita* has answered the question in decisive language: "By desireless action; by renouncing fruits of action; by dedicating all activities to God, i.e., by surrendering oneself to Him body and soul."

16. But desirelessness or renunciation does not come for the mere talking about it. It is not attained by intellectual feat. It is attainable only by a constant heart-churn. Right knowledge is necessary for attaining renunciation. Learned men possess a knowledge of a kind. They may recite the Vedas from memory, yet they may be steeped in self-indulgence. In order that knowledge may not run riot, the author of the *Gita* has insisted on devotion accompanying it and has given it the first place. Knowledge without devotion will be like a misfire. Therefore, says the *Gita*, "Have devotion, and knowledge will follow." This devotion is not mere lip worship, it is a wrestling with death. Hence, the *Gita*'s assessment of the devotee's quality is similar to that of the sage.

17. Thus the devotion required by the *Gita* is no soft-hearted effusiveness. It certainly is not blind faith. The devotion of the *Gita* has the least to do with the externals. A devotee may use, if he likes, rosaries, forehead marks, make offerings, but these things are no test of his devotion. He is the devotee who is jealous of none, who is a fount of mercy, who is without egotism, who is selfless, who treats alike cold and heat, happiness and misery, who is ever forgiving, who is always contented, whose resolutions are firm, who has dedicated mind and soul to God, who causes no dread, who is not afraid of others, who is free from exultation, sorrow and fear, who is pure, who is versed in action and yet remains unaffected by it, who renounces all fruit, good or bad, who treats friend and foe alike, who is untouched by respect or disrespect,

who is not puffed up by praise, who does not go under when people speak ill of him who loves silence and solitude, who has a disciplined reason. Such devotion is inconsistent with the existence at the same time of strong attachments.

18. We thus see that to be a real devotee is to realize oneself. Self-realization is not something apart. One rupee can purchase for us poison or nectar, but knowledge or devotion cannot buy us salvation or bondage. These are not media of exchange. They are themselves the thing we want. In other words, if the means and the end are not identical, they are almost so. The extreme of means is salvation. Salvation of the *Gita* is perfect peace.

19. But such knowledge and devotion, to be true, have to stand the test of renunciation of fruits of action. Mere knowledge of right and wrong will not make one fit for salvation. According to common notions, a mere learned man will pass as a *pandit*. He need not perform any service. He will regard as bondage even to lift a little *lota*. Where one test of knowledge is non-liability for service, there is no room for such mundane work as the lifting of a *lota*.

20. Or take *bhakti*. The popular notion of *bhakti* is soft-heartedness, telling beads and the like, and disdaining to do even a loving service, least the telling of beads etc. might be interrupted. This *bhakti*, therefore, leaves the rosary only for eating, drinking and the like, never for grinding corn or nursing patients.

21. But the *Gita* says: No one has attained his goal without action. Even men like Janaka attained salvation through action. If even I were lazily to cease working, the world would not perish. How much more necessary then for the people at large to engage in action.

22. While on the one hand it is beyond dispute that all action binds, on the other hand it is equally true that all living beings have to do some work, whether they will or no. Here all activity, whether mental or physical is to be included in the term action. Then how is one to be free from the bondage of action, even though he may be acting? The manner in which the *Gita* has solved the problem is to my knowledge unique. The *Gita* says: 'Do your allotted work but renounce its fruit — be detached and work have no desire for reward and work.'

This is the unmistakable teaching of the *Gita*. He who gives up action falls. He who gives up only the reward rises. But renunciation of fruit in no way means indifference to the result. In regard to every action one must know the result that is expected to follow, the means thereto, and the capacity for it. He, who, being thus equipped, is without desire for the result and is yet wholly engrossed in the due fulfillment of the task before him is said to have renounced the fruits of his action.

23. Again let no one consider renunciation to mean want of fruit for the renouncer. The *Gita* reading does not warrant such a meaning. Renunciation means absence of hankering after fruit. As a matter of fact, he who renounces reaps a thousandfold. The renunciation of the *Gita* is the acid test of faith. He who is ever brooding over result often loses nerve in the performance of his duty. He becomes impatient and then gives vent to anger and begins to do unworthy things; he jumps from action to action never remaining faithful to any. He who broods over results is like a man given to objects of senses; he is ever distracted, he says goodbye to all scruples, everything is right in his estimation and he therefore resorts to means fair and foul to attain his end.

24. From the bitter experiences of desire for fruit the author of the *Gita* discovered the path of renunciation of fruit and put it before the world in a most convincing manner. The common belief is that religion is always opposed to material good. "One cannot act religiously in mercantile and such other matters. There is no place for religion in such pursuits; religion is only for attainment of salvation," we here many worldly-wise people say. In my opinion the author of the *Gita* has dispelled this delusion. He has drawn no line of demarcation between salvation and worldly pursuits. On the contrary he has shown that religion must rule even our worldly pursuits. I have felt that the *Gita* teaches us that what cannot be followed out in day-to-day practice cannot be called religion. Thus, according to the *Gita*, all acts that are incapable of being performed without attachment are taboo. This golden rule saves mankind from many a pitfall. According to this interpretation murder, lying, dissoluteness and the like must be regarded as sinful and therefore taboo. Man's life then becomes simple, and from that simpleness springs peace.

25. Thinking along these lines, I have felt that in trying to enforce in one's life the central teaching of the *Gita*, one is bound to follow Truth and *ahimsa*. When there is no desire for fruit, there is no temptation for untruth or *himsa*. Take any instance of untruth or violence, and it will be found that at its back was the desire to attain the cherished end. But it may be freely admitted that the *Gita* was not written to establish *ahimsa*. It was an accepted and primary duty even before the *Gita* age. The *Gita* had to deliver the message of renunciation of fruit. This is clearly brought out as early as the second chapter.

26. But if the *Gita* believed in *ahimsa* or it was included in desirelessness, why did the author take a warlike illustration? When the *Gita* was written, although people believed in *ahimsa*, wars were not only not taboo, but nobody observed the contradiction between them and *ahimsa*.

27. In assessing the implications of renunciation of fruit, we are not required to probe the mind of the author of the *Gita* as to his limitations of *ahimsa* and the like. Because a poet puts a particular truth before the world, it does not necessarily follow that he has known or worked out all its great consequences or that having done so, he is able always to express them fully. In this perhaps lies the greatness of the poem and the poet. A poet's meaning is limitless. Like man, the meaning of great writings suffers evolution. On examining the history of languages, we noticed that the meaning of important words has changed or expanded. This is true of the *Gita*. The author has himself extended the meanings of some of the current words. We are able to discover this even on superficial examination. It is possible that, in the age prior to that of the *Gita*, offering of animals as sacrifice was permissible. But there is not a trace of it in the sacrifice in the *Gita* sense. In the *Gita* continuous concentration on God is the king of sacrifices. The third chapter seems to show that sacrifice chiefly means body-labour for service. The third and fourth chapters read together will use other meanings for sacrifice, but never animal-sacrifice. Similarly has the meaning of the word *sannyasa* undergone, in the *Gita*, a transformation. The *sannyasa* of the *Gita* will not tolerate complete cessation of all activity. The *sannyasa* of the *Gita* is all work and yet no work. Thus the author of the *Gita*, by extending meanings of words, has taught us to imitate him. Let it be granted, that according

to the letter of the *Gita* it is possible to say that warfare is consistent with renunciation of fruit. But after forty years' unremitting endeavor fully to enforce the teaching of the *Gita* in my own life, I have in all humility felt that perfect renunciation is impossible without perfect observance of *ahimsa* in every shape and form.

28. The *Gita* is not an aphoristic work; it is a great religious poem. The deeper you dive into it, the richer the meanings you get. It being meant for the people at large, there is pleasing repetition. With every age the important words will carry new and expanding meanings. But its central teaching will never vary. The teacher is at liberty to extract from this treasure any meaning he likes so as to enable him to enforce in his life the central teaching.

29. Nor is the *Gita* a collection of Do's and Dont's. What is lawful for one may be unlawful for another. What may be permissible at one time, or in one place, may not be so at another time, and in another place. Desire for fruit is the only universal prohibition. Desirelessness is obligatory.

30. The *Gita* has sung the praises of Knowledge, but it is beyond the mere intellect; it is essentially addressed to the heart and capable of being understood by the heart. Therefore the *Gita* is not for those who have no faith. The author makes Krishna say:

"Do not entrust this treasure to him who is without sacrifice, without devotion, without the desire for this teaching and who denies Me. On the other hand, those who will give this precious treasure to My devotees will, by the fact of this service, assuredly reach me. And those who, being free from malice, will with faith absorb this teaching, shall, having attained freedom, live where people of true merit go after death.

Discource 1

No knowledge is to be found without seeking, no tranquility with-out travail, no happiness except through tribulation. Every seeker has, at one time or another, to pass through a conflict of duties, a heart-churning.

DHRITARASHTRA SAID :

1. Tell me, O Sanjaya, what my sons and Pandu's assembled, on battle intent, did on the field of Kuru, the field of duty.

   The human body is the battlefield where the eternal duel between right and wrong goes on. Therefore it is capable of being turned into a gateway to Freedom. It is born in sin and becomes the seed-bed of sin. Hence it is also called the field of Kuru. The Kuravas represent the forces of Evil, the Pandavas the forces of Good. Who is there that has not experienced the daily conflict within himself between the forces of Evil and the forces of Good?

SANJAYA SAID :

2. On seeing the Pandava's army drawn up in battle array, King Duryo-dhana approached Drona, the preceptor, and addressed him.

3. Behold, O preceptor, this mighty army of the sons of Pandu, set in array by the son of Drupada, thy wise disciple.

4. Here are brave bowmen, peers of Bhima and Arjuna in fighting: Yuyudhana and Virata, and the 'Maharatha' Drupada.

5. Dhrishtaketu, Chekitana, valorous Kashiraja, Purujit the Kuntibhoja, and Shaibya, chief among men;

6. Valiant Yudhamanyu, valorous Uttamaujas, Subhadra's son, and the sons of Draupadi — each one of them a 'Maharatha'.

7. Acquaint thyself now, O best of *Brahmanas*, with the distinguished among us. I mention for thy information, the names of the captains of my army.

8. Thy noble self, Bhishma, Karna, and Kripa, victorious in battle, *Ashvatthaman*, Vikarna, also Somadatta's son.

9. There is many another hero, known for his skill in wielding diverse weapons, pledged to lay down his life for my sake, and all adepts in war.

10. This our force, commanded by Bhishma, is all too inadequate; while theirs, commanded by Bhima, is quite adequate.

11. Therefore, let each of you, holding your appointed places, at every entrance, guard only Bhishma.

12. At this, the heroic grandsire, the grand old man of the Kurus, gave a loud lion's roar and blew his conch to hearten Duryodhana.

13. Thereupon, conches, drums, cymbals and trumpets were sounded all at once. Terrific was the noise.

14. Then Madhava and Pandava, standing in their great chariot yoked with white steeds, blew their divine conches.

15. Hrishikesha blew the Panchajanya and Dhananjaya the Devadatta; while the wolf-bellied Bhima of dread deeds sounded his great conch Paundra.

16. King Yudhishthira, Kunti's son, blew the Anantavijaya, and Nakula and Sahadeva their conches, Sughosha and Manipushpaka.

17. And Kashiraja, the great bowman, Shikhandi the 'Maharatha', Dhrishtadyumna, Virata and Satyaki, the unconquerable.

18. Drupada, Draupadi's sons, the strong-armed son of Subhadra, all these, O King, blew each his own conch.

19. That terrifying tumult, causing earth and heaven to resound, rent the hearts of Dhritarashtra's sons.

20-21. Then, O King, the ape-bannered Pandava, seeing Dhritarashtra's sons arrayed and flight of arrows about to begin, took up his bow, and spoke thus to Hrishikesha: "Set my chariot between the two armies, O Achyuta!"

22. That I may behold them drawn up, on battle intent, and know whom I have to engage in this fearful combat.

23. And that I may survey the fighters assembled here anxious to fulfill in battle perverse Duryodhana's desire.

SANJAYA SAID :

24-25. Thus addressed by Gudakesha, O King, Hrishikesha set the unique chariot between the two armies in front of Bhishma, Drona and all the kings and said: Behold, O Partha, the Kurus assembled yonder.

26-28. Then did Partha see, standing there, sires, grandsires, preceptors, uncles, brothers, sons, grandsons, comrades, fathers-in-law and friends in both armies. Beholding all these kinsmen ranged before him, Kaunteya was overcome with great compassion and spake thus in anguish:

ARJUNA SAID :

28-29. As I look upon these kinsmen, O Krishna, assembled here eager to fight, my limbs fail, my mouth is parched, a tremor shakes my frame and my hair stands on end.

30. Gandiva slips from my hand, my skin is on fire, I cannot keep my feet, and my mind reels.

31. I have unhappy forebodings, O Keshava; and I see no good in slaying kinsmen in battle.

32. I seek not victory, nor sovereign power, nor earthly joys. What good are sovereign power, worldly pleasures and even life to us, O Govinda?

33. Those for whom we would desire sovereign power, earthly joys and delights are here arrayed in battle, having renounced life and wealth.

34. Preceptors, sires, grandsires, sons and even grandsons, uncles, fathers-in-law, brothers-in-law, and other kinsmen.

35. These I would not kill, O Madhusudana, even though they slay me, not even for kingship of the three worlds, much less for an earthly kingdom.

36. What pleasure can there be in slaying these sons of Dhritarashtra, O Janardana? Sin only can be our lot, if we slay these, usurpers though they be.

37. It does not therefore behove us to kill our kinsmen, these sons of Dhritarashtra. How may we be happy, O Madhava, in killing our own kins?

38. Even though these, their wits warped by greed, see not the guilt that lies in destroying the family, nor the sin of treachery to comrades;

39. How can we, O Janardana, help recoiling from this sin, seeing clearly as we do the guilt that lies in such destruction?

40. With the destruction of the family perish the eternal family virtues, and with the perishing of these virtues unrighteousness seizes the whole family.

41. When unrighteousness prevails, O Krishna, the women of the family become corrupt, and their corruption, O Varshneya, causes a confusion of *varnas*.

42. This confusion verily drags the family-slayer, as well as the family, to hell, and for want of obsequies offerings and rites their departed sires fall from blessedness.

43. By the sins of these family-slayers resulting in confusion of *varnas*, the eternal tribal and family virtues are brought to naught.

44. For we have had it handed down to us, O Janardana, that the men whose family virtues have been ruined are doomed to dwell in hell.

45. Alas! What a heinous sin we are about to commit, in that, from greed of the joy of sovereign power, we are prepared to slay our kith and kin!

46. Happier far would it be for me if Dhritarashtra's sons, weapons in hand, should strike me down on the battlefield, unresisting and unarmed.

SANJAYA SAID:

47. Thus spake Arjuna on the field of battle, and dropping his bow and arrows sank down on his seat in the chariot, overwhelmed with anguish.

Thus ends the first discourse, entitled *'Arjuna Vishada Yoga'* in the converse of Lord Krishna and Arjuna, on the science of Yoga as part of the knowledge of Brahman in the Upanishad called the *Bhagawadgita.*

Discource 2

By reason of delusion, man takes wrong to be right. By reason of delusion was Arjuna led to make a difference between kinsmen and non-kinsmen. To demonstrate that this is a vain distinction, Lord Krishna distinguishes between body (not-Self) and Atman (Self) and shows that whilst bodies are impermanent and several, Atman is permanent and one. Effort is within man's control, not the fruit thereof. All he has to do, therefore, is to decide his course of conduct or duty on each occasion and persevere in it, unconcerned about the result. Fulfillment of one's duty in the spirit of detachment or selflessness leads to Freedom.

SANJAYA SAID :

1. To Arjuna, thus overcome with compassion, sorrowing, and his eyes obscured by flowing tears, Madhusudana spake these words:

THE LORD SAID :

2. How is it that at this perilous moment this delusion, unworthy of the noble, leading neither to heaven nor to glory, has overtaken thee?
3. Yield not to unmanliness, O Partha; it does not become thee. Shake off this miserable faint-heartedness and arise, O Parantapa!

ARJUNA SAID :

4. How shall I, with arrows, engage Bhishma and Drona in battle, O Madhusudana, they who are worthy of reverence, O Arisudana?

5. It were better far to live on alms of this world than to slay these venerable elders. Having slain them I should but have blood-stained enjoyments.

6. Nor do we know which is better for us, that we conquer them or that they conquer us, for here stand before us Dhritarashtra's sons having killed whom we should have no desire to live.

7. My being is paralysed by faint-heartedness; my mind discerns not duty; hence I ask thee; tell me, I pray thee, in no uncertain language, wherein lies my good. I am thy disciple; guide me; I see refuge in thee.

8. For I see nothing that can dispel the anguish that shrivels up my senses even if I should win on earth uncontested sovereignty over a thriving kingdom or lordship over the gods.

SANJAYA SAID :

9. Thus spoke Gudakesha Parantapa to Hrishikesha Govinda, and with the words 'I will not fight' became speechless.

10. To him thus stricken with anguish, O Bharata! between the two armies, Hrishikesha, as though mocking, addressed these words:

THE LORD SAID :

11. Thou mournest for them whom thou shouldst not mourn and utterest vain words of wisdom. The wise mourn neither for the living nor for the dead.

12. For never was I not, nor thou, nor these kings; nor will any of us cease to be hereafter.

13. As the embodied one has, in the present body, infancy, youth and age, even so does he receive another body. The wise man is not deceived therein.

14. O Kaunteya! contacts of the senses with their objects bring cold and heat, pleasure and pain; they come and go and are transient. Endure them, O Bharata.

15. O noblest of men, the wise man who is not disturbed by these, who is unmoved by pleasure and pain, he is fitted for immortality.

16. What is non-Being is never known to have been, and what is Being is never known not to have been. Of both these the secret has been seen by the seers of the Truth.

17. Know that to be imperishable whereby all this is pervaded. No one can destroy that immutable being.

18. These bodies of the embodied one who is eternal, imperishable and immeasurable are finite. Fight, therefore, O Bharata.

19. He who thinks of This (*Atman*) as slayer and he who believes This to be slain, are both ignorant. This neither slays nor is ever slain.

20. This is never born nor ever dies, nor having been will ever not be any more; unborn, eternal, everlasting, ancient, This is not slain when the body is slain.

21. He who knows This, O Partha, to be imperishable, eternal, unborn, and immutable—whom and how can that man slay or cause to be slain?

22. As a man casts off worn-out garments and takes others that are new, even so the embodied one casts off worn-out bodies and passes on to others new.

23. This no weapons wound, This no fire burns, This no waters wet, This no wind doth dry.

24. Beyond all cutting, burning, wetting and drying is This-eternal, all-pervading, stable, immovable, everlasting.

25. Perceivable neither by the senses nor by the mind, This is called unchangeable; therefore knowing This as such thou shouldst not grieve.

26. And if thou deemest This to be always coming to birth and always dying, even then, O Mahabahu, thou shouldst not grieve.

27. For certain is the death of the born, and certain is the birth of the dead; therefore what is unavoidable thou shouldst not regret.

28. The state of all beings before birth is unmanifest; their middle state manifest; their state after death is again unmanifest. What occasion is there for lament, O Bharata?

29. One looks upon This as a marvel; another speaks of This as such; another hears thereof as a marvel; yet having heard This none truly knows This.

30. This embodied one in the body of every being is ever beyond all harm, O Bharata; thou shouldst not, therefore, grieve for any one. Thus far Lord Krishna, by force of argument based on pure reason, has demonstrated that *Atman* is abiding while the physical body is fleeting, and has explained that if, under certain circumstances, the destruction of a physical body is deemed justifiable, it is delusion to imagine that the Kauravas should not be slain because they are kinsmen. Now he reminds Arjuna of the duty of a *Kshatriya*.

31. Again, seeing thine own duty thou shouldst not shrink from it; for there is no higher good for a *Kshatriya* than a righteous war.

32. Such a fight, coming unsought, as a gateway to heaven thrown open, falls only to the lot of happy *Kshatriyas*, O Partha.

33. But if thou wilt not fight this righteous fight, then failing in thy duty and losing thine honour thou wilt incur sin.

34. The world will forever recount the story of thy disgrace; and for a man of honour disgrace is worse than death.

35. The *Maharathas* will think that fear made thee retire from battle; and thou wilt fall in the esteem of those very ones who have held thee high.

36. Thine enemies will deride thy prowess and speak many unspeakable words about thee. What can be more painful than that?

37. Slain, thou shalt gain heaven; victorious, thou shall inherit the earth: therefore arise, O Kaunteya, determined to fight.

Having declared the highest truth, viz. the immortality of the eternal *Atman* and the fleeting nature of the physical body (11-30), Krishna reminds Arjuna that a *Kshatriya* may not flinch from a fight which comes unsought (31-32). He then (33-37) shows how the highest truth and the performance of duty incidentally coincide with expediency. Next he proceeds to foreshadow the central teaching of the *Gita* in the following *shloka*.

38. Hold alike pleasure and pain, gain and loss, victory and defeat, and gird up thy loins for the fight; so doing thou shalt not incur sin.

39. Thus have I set before thee the attitude of Knowledge; hear now the attitude of Action; resorting to this attitude thou shalt cast off the bondage of action.

40. Here no effort undertaken is lost, no disaster befalls. Even a little of this righteous course delivers one from great fear.

41. The attitude, in this matter, springing, as it does, from fixed resolve is but one, O Kurunandana; but for those who have no fixed resolve the attitudes are many-branched and unending. When the attitude ceases to be one and undivided and becomes many and divided, it ceases to be one settled will, and is broken up into various wills of desires between which man is tossed about.

42-44. The ignorant, revelling in the letter of the Vedas, declare that there is naught else; carnally-minded, holding heaven to be their goal, they utter swelling words which promise birth as the fruit of action and which dwell on the many and varied rites to be performed for the sake of pleasure and power; intent, as they are, on pleasure and power their swelling words rob them of their wits, and they have no settled attitude which can be centered on the supreme goal.

The Vedic ritual, as opposed to the doctrine of *Yoga* laid down in the *Gita*, is alluded to here. The Vedic ritual lays countless ceremonies and rites with a view to attaining merit and heaven. These, divorced as they are from the essence of the Vedas and short-lived in their result, are worthless.

45. The Vedas have as their domain the three *gunas*; eschew them, O Arjuna. Free thyself from the pairs of opposites, abide in eternal truth, scorn to gain or guard anything, remain the master of thy soul.

46. To the extent that a well is of use when there is a flood of water on all sides, to the same extent are all the Vedas of use to an enlightened *Brahmana*.

47. Action alone is thy province, never the fruits thereof; let not thy motive be the fruit of action, nor shouldst thou desire to avoid action.

48. Act thou, O Dhananjaya, without attachment, steadfast in *Yoga*, even-minded in success and failure. Even-mindedness is *Yoga*.

49. For action, O Dhananjaya, is far inferior to unattached action; seek refuge in the attitude of detached action. Pitiable are those who make fruit their motive.

50. Here in this world a man gifted with that attitude of detachment escapes the fruit of both good and evil deeds. Gird thyself up for *Yoga*, therefore. *Yoga* is skill in action.

51. For sages, gifted with the attitude of detachment, who renounce the fruit of action, are released from the bondage of birth and attain to the state which is free from all ills.

52. When thy understanding will have passed through the slough of delusion, then wilt thou be indifferent alike to what thou hast heard and wilt hear.

53. When thy understanding, distracted by much hearing, will rest steadfast and unmoved in concentration, then wilt thou attain *Yoga*.

ARJUNA SAID :

54. What, O Keshava, is the mark of the man whose understanding is secure, whose mind is fixed in concentration? How does he talk? How sit? How move.

THE LORD SAID :

55. When a man puts away, O partha, all the cravings that arise in the mind and finds comfort for himself only from *Atman*, then he is called the man of secure understanding.

    To find comfort for oneself from *Atman* means to look to the spirit within for spiritual comfort, not to outside objects which in their very nature must give pleasure as well as pain. Spiritual comfort or bliss must be distinguished from pleasure or happiness. The pleasure I may derive from the possession of wealth, for instance, is delusive; real spiritual comfort or bliss can be attained only if I rise superior to every temptation even though troubled by the pangs of poverty and hunger.

.

56. Whose mind is untroubled in sorrows and longeth not for joys, who is free from passion, fear and wrath—he is called the ascetic of secure understanding.

57. Who owns attachment nowhere, who feels neither joy nor resentment whether good or bad comes his way—that man's understanding is secure.

58. And when, like the tortoise drawing in its limbs from every side, this man draws in his senses from their objects, his understanding is secure.

59. When a man starves his senses, the objects of those senses disappear from him, but not the yearning for them; the yearning too departs when he beholds the Supreme. The *shloka* does not rule out fasting and other forms of self-restraint, but indicates their limitations, these restraints are needed for subduing the desire for sense-objects, which however is rooted out only when one has a vision of the Supreme. The higher yearning conquers all the lower yearnings.

60. For, in spite of the wise man's endeavour, O Kaunteya, the unruly senses distract his mind perforce.

61. Holding all these in check, the *yogi* should sit intent on Me; for he whose senses are under control is secure of understanding.

    This means that without devotion and the consequent grace of God, man's endeavour is vain.

62. In a man brooding on objects of the senses, attachment to them springs up; attachment begets craving and craving begets wrath.

    Craving cannot but lead to resentment, for it is unending and unsatisfied.

63. Wrath breeds stupefaction, stupefaction leads to loss of memory, loss of memory ruins the reason, and the ruin of reason spells utter destruction.

64. But the disciplined soul, moving among sense-objects with the senses weaned from likes and dislikes and brought under the control of *Atman*, attains peace of mind.

65. Peace of mind means the end to all ills, for the understanding of him whose mind is at peace stands secure.

66. The undisciplined man has neither understanding nor devotion; for him who has no devotion there is no peace, and for him who has no peace whence happiness?

67. For when his mind runs after any of the roaming senses, it sweeps away his understanding, as the wind a vessel upon the waters.

68. Therefore, O Mahabahu, he, whose senses are reined in on all sides from their objects, is the man of secure understanding.

69. When it is night for all other beings, the disciplined soul is awake; when all other beings are awake, it is night for the seeing ascetic.

This verse indicates the divergent paths of the discipline ascetic and sensual man. Whereas the ascetic is dead to the things of the world and lives in God, the sensual man is alive only to the things of the world and dead to the things of the spirit.

70. He in whom all longings subside, even as the waters subside in the ocean which, though ever being filled by them, never overflows—that man finds peace; not he who cherishes longing.

71. The man who sheds all longing and moves without concern, free from the sense of 'I' and 'Mine'—he attains peace.

72. This is the state, O partha, of the man who rests in *Brahman*; having attained to it, he is not deluded. He who abides in this state even at the hour of death passes into oneness with *Brahman*.

Thus ends the second discourse, entitled *'Sankhya Yoga'* in
the converse of Lord Krishna and Arjuna, on the science
of *Yoga* as part of the knowledge of *Brahman* in the
Upanishad called the *Bhagawadgita*.

Discource 3

This discourse may be said to be the key to the essence of the Gita. It makes absolutely clear the spirit and the nature of right action and shows how true knowledge must express itself in acts of selfless service.

ARJUNA SAID :

1. If, O Janardana, thou holdest that the attitude of detachment is superior to action, then why, O Keshava, dost thou urge me to dreadful action?

2. Thou dost seem to confuse my understanding with perplexing speech; tell me, therefore, in no uncertain voice, that alone whereby I may attain salvation.

   Arjuna is sore perplexed, for whilst on the one hand he is rebuked for his faint-heartedness, on the other he seems to be advised to refrain from action (II.49-50). But this, in reality, is not the case as the following *shlokas* will show.

THE LORD SAID :

3. I have spoken, before, O sinless one, of two attitudes in this world— the *Sankhayas*', that of *Jnana yoga* and the *Yogins*', that of *Karma yoga*.

4. Never does man enjoy freedom from action by not undertaking action, nor does he attain that freedom by mere renunciation of action.

'Freedom from action' is freedom from the bondage of action. This freedom is not to be gained by cessation of all activity, apart from the fact that this cessation is in the very nature of things impossible (see following *shloka*). How then may it be gained? The following *shlokas* will explain.

5. For none ever remains inactive even for a moment; for all are compelled to action by the *gunas* inherent in *prakriti*.

6. He who curbs the organs of action but allows the mind to dwell on the sense-objects,—such a one, wholly deluded, is called a hypocrite.

The man who curbs his tongue but mentally swears at another is a hypocrite. But that does not mean that free rein should be given to the organs of action so long as the mind cannot be brought under control. Self-imposed physical restraint is a condition precedent to mental restraint. Physical restraint should be entirely self-imposed and not super-imposed from outside, e.g. by fear. The hypocrite who is held up to contempt here is not the humble aspirant after self-restraint. The *shloka* has reference to the man who curbs the body because he cannot help it while indulging the mind, and who would indulge the body too if he possibly could. The next *shloka* puts the thing conversely.

7. But he, O Arjuna, who keeping all the senses under control of the mind, engages the organs in *Karma yoga*, without attachment—that man excels.

The mind and body should be made to accord well. Even with the mind kept in control, the body will be active in one way or another. But he whose mind is truly restrained will, for instance, close his ears to foul talk and open them only to listen to the praise of God or of good men. He will have no relish for sensual pleasures and will keep himself occupied with such activity as ennobles the soul. That is the path of action. *Karma yoga* is the *yoga* (means) which will deliver the self from the bondage of the body, and in it there is no room for self-indulgence.

8. Do thou thy allotted task; for action is superior to inaction; with inaction even life's normal course is not possible.

9. This world of men suffers bondage from all action save that which is done for the sake of sacrifice; to this end, O Kaunteya, perform action without attachment.

   'Action for the sake of sacrifice' means acts of selfless service dedicated to God.

10. Together with sacrifice did the Lord of beings create, of old, mankind, declaring:

    "By this shall ye increase; may this be to you the giver of all your desires.

11. "With this may you cherish the gods and may the gods cherish you; thus cherishing one another may you attain the highest good.

12. "Cherished with sacrifice, the gods will bestow on you the desired boons." He who enjoys their gifts without rendering aught unto them is verily a thief.

    "Gods" in *shlokas* 11 and 12 must be taken to mean the whole creation of God. The service of all created beings is the service of the gods and the same is sacrifice.

13. The righteous men who eat the residue of the sacrifice are freed from all sin, but the wicked who cook for themselves eat sin.

14. From food springs all life, from rain is born food; from sacrifice comes rain and sacrifice is the result of action.

15. Know that action springs from *Brahman* and *Brahman* from the Imperishable; hence the all-pervading *Brahman* is ever firm-founded on sacrifice.

16. He who does not follow the wheel thus set in motion here below, he, living in sin, sating his senses, lives, O Partha, in vain.

17. But the man who revels in *Atman*, who is content in *Atman* and who is satisfied only with *Atman*, for him no action exists.

18. He has no interest whatever in anything done, nor in anything not done, nor has he need to rely on anything for personal ends.

19. Therefore, do thou ever perform without attachment the work that thou must do; for performing action without attachment man attains the Supreme.

20. For through action alone Janaka and others achieved perfection; even with a view to the guidance of mankind thou must act.

21. Whatever the best man does, is also done by other men, what example he sets, the world follows.

22. For me, O Partha, there is naught to do in the three worlds, nothing worth gaining that I have not gained; yet I am ever in action.

An objection is sometimes raised that God being impersonal is not likely to perform any physical activity, at best He may be supposed to act mentally. This is not correct. For the unceasing movement of the sun, the moon, the earth etc. signifies God in action. This is not mental but physical activity. Though God is without form and impersonal, He acts as though He had form and body. Hence though He is ever in action, He is free from action, unaffected by action. What must be borne in mind is that, just as all Nature's movements and processes are mechanical and yet guided by Divine Intelligence or Will, even so man must reduce his daily conduct to mechanical regularity and precision, but he must do so intelligently. Man's merit lies in observing divine guidance at the back of these processes and in an intelligent imitation of it rather than in emphasizing the mechanical nature thereof and reducing himself to an automation. One has but to withdraw the self, withdraw attachment to fruit from all action, and then not only mechanical precision but security from all wear and tear will be ensured. Acting thus man remains fresh until the end of his days. His body will perish in due course, but his soul will remain evergreen without a crease or a wrinkle.

23. Indeed, for were I not, unslumbering, ever to remain in action, O Partha, men would follow my example in every way.

24. If I were not to perform my task, these worlds would be ruined; I should be the same cause of chaos and of the end of all mankind.

25. Just as, with attachment, the unenlightened perform all actions, O Bharata, even so, but unattached, should the enlightened man act, with a desire for the welfare of humanity.

26. The enlightened may not confuse the mind of the unenlightened, who are attached to action; rather must he perform all actions unattached, and thus encourage them to do likewise.

27. All action is entirely done by the *gunas* of *prakriti*. Man, deluded by the sense of 'I', thinks, 'I am the doer'.

28. But he, O Mahabahu, who understands the truth of the various *gunas* and their various activities, knows that it is the *gunas* that operate on the *gunas*; he does not claim to be the doer.

    As breathing, winking and similar processes are automatic and man claims no agency for them, he being conscious of the processes only when disease or similar cause arrests them, in a similar manner all his acclivities should be automatic, without his arrogating to himself the agency or responsibility thereof. A man of charity does not even know that he is doing charitable acts, it is his nature to do so, he cannot help it. This detachment can only come from tireless endeavour and God's grace.

29. Deluded by the *gunas* of *prakriti* men become attached to the activities of the *gunas*; he who knows the truth of things should not unhinge the slow-witted who have not the knowledge.

30. Cast all thy acts on Me, with thy mind fixed on the indwelling *Atman*, and without any thought of fruit, or sense of 'mine' shake off thy fever and fight!

    He who knows the *Atman* inhabiting the body and realizes Him to be a part of the supreme *Atman* will dedicate everything to Him, even as a faithful servant acts as a mere shadow of his master and dedicates to him all that he does. For the master is the real doer, the servant but the instrument.

31. Those who always act according to the rule I have here laid down, in faith and without cavilling—they too are released from the bondage of their actions.

32. But those who cavil at the rule and refuse to conform to it are fools, dead to all knowledge; know that they are lost.

33. Even a man of knowledge acts according to his nature; all creatures follow their nature; what then will constraint avail?

    This does not run counter to the teaching in II. 61 and II. 68. Self-restraint is the means of salvation (VI. 35; XIII. 7). Man's energies should be bent towards achieving complete self-restraint until the end of his days. But if he does not succeed, neither will constraint help him. The *shloka* does not rule out restraint but explains that nature prevails. He who justifies himself saying, 'I cannot do this, it is not in my nature,' misreads the *shloka*. True we do not know our nature, but habit is not nature. Progress, not decline, ascent, not descent, is the nature of the soul, and therefore every threatened decline or descent ought to be resisted. The next verse makes this abundantly clear.

34. Each sense has its settled likes and dislikes towards its objects; man should not come under the sway of these, for they are his besetters.

Hearing, for instance, is the object of the ears which may be inclined to hear something and disinclined to hear something else. Man may not allow himself to be swayed by these likes and dislikes, but must decide for himself what is conducive to his growth, his ultimate end being to reach the state beyond happiness and misery.

35. Better one's own duty, bereft of merit, than another's well-performed; better is death in the discharge of one's duty; another's duty is fraught with danger.

One man's duty may be to serve the community by working as a sweeper, another's may be to work as an accountant. An accountant's work may be more inviting, but that need not draw the sweeper away from his work. Should he allow himself to be drawn away he would himself be lost and put the community into danger. Before God the work of man will be judged by the spirit in which it is done, not by the nature of the work which makes no difference whatsoever. Whoever acts in a spirit of dedication fits himself for salvation.

ARJUNA SAID :

36. Then what impels man to sin, O Varshneya, even against his will, as though by force compelled?

THE LORD SAID :

37. It is Lust, it is Wrath, born of the *guna* — *Rajas*. It is the arch-devourer, the arch-sinner. Know this to be man's enemy here.

38. As fire is obscured by smoke, a mirror by dirt, and the embryo by the amnion, so is knowledge obscured by this.

39. Knowledge is obscured, O Kaunteya, by this eternal enemy of the wise man, in the form of Lust, the insatiable fire.

40. The senses, the mind and the reason are said to be its great seat; by means of these it obscures knowledge and stupefies man.

    When Lust seizes the senses, the mind is corrupted, discrimination is obscured and reason ruined. See II. 62-64.

41. Therefore, O Bharatarshabha, bridle thou first the senses and then rid thyself of this sinner, the destroyer of knowledge and discrimination.

42. Subtle, they say, are the senses; subtler than the senses is the mind; subtler than the mind is the reason; but subtler even than the reason is He.

43. Thus realizing Him to be subtler than the reason, and controlling the self by the Self (*Atman*), destroy, O Mahabahu, this enemy—Lust, so hard to overcome.

    When man realizes Him, his mind will be under his control, not swayed by the senses. And when the mind is conquered, what power has Lust? It is indeed a subtle enemy, but when once the senses, the mind and the reason are under the control of the subtlemost Self, Lust is extinguished.

Thus ends the third discourse entitled *'Karma Yoga'* in
the converse of Lord Krishna and Arjuna, on the
science of *Yoga*, as part of the knowledge of Brahman
in the Upanishad called the *Bhagawadgita*.

Discourse 4

This discourse further explains the subject-matter of the third and describes the various kinds of sacrifice.

THE LORD SAID:

1. I expounded this imperishable *yoga* to Vivasvat; Vivasvat communicated it to Manu, and Manu to Ikshvaku.

2. Thus handed down in succession, the royal sages learnt it; with long lapse of time it dwindled away in this world, O Parantapa.

3. The same ancient *yoga* have I expounded to thee today; for thou art My devotee and My friend, and this is the supreme mystery.

ARJUNA SAID:

4. Later was Thy birth, my Lord, earlier that of Vivasvat. How then am I to understand that Thou didst expound it in the beginning?

THE LORD SAID:

5. Many births have we passed through, O Arjuna, both thou and I; I know them all, thou knowest them not, O Parantapa.

6. Though unborn and inexhaustible in My essence, though Lord of all beings, yet assuming control over My Nature, I come into being by My mysterious power.

7. For whenever Right declines and Wrong prevails, then O Bharata, I come to birth.

8. To save the righteous, to destroy the wicked, and to re-establish Right I am born from age to age.

   Here is comfort for the faithful and affirmation of the truth that Right ever prevails. An eternal conflict between Right and Wrong goes on. Sometimes the latter seems to get the upper hand, but it is Right which ultimately prevails. The good are never destroyed, for Right—which is Truth—cannot perish; the wicked are destroyed, because Wrong has no independent existence. Knowing this let man cease to arrogate to himself authorship and eschew untruth, violence and evil. Inscrutable Providence—the unique power of the Lord—is ever at work. This in fact is avatara, incarnation. Strictly speaking there can be no birth for God.

9. He who knows the secret of this My divine birth and action is not born again, after leaving the body; he comes to Me, O Arjuna.

   For when a man is secure in the faith that Right always prevails, he never swerves therefrom, pursuing to the bitterest end and against serious odds, and as no part of the effort proceeds from his ego, but all is dedicated to Him, being ever one with Him, he is released from birth to death.

10. Freed from passion, fear and wrath, filled full with Me, relying on Me, and refined by the fiery ordeal of knowledge, many have become one with Me.

11. In whatever way men resort to Me, even so do I render to them. In every way, O Partha, the path men follow is Mine.

    That is, the whole world is under His ordinance. No one may break God's law with impunity. As we sow, so shall we reap. This law operates inexorably without fear or favor.

12. Those who desire their actions to bear fruit worship the gods here; for in this world of men the fruit of action is quickly obtainable.

    Gods, as indicated before, must not be taken to mean the heavenly beings of tradition, but whatever reflects the divine. In that sense man is also a god. Steam, electricity and the other great forces of Nature are all gods. Propitiation of these forces quickly bears fruit, as we well know, but it is short-lived. It fails to bring comfort to the soul and it certainly does not take one even a short step towards salvation.

13. The order of the four *varnas* was created by Me according to the different *gunas* and *karma* of each; yet know that though, therefore, author thereof, being changeless I am not the author.

14. Actions do not affect Me, nor am I concerned with the fruits thereof. He who recognizes Me as such is not bound by actions.

For man has thus before him the supreme example of one who though in action is not the doer thereof. And when we are but instruments in His hands, where then is the room for arrogating responsibility for action?

15. Knowing this did men of old, desirous of freedom, perform action; do thou, then, just as they did—the men of old in days gone by.

16. 'What is action? What is inaction?'—here even the wise are perplexed. I will then expound to thee that action knowing which thou shalt be saved from evil.

17. For it is meet to know the meaning of action, of forbidden action, as also inaction. Impenetrable is the secret of action.

18. Who sees action in action and action in inaction, he is enlightened among men, he is a *yogi*, he has done all he need do.

The 'action' of him who, though ever active, does not claim to be the doer, is inaction; and the 'inaction' of him who, though outwardly avoiding action, is always building castles in his own mind, is action. The enlightened man who has grasped the secret of action knows that no action proceeds from him, all proceeds from God and hence he selflessly remains absorbed in action. He is the true *yogi*. The man who acts self-fully misses the secret of action and cannot distinguish between Right and Wrong. The soul's natural progress is towards selflessness and purity and one might, therefore, say that the man who strays from the path of purity strays from selflessness. All actions of the selfless man are naturally pure.

19. He whose every undertaking is free from desire and selfish purpose, and he who has burnt all his actions in the fire of knowledge—such an one the wise call a *pandita*.

20. He who has renounced attachment to the fruit of action, who is ever content, and free from all dependence,—he, though immersed in action, yet acts not.

That is, his action does not bind him.

21. Expecting naught, holding his mind and body in check, putting away every possession, and going through action only in the body he incurs no stain.

The purest act, if tainted by 'self', binds. But when it is done in a spirit of dedication, it ceases to bind. When 'self' has completely subsided, it is only the body that works. For instance, in the case of a man who is asleep his body alone is working. A prisoner doing his prison tasks has surrendered his body to the prison authorities and only his body, therefore, works. Similarly, he who has voluntarily made himself God's prisoner, does nothing himself. His body mechanically acts, the doer is God, hot he. He has reduced himself to nothingness.

22. Content with whatever chance may bring, rid of the pairs of opposites, free from ill-will, even-minded in success and failure, he is not bound though he acts.

23. Of the free soul who has shred all attachment, whose mind is firmly grounded in knowledge, who acts only for sacrifice, all *karma* is extinguished.

24. The offering of sacrifice is *Brahman;* the oblation is *Brahman;* it is offered by *Brahman* in the fire that is *Brahman;* thus he whose mind is fixed on acts dedicated to *Brahman* must needs pass on to *Brahman.*

25. Some *yogins* perform sacrifice in the form of worship of the gods, others offer sacrifice of sacrifice itself in the fire that is *Brahman.*

26. Some offer as sacrifice the sense of hearing and the other senses in the fires of restraint; others sacrifice sound and the other objects of sense in the fires of the senses.

The restraint of the senses—hearing and others—is one thing; and directing them only to legitimate objects, e.g. listening to hymns in the praise of god, is another, although ultimately both amount to the same thing.

27. Others again sacrifice all the activities of the senses and of the vital
    energy in the *yogic* fire of self-control kindled by knowledge.

    That is to say, they lose themselves in the contemplation of the
    Supreme.

28. Some sacrifice with material gifts; with austerities; with *yoga*; some
    with the acquiring and some with the imparting of knowledge. All
    these are sacrifices of stern vows and serious endeavour.

29. Others absorbed in the practices of the control of the vital energy
    sacrifice the outward in the inward and the inward in the outward, or
    check the flow of both the inward and the outward vital airs.

    The reference here is to the three kinds of practices of the control
    of vital energy—*puraka, rechaka,* and *kumbhaka.*

30. Yet others, abstemious in food, sacrifice one form of vital energy in
    another. All these know what sacrifice is and purge themselves of all
    impurities by sacrifice.

31. Those who partake of the residue of sacrifice—called *amrita* (ambro-
    sia)—attain to everlasting *Brahman.* Even this world is not for a
    non-sacrificer; how then the next, O Kurusattama?

32. Even so various sacrifices have been described in the Vedas; know
    them all to proceed from action; knowing this thou shalt be released.

    Action here means mental, physical and spiritual action. No
    sacrifice is possible without this triple action and no salvation with-
    out sacrifice. To know this and to put the knowledge into practice is
    to know the secret of sacrifice. In fine, unless man uses all his phys-
    ical, mental and spiritual gifts in the service of mankind, he is a thief
    unfit for Freedom. He who uses his intellect only and spares his
    body is not a full sacrificer. Unless the mind and the body and the
    soul are made to work in unison, they cannot be adequately used for
    the service of mankind. Physical, mental and spiritual purity is essen-
    tial for the harmonious working. Therefore man should concentrate
    on developing, purifying, and turning to the best of all his faculties.

33. Knowledge-sacrifice is better, O-Parantapa, than material sacrifice, for
    all action which does not bind finds its consummation in Knowledge
    (*jnana*).

Who does not know that works of charity performed without knowledge often result in great harm? Unless every act, however nobel its motive, is informed with knowledge, it lacks perfection. Hence the complete fulfillment of all action is in knowledge.

34. The masters of knowledge who have seen the Truth will impart to thee this Knowledge; learn it through humble homage and service and by repeated questioning.

The three conditions of knowledge—homage, repeated questioning and service—deserve to be carefully borne in mind in this age. Homage or obeisance means humility and service is a necessary accompaniment; else it would be mock homage. Repeated questioning is equally essential, for without a keen spirit of inquiry, there is no knowledge. All this presupposes devotion to and faith in the person approached. There can be no humility, much less service, without faith.

35. When thou hast gained this knowledge, O Pandava, thou shalt not again fall into such error; by virtue of it thou shalt see all beings without exception in thyself and thus in Me.

The adage '*Yatha pinde tatha brahmande*'—'as with the self so with the universe') means the same thing. He who has attained Self-realization sees no difference between himself and others.

36. Even though thou be the most sinful of sinners, thou shalt cross the ocean of sin by the boat of knowledge.

37. As a blazing fire turns its fuel to ashes, O Arjuna, even so the fire of Knowledge turns all actions to ashes.

38. There is nothing in this world so purifying as Knowledge. He who is perfected by *yoga* finds it in himself in the fullness of time.

39. It is the man of faith who gains knowledge—the man who is intent on it and who has mastery over his senses; having gained knowledge, he comes ere long to the supreme peace.

40. But the man of doubt, without knowledge and without faith, is lost; for him who is given to doubt there is neither this world nor that beyond, nor happiness.

41. He who has renounced all action by means of *yoga*, who has severed all doubt by means of knowledge—him self-possessed, no actions bind, O Dhananjaya!

42. Therefore, with the sword of Self-realization sever thou this doubt, bred of ignorance, which has crept into thy heart! Betake thyself to *yoga* and arise, O Bharata!

Thus ends the fourth discourse, entitled *'Jnana-Karma-Sannyasa-Yoga'* in the converse of Lord Krishna and Arjuna, on the science of *Yoga*, as part of the knowledge of Brahman in the Upanishad called the *Bhagawadgita*.

Discource 5

This discourse is devoted to showing that renunciation of action as such is impossible without the discipline of selfless action and that both are ultimately one.

Arjuna Said :

1. Thou laudest renunciation of actions, O Krishna, whilst at the same time thou laudest performance of action; tell me for a certainty which is the better.

The Lord Said :

2. Renunciation and performance of action both lead to salvation; but of the two, *karmayoga* (performance) is better than *sannyasa* (renunciation).

3. Him one should know as ever renouncing who has no dislikes and likes; for he who is free from the pairs of opposites is easily released from bondage.

    That is, not renunciation of action but of attachment to the pairs determines true renunciation. A man who is always in action may be a good *sannyasa* (renouncer) and another who may be doing no work may well be a hypocrite. See III. 6.

4. It is the ignorant who speak of *sankhya* and *yoga* as different, not so those who have knowledge. He who is rightly established even in one wins to the fruit of both.

The *yogi* engrossed in *sankhya* (knowledge) lives even in thought for the good of the world and attains the fruit of *karmayoga* by the sheer power of his thought. The *karmayogi* ever engrossed in unattached action naturally enjoys the peace of the *jnanayogi*.

5. The goal that the *sankhya*s attain is also reached by the *yogins*. He sees truly who sees both *sankhya* and *yoga* as one.

6. But renunciation, O Mahabahu, is hard to attain except by *yoga;* the ascetic equipped with *yoga* attains *Brahman* ere long.

7. The *yogi* who has cleared himself, has gained mastery over his mind and all his senses, who has become one with the *Atman* in all creation, although he acts he remains unaffected.

8. The *yogi* who has seen the Truth knows that it is not he that acts whilst seeing, hearing, touching, smelling, eating, walking, sleeping, or breathing.

9. Talking, letting go, holding fast, opening or closing the eyes—in the conviction that is the senses that are moving in their respective spheres.

   So long as 'self' endures, this detachment cannot be achieved. A sensual man therefore may not shelter himself under the pretence that it is not he but his senses that are acting. Such a mischievous interpretation betrays a gross ignorance of the *Gita* and right conduct. The next *shloka* makes this clear.

10. He who dedicates his actions to *Brahman* and performs them without attachment is not smeared by sin, as the lotus-leaf by water.

11. Only with the body, mind and intellect and also with the senses, do the *yogins* perform action without attachment for the sake of self-purification.

12. A man of *yoga* obtains everlasting peace by abandoning the fruit of action; the man ignorant of *yoga*, selfishly attached to fruit, remains bound.

13. Renouncing with the mind all actions, the dweller in the body, who is master of himself, rests happily in his city of nine gates, neither doing nor getting anything done.

    The principal gates of the body are the two eyes, the two nostrils, the two ears, the mouth, and the two organs of excretion—though really speaking the countless pores of the skin are no less gates. If the gatekeeper always remains on the alert and performs his task, letting in or out only the objects that deserve ingress or egress, then of him it can truly be said that he has no part in the ingress or egress, but that he is a passive witness. He thus does nothing nor gets anything done.

14. The Lord creates neither agency nor action for the world; neither does he connect action with its fruit. It is nature that is at work.

    God is no doer. The inexorable law of *karma* prevails, and in the very fulfillment of the law—giving everyone his deserts, making everyone reap what he sows—lies God's abounding mercy and justice. In undiluted justice is mercy. Mercy which is inconsistent with justice is not mercy but it's opposite. But man is not a judge knowing past, present, and future. So for him the law is reversed and mercy or forgiveness is the purest justice. Being himself ever liable to be judged he must accord to others what he would accord to himself, viz. forgiveness. Only by cultivating the spirit of forgiveness can he reach the state of a *yogi*, whom no actions bind, the man of even-mindedness, the man skilled in action.

15. The Lord does not take upon Himself anyone's vice or virtue; it is ignorance that veils knowledge and deludes all creatures.

    The delusion lies in man arrogating to himself the authorship of action and the attributing to God the consequences thereof—punishment or reward as the case may be.

16. But to them whose ignorance is destroyed by the knowledge of *Atman*, this their knowledge, like the sun, reveals the Supreme.

17. Those whose intellect is suffused with That, whose self has become one with That, who abide in That, and whose end and aim is that, wipe out their sins with knowledge, and go whence there is no return.

18. The men of Self-realization look with an equal eye on a *brahmana* possessed of learning and humility, a cow, an elephant, a dog and even a dog-eater.

    That is to say, they serve every one of them alike, according to the needs of each. Treating a *brahmana* and *shwapaka* (dog-eater) alike means that the wise man will suck the poison off a snake-bitten *shwapaka* with as much eagerness and readiness as he would from a snake-bitten *brahmana*.

19. In this very body they have conquered the round of birth and death, whose mind is anchored in sameness; for perfect *Brahman* is same to all, therefore in *Brahman* they rest.

    As a man thinks, so he becomes, and therefore those whose minds are bent on being the same to all achieve that sameness and become one with *Brahman*.

20. He whose understanding is secure, who is undeluded, who knows *Brahman* and who rests in *Brahman*, will neither be glad to get what is pleasant, nor sad to get what is unpleasant.

21. He who has detached himself from contacts without, finds bliss in *Atman*; having achieved union with *Brahman* he enjoys eternal bliss.

    He who has weaned himself from outward objects to the inner *Atman* is fitted for union with *Brahman* and the highest bliss. To withdraw oneself from contacts without and to bask in the sunshine of union with *Brahman* are two aspects of the same state, two sides of the same coin.

22. For the joys derived from sense-contacts are nothing but mines of misery; they have beginning and end, O Kaunteya; the wise man does not revel therein.

23. The man who is able even here on earth, ere he is released from the body, to hold out against the floodtide of lust and wrath,—he is a *yogi*, he is happy.

    As a corpse has no likes and dislikes, no sensibility to pleasure and pain, even so he who though alive is dead to these, he truly lives, he is truly happy.

24. He who finds happiness only within, rest only within, light only within,—that *yogi*, having become one with nature, attains to oneness with *Brahman*.

25. They win oneness with *Brahman*—the seers whose sins are wiped out, whose doubts are resolved, who have mastered themselves, and who are engrossed in the welfare of all beings.

26. Rid of lust and wrath, masters of themselves, the ascetics who have realized *Atman* find oneness with *Brahman* everywhere around them.

27-28. That ascetic is ever free—who, having shut out the outward sense-contacts, sits with his gaze fixed between the brows, outward and inward breathing in the nostrils made equal; his senses, mind, and reason held in check; rid of longing, fear and wrath; and intent on Freedom.

These *shlokas* refer to some of the *yogic* practices laid down in the *Yoga-sutras*. A word of caution is necessary regarding these practices. They serve for the *yogin* the same purpose as athletics and gymnastics do for the *bhogin* (who pursues worldly pleasures). His physical exercises help the latter to keep his senses of enjoyment in full vigour. The *yogic* practices help the *yogin* to keep his body in condition and his senses in subjection. Men versed in these practices are rare in these days, and few of them turn them to good account. He who has achieved the preliminary stage on the path to self-discipline, he who has a passion for Freedom, and who having rid himself of the pairs of opposites has conquered fear, would do well to go in for these practices which will surely help him. It is such a disciplined man alone who can, through these practices, render his body a holy temple of God. Purity both of the mind and body is a sine qua non, without which these processes are likely, in the first instance, to lead a man astray and then drive him deeper into the slough of delusion. That this has been the result in some cases many know from actual experience. That is why that prince of *yogins*, Patanjali gave the first place to *yamas* (cardinal vows) and *niyamas* (casual vows), and held as eligible for *yogic* practices only those who have gone through the preliminary discipline.

The five cardinal vows are: non-violence, truth, non-stealing, celibacy, non-possession. The five casual vows are: bodily purity, contentment, the study of the scriptures, austerity, and meditation of God.

29. Knowing Me as the Acceptor of sacrifice and austerity, the great Lord of all the worlds, the Friend of all creation, the *yogi* attains to peace.

This *shloka* may appear to be in conflict with *shlokas* 14 and 15 of this discourse and similar ones in other discourses. It is not really so.

Almighty God is Doer and non-Doer, Enjoyer and non-Enjoyer both. He is indescribably, beyond the power of human speech. Man somehow strives to have a glimpse of Him and in so doing invests Him with diverse and even contradictory attributes.

Thus ends the fifth discourse, entitled *'Sannyasa Yoga'* in the converse of Lord Krishna and Arjuna, on the science of *Yoga*, as part of the knowledge of Brahman, in the Upanishad called the *Bhagawadgita*.

Discource 6

This discourse deals with some of the means for the accomplishment of Yoga or the discipline of the mind and its activities.

THE LORD SAID :

1. He who performs all obligatory action, without depending on the fruit thereof, is a *sannyasin* and a *yogin*—not the man who neglects the sacrificial fire nor he who neglects action. Fire here may be taken to mean all possible instruments of action.

   Fire was needed when sacrifices used to be performed with its help. Assuming that spinning were a means of universal service in this age, a man by neglecting the spinning wheel would not become a *sannyasi*.

2. What is called *sannyasa*, know thou to be *yoga*, O Pandava; for none can become a *yogin* who has not renounced selfish purpose.

3. For the man who seeks to scale the heights of *yoga*, action is said to be the means; for the same man, when he has scaled those heights, repose is said to be the means.

   He who has purged himself of all impurities and who has achieved even-mindedness will easily achieve Self-realization. But this does not mean that he who has scaled the heights of *yoga* will disdain to work for the guidance of the world. On the contrary that work will be to him not only the breath of his nostrils, but also as natural to him as breathing. He will do so by the sheer force of will. See V. 4.

4. When a man is not attached either to the objects of sense or to actions and sheds all selfish purpose, then he is said to have scaled the heights of *yoga*.

5. By one's Self should one raise oneself, and not allow oneself to fall; for *Atman* (Self) alone is the friend of self, and Self alone is self's foe.

6. His Self alone is friend, who has conquered himself by his Self: but to him who has not conquered himself and is thus inimical to himself, even his Self behaves as foe.

7. Of him who has conquered himself and who rests in perfect calm the self is completely composed, in cold and heat, in pleasure and pain, in honour and dishonour.

8. The *yogin* who is filled with the contentment of wisdom and discriminative knowledge, who is firm as a rock, who has mastered his senses, and to whom a clod of earth, a stone and gold are the same, is possessed of *yoga*.

9. He excels who regards alike the boon companion, the friend, the enemy, the stranger, the mediator, the alien and the ally, as also the saint and the sinner.

10. Let the *yogi* constantly apply his thought to *Atman* remaining alone in a scheduled place, his mind and body in control, rid of desires and possessions.

11. Fixing for himself, in a pure spot, a firm seat, neither too high nor yet too low, covered with *kusha* grass, thereon a deerskin, and thereon a cloth;

12. Sitting on that seat, with mind concentrated, the functions of thought and sense of control, he should set himself to the practice of *yoga* for the sake of self-purification.

13. Keeping himself steady, holding the trunk, the neck and the head in a straight line and motionless, fixing his eye on the tip of his nose, and looking not around.

14. Tranquil in spirit, free from fear, steadfast in the vow of *brahmacharya*, holding his mind in control, the *yogi* should sit, with all his thoughts on Me, absorbed in Me.

    Brahmacharya (usually translated 'celibacy') means not only sexual continence but observance of all the cardinal vows for the attainment of *Brahman*.

15. The *yogi*, who ever thus, with mind controlled, unites himself to *Atman*, wins the peace which culminates in Nirvana, the peace that is in Me.

16. *Yoga* is not for him who eats too much, nor for him who fasts too much, neither for him who sleeps too much, nor yet for him who is too wakeful.

17. To him who is disciplined in food and recreation, in effort in all activities, and in sleep and waking, *yoga* (discipline) becomes a relief from all ills.

18. When one's thought, completely controlled, rests steadily on only *Atman*, when one is free from longing for all objects of desire, then one is called a *yogin*.

19. As a taper in a windless spot flickers not, even so is a *yogin*, with his thought controlled, seeking to unite himself with *Atman*.

20. Where thought curbed by the practice of *yoga* completely ceases, where a man sits content within himself, *Atman* having seen *Atman*;

21. Where he experiences that endless bliss beyond the senses which can be grasped by reason alone; wherein established he swerves not from the Truth;

22. Where he holds no other gain greater than that which he has gained; and where, securely seated, he is not shaken by any calamity however great;

23. That state should be known as *yoga* (union with the Supreme), the disunion from all union with pain. This *yoga* must one practice with firm resolve and unwearying zeal.

24. Shaking oneself completely free from longings born of selfish purpose; reining in the whole host of senses, from all sides, with the mind itself;

25. With reason held securely by the will, he should gradually attain calm and with the mind established in *Atman* think of nothing.

26. Wherever the fickle and unsteady mind wanders, thence should it be reined and brought under the sole sway of *Atman*.

27. For, supreme bliss comes to this *yogin*, who, with mind becalmed, with passions stilled, has become one with *Brahman*, and is purged of all stain.

28. The *yogin*, cleansed of all stain, unites himself ever thus to *Atman*, easily enjoys the endless bliss of contact with *Brahman*.

29. The man equipped with *yoga* looks on all with an impartial eye, seeing *Atman* in all beings and all beings in *Atman*.

30. He who sees Me everywhere and everything in Me, never vanishes from Me nor I from him.

31. The *yogin* who, anchored in unity, worships Me abiding in all beings, lives and moves in me, no matter how he live and move.

So long as 'self' subsists, the Supreme Self is absent; when 'self' is extinguished, the Supreme Self is seen everywhere. Also see note on XIII. 23.

32. He who, by likening himself with others, senses pleasure and pain equally for all as for himself, is deemed to be the highest *yogi*, O Arjuna.

ARJUNA SAID :

33. I do not see, O Madhusudana, how this *yoga*, based on the equal-mindedness that Thou hast expounded to me, can steadily endure, because of fickleness (of the mind).

34. For fickle is the mind, O Krishna, unruly, overpowering and stubborn; to curb it is, I think, as hard as to curb the wind.

THE LORD SAID :

35. Undoubtedly, O Mahabahu, the mind is fickle and hard to curb; yet, O Kaunteya, it can be held in check by constant practice and dispassion.

36. Without self-restraint, *yoga*, I hold, is difficult to attain; but the self-governed soul can attain it by proper means, if he strives for it.

ARJUNA SAID :

37. If one, possessed of faith, but slack of effort, because of his mind straying from *yoga*, reach not perfection in *yoga*, what end does he come to, O Krishna?

38. Without a foothold, and floundering in the path to *Brahman* fallen from both, is he indeed not lost, O Mahabahu, like a dissipated cloud?

39. This my doubt, O Krishna, do thou dispel utterly; for there is to be found none other than thou to banish this doubt.

THE LORD SAID :

40. Neither in this world, nor in the next, can there be ruin for him, O Partha; no well-doer, oh loved one, meets with a sad end.

41. Fallen from *yoga*, a man attains the worlds of righteous souls, and having dwelt there for numberless years is then born in a house of pure and gentle blood.

42. Or he may even be born into a family of *yogins*, though such birth as this is all too rare in this world.

43. There, O Kurunandana, he discovers the intellectual stage he had reached in previous birth, and thence he stretches forward again towards perfection.

44. By virtue of that previous practice he is borne on, whether he will it or not, even he with a desire to know *yoga* passes beyond the Vedic ritual.

45. But the *yogi* who perseveres in his striving, cleansed of sin, perfected through many births, reaches the highest state.

46. The *yogin* is deemed higher than the man of austerities; he is deemed also higher than the man of knowledge; higher is he than the man engrossed in ritual; therefore be thou a *yogin*, O Arjuna!

47. And among all *yogins*, he who worships Me with faith, his inmost self all rapt in Me, is deemed by me to be the best *yogin*.

Thus ends the sixth discourse entitled '*Dhyana Yoga*' in
the converse of Lord Krishna and Arjuna, on the
science of *Yoga*, as part of the knowledge of *Brahman* in
the Upanishad called the *Bhagawadgita*.

Discource 7

With this discourse begins an exposition of the nature of Reality and the secret of devotion.

THE LORD SAID :

1. Hear, O Partha, how, with thy mind rivetted on me, by practicing *yoga* and making me the sole refuge, thou shalt, without doubt, know me fully.

2. I will declare to thee, in its entirety, this knowledge, combined with discriminative knowledge, which when thou hast known there remains here nothing more to be known.

3. Among thousands of men hardly one strives after perfection; among those who strive hardly one knows Me in truth.

4. Earth, Water, Fire, Air, Ether, Mind, Reason and Ego—thus eightfold is my *prakriti* divided.

   The eightfold *prakriti* is substantially the same as the field described in XIII. 5 and the perishable Being in XV. 16.

5. This is My lower aspect; but know thou My other aspect, the higher— which is *Jiva* (the Vital Essence) by which, O Mahabahu, this world is sustained.

6. Know that these two compose the source from which all beings spring; I am the origin and end of the entire universe.

7. There is nothing higher than I, O Dhananjaya; all this is strung on Me as a row of gems upon a thread.

8. In water I am the savour, O Kaunteya; in the sun and the moon I am the light; the syllable *AUM* in all the Vedas; the sound in ether, and manliness in men.

9. I am the sweet fragrance in earth; the brilliance in fire; the life in all beings; and the austerity in ascetics.

10. Know Me, O Partha, to be the primeval seed of all beings; I am the reason of rational beings and the splendour of the splendid.

11. Of the strong, I am the strength, divorced from lust and passion; in beings I am desire undivorced from righteousness.

12. Know that all the manifestations of the three *gunas*, *sattva*, *rajas*, and *tamas*, proceed from none but Me; yet I am not in them; they are in Me.

    God is not dependent on them, they are dependent on Him. Without Him those various manifestations would be impossible.

13. Befogged by these manifestations of the three *gunas*, the entire world fails to recognize Me, the imperishable, as transcending them.

14. For this My divine delusive mystery made up of the three *gunas* is hard to pierce; but those who make Me their sole refuge pierce the veil.

15. The deluded evil-doers, lowest of men, do not see refuge in Me; for, by reason of this delusive mystery, they are bereft of knowledge and given to devilish ways.

16. Four types of well-doers are devoted to Me, O Arjuna; they are, O Bharatarshabha, the afflicted, the spiritual seeker, the material seeker, and the enlightened.

17. Of these the enlightened, ever attached to Me in single-minded devotion, is the best; for to the enlightened I am exceedingly dear and he is dear to Me.

18. All these are estimable indeed, but the enlightened I hold to be My very self; for he, the true *yogi*, is stayed on Me alone, the supreme goal.

19. At the end of many births the enlightened man finds refuge in Me; rare indeed is this great soul to whom 'Vasudeva is all'.

20. Men, bereft of knowledge by reason of various longings, seek refuge in other gods, pinning their faith on diverse rites, guided by their own nature.

21. Whatever form one desires to worship in faith and devotion, in that very form I make that faith of his secure.

22. Possessed of that faith he seeks a propitiate that one, and obtains there through his longings, dispensed in truth by none but Me.

23. But limited is the fruit that falls to those short-sighted ones; those who worship the gods go to the gods, those who worship Me come unto Me.

24. Not knowing My transcendent, imperishable, supreme character, the undiscerning think Me who am unmanifest to have become manifest.

25. Veiled by the delusive mystery created by My unique power, I am not manifest to all; this bewildered world does not recognize Me, birthless and changeless.

Having the power to create this world of sense and yet unaffected by it, He is described as having unique power.

26. I know, O Arjuna, all creatures past, present and to be; but no one knows Me.

27. All creatures in this universe are bewildered, O Parantapa, by virtue of the delusion of the pairs of opposite sprung from likes and dislikes, O Bharata.

28. But those virtuous men whose sin has come to an end, freed from delusion and of the pairs of opposites, worship Me in steadfast faith.

29. Those who endeavour for freedom from age and death by taking refuge in Me, know in full that *Brahman*, *Adhyatma* and all *Karma*.

30. Those who know Me, including *Adhibhuta*, *Adhidaiva*, *Adhiyajna*, possessed of even-mindedness, they know Me even at the time of passing away.

The terms in italics are defined in the next discourse the subject of which is indicated in 29-30. The sense is that every nook and cranny of the universe is filled with *Brahman*, that He is the sole Agent of all action, and that the man who imbued to Him, becomes one with Him at the time of passing hence. All his desires are extinguished in his vision of Him and he wins his freedom.

Thus ends the seventh discourse, entitled *'Jananvijnana Yoga'* in the converse of Lord Krishna and Arjuna, on the science of *Yoga,* as part of the knowledge of *Brahman* in the Upanishad called the *Bhagawadgita.*

Discource 8

The nature of the Supreme is further expounded in this discourse.

ARJUNA SAID:

1. What is that *Brahman?* What is *Adhyatma?* What *Karma*, O *Purushottama?* What is called *Adhibhuta?* And what *Adhidaiva?*

2. And who here in this body is *Adhiyajna* and how? And how at the time of death art Thou to be known by the self-controlled?

THE LORD SAID:

3. The Supreme, the Imperishable is *Brahman;* its manifestation is *Adhyatma;* the creative process whereby all beings are created is called *Karma.*

4. *Adhibhuta* is My perishable form; *Adhidaivata* is the individual self in that form; and O best among the embodied, *Adhiyajna* am I in this body, purified by sacrifice. That is, from Imperishable Unmanifest down to the perishable atom everything in the universe is the Supreme and an expression of the Supreme. Why then should mortal man arrogate to himself authorship of anything rather than do His bidding and dedicate all action to Him?

5. And he who, at the last hour remembering Me only, departs leaving the body, enters into Me; of that there is no doubt.

6. Or whatever form a man continually contemplates, that same he remembers in the hour of death, and to that very form he goes, O Kaunteya.

7. Therefore at all times remember Me and fight on; thy mind and reason thus on Me fixed thou shalt surely come to Me.

8. With thought steadied by constant practice, and wandering nowhere, he who meditates on the Supreme Celestial Being, O Partha, goes to Him.

9-10. Whoso, at the time of death, with unwavering mind, with devotion, and fixing the breath rightly between the brows by the power of *yoga*, meditates on the Sage, the Ancient, the Ruler, subtler than the subtlest, the Supporter of all, the Inconceivable, glorious as the sun beyond the darkness,—he goes to that Supreme Celestial Being.

11. That which the knowers of the Vedas call the Imperishable (or that word which the knowers of the Vedas repeat), wherein the ascetics freed from passion enter and desiring which they practice *brahmacharya*, that Goal (or Word) I will declare to thee in brief.

12. Closing all the gates, locking up the mind in the *hridaya*, fixing his breath within the head, rapt in *yogic* meditation;

13. Whoso departs leaving the body uttering *AUM—Brahman* in one syllable—repeatedly thinking on Me, he reaches the highest state.

14. That *yogi* easily wins to Me, O Partha, who, ever attached to Me, constantly remembers Me with undivided mind.

15. Great souls, having come to Me, reach the highest perfection; they come not again to birth, unlasting and (withal) an abode of misery.

16. From the world of Brahma down, all the worlds are subject to return, O Arjuna; but on coming to Me there is no rebirth.

17. Those men indeed know what is Day and what is Night, who know that Brahma's day lasts a thousand yugas and that his night too is a thousand yugas long.

That is to say, our day and night of a dozen hours each are less than the infinitesimal fraction of a moment in that vast cycle of time. Pleasures pursued during these incalculably small moments are as illusory as a mirage. Rather than waste these brief moments, we should devote them to serving God through service of mankind. On the other hand, our time is such a small drop in the ocean of eternity that if we fail of our object here, viz. Self-realization, we need not despair. She should bide our time.

18. At the coming of Day all the manifest spring forth from the Unmanifest, and at the coming of Night they are dissolved into that same Unmanifest.

   Knowing this too, man should understand that he has very little power over things, the round of birth and death is ceaseless.

19. This same multitude of creatures come to birth, O Partha, again and again; they are dissolved at the coming of Night, whether they will or not; and at the break of Day they are re-born.

20. But higher than the Unmanifest is another Unmanifest Being, everlasting, which perisheth not when all creatures perish.

21. This Unmanifest, named the Imperishable, is declared to be the highest goal. For those who reach it there is no return. That is my highest abode.

22. This Supreme Being, O Partha, may be won by undivided devotion; in It all beings dwell, by It all is pervaded.

23. Now I will tell thee, Bharatarshabha, the conditions which determine the exemption from return, as also the return, of *yogins* after they pass away hence.

24. Fire, Light, Day, the Bright Fortnight, the six months of the Northern Solstice—through these departing men knowing *Brahman* go to *Brahman*.

25. Smoke, Night, the Dark Fortnight, the six months of the Southern Solstice—There through the *yogin* attains to the lunar light and thence returns.

   I do not understand the meaning of these two *shlokas*. They do not seem to me to be consistent with the teaching of the *Gita*. The *Gita* teaches that he whose heart is meek with devotion, who is devoted to unattached action and has seen the Truth must win salvation, no matter when he dies. These *shlokas* seem to run counter to this. They may perhaps be stretched to mean broadly that a man of sacrifice, a man of light, a man who has known *Brahman* finds release from birth if he retains that enlightenment at the time of death, and that on the contrary the man who has none of these attributes goes to the world of the moon—not at all lasting—and returns to birth. The moon, after all, shines with borrowed light.

26. These two paths—bright and dark—are deemed to be the eternal paths of the world; by the one a man goes to return not, by the other he returns again.

    The Bright one may be taken to mean the path of knowledge and the dark one that of ignorance.

27. The *Yogin* knowing these two paths falls not into delusion, O Partha; therefore, at all times, O Arjuna, remain steadfast in *yoga*.

    "Will not fall into delusion" means that he who knows the two paths and has known the secret of even-mindedness will not take the path of ignorance.

28. Whatever fruit of good deeds is laid down as accruing from (a study of) the Vedas, from sacrifices, austerities, and acts of charity—all that the *yogin* transcends, on knowing this, and reaches the Supreme and Primal Abode.

    He who has achieved even-mindedness by dint of devotion, knowledge and service not only obtains the fruit of all his good actions, but also wins salvation.

Thus ends the eighth discourse entitled *'Brahma Yoga'* in
the converse of Lord Krishna and Arjuna, on the science
of *Yoga*, as part of the knowledge of *Brahman* in the
Upanishad called the *Bhagawadgita*.

Discource 9

This discourse reveals the glory of devotion.

THE LORD SAID :

1. I will now declare to thee, who art uncensorious, this mysterious knowledge, together with discriminative knowledge, knowing which thou shalt be released from ill.

2. This is the king of sciences, the king of mysteries, pure and sovereign, capable of direct comprehension, the essence of *dharma*, easy to practice, changeless.

3. Men who have no faith in this doctrine, O Parantapa, far from coming to Me, return repeatedly to the path of this world of death.

4. By Me, unmanifest in form, this whole world is pervaded; all beings are in Me, I am not in them.

5. And yet those beings are not in Me. That indeed is My unique power as Lord! Sustainer of all beings, I am not in them; My Self brings them into existence.

   The sovereign power of God lies in this mystery, this miracle, that all beings are in Him and yet not in Him, He in them and yet not in them. This is the description of God in the language of mortal man. Indeed He soothes man by revealing to him all His aspects by using all kinds of paradoxes. All beings are in him inasmuch as all creation is His; but as He transcends it all, as He really is not the author of it all, it may be said with equal truth that the beings are not in Him. He really is in all His true devotees, He is not, according to them, in those who deny Him. What is this if not a mystery, a miracle of God?

6. As the mighty wind, moving everywhere, is ever contained in ether, even so know that all beings are contained in Me.

7. All beings, O Kaunteya, merge into my *prakriti*, at the end of a *kalpa*, and I send them forth again when a *kalpa* begins.

8. Resorting to my *prakriti*, I send forth again and again this multitude of beings, powerless under the sway of *prakriti*.

9. But all this activity, O Dhananjaya, does not bind Me, seated as one indifferent, unattached to it.

10. With me as Presiding Witness, *prakriti* gives birth to all that moves and does not move; and because of this, O Kaunteya, the wheel of the world keeps going.

11. Not knowing My transcendent nature as the sovereign Lord of all beings, fools condemn Me incarnated as man.

    For they deny the existence of God and do not recognize the Director in the human body.

12. Vain are the hopes, actions and knowledge of those witless ones who have resorted to the delusive nature of monsters and devils.

13. But those great souls who resort to the divine nature, O Partha, know Me as the Imperishable Source of all beings and worship Me with an undivided mind.

14. Always declaring My glory, striving in steadfast faith, they do Me devout homage; ever attached to Me, they worship Me.

15. Yet others, with knowledge-sacrifice, worship Me, who am to be seen everywhere, as one, as different or as many.

16. I am the sacrificial vow; I am the sacrifice; I the ancestral oblation; I the herb; I the sacred text; I the clarified butter; I the fire; I the burnt offering.

17. Of this universe I am the Father, Mother, Creator, Grandsire: I am what is to be known, the sacred syllable *AUM*; the *Rig*, the *Saman* and the *Yajus*;

18. I am the Goal, the Sustainer, the Lord, the Witness, the Abode, the Refuge, the Friend; the Origin, the End the Preservation, the Treasure house, the Imperishable Seed.

19. I give heat; I hold back and pour forth rain; I am deathlessness and also death. O Arjuna, Being and not-Being as well.

20. Followers of the three Vedas, who drink the *soma* juice and are purged of sin, worship Me with sacrifice and pray for going to heaven; they reach the holy world of the gods and enjoy in heaven the divine joys of the gods.

    The reference is to the sacrificial ceremonies and rites in vogue in the days of the *Gita*. We cannot definitely say what they were like nor what the soma juice exactly was.

21. They enjoy the vast world of heaven, and their merit spent, they enter the world of the mortals; thus those who, following the Vedic law, long for the fruit of their action earn but the round of birth and death.

22. As for those who worship Me, thinking on Me alone and nothing else, ever attached to Me, I bear the burden of getting them what they need.

    There are thus three unmistakable marks of a true *yogi* or *bhakta*— even-mindedness, skill in action, undivided devotion. These three must be completely harmonized in a *yogi*. Without devotion there is no even-mindedness, without even-mindedness no devotion, and without skill in action devotion and even-minded might well be a pretense.

23. Even those who, devoted to other gods, worship them in full faith, even they, O Kaunteya, worship none but Me, though not according to the rule.

    'Not according to the rule' means not knowing Me as the Impersonal and the Absolute.

24. For I am the Acceptor and the Director of all sacrifices; but not recognizing Me as I am, they go astray.

25. Those who worship the gods go to the gods; those who worship the manes go to the manes; those who worship the spirits go to the spirits; but those who worship Me come to Me.

26. Any offering of leaf, flower, fruit or water, made to Me in devotion, by an earnest soul, I lovingly accept.

   That is to say, it is the Lord in every being whom we serve with devotion who accepts the service.

27. Whatever thou doest, whatever thou eatest, whatever thou offerest as sacrifice or gift, whatever austerity thou dost perform, O kaunteya, dedicate all to Me.

28. So doing thou shalt be released from the bondage of action, yielding good and evil fruit; having accomplished both renunciation and performance, thou shalt be released (from birth and death) and come unto Me.

29. I am the same to all beings; with Me there is non disfavoured, none favoured; but those who worship Me with devotion are in Me and I in them.

30. A sinner, howsoever great, if he turns to Me with undivided devotion, must indeed be counted a saint; for he has a settled resolve. The undivided devotion subdues both his passions and his evil deeds.

31. For soon he becomes righteous and wins everlasting peace; know for a certainty, O Kaunteya, that my *bhakta* never perishes.

32. For finding refuge in Me, even those who though are born of the womb of sin, women, *vaishyas*, and *shudras* too, reach the supreme goal.

33. How much more then, the pure *brahmanas* and seer-kings who are my devotees? Do thou worship Me, therefore, since thou hast come to this fleeting and joyless world.

34. On Me fix thy mind, to Me bring thy devotion, to Me offer thy sacrifice, to Me make thy obeisance; thus having attached thyself to Me and made Me thy end and aim, to Me indeed shalt thou come.

Thus ends the ninth discourse entitled *'Rajavidya-rajaguhya Yoga'* in the converse of Lord Krishna and Arjuna, on the science of *Yoga*, as part of the knowledge of *Brahman* in the Upanishad called the *Bhagawadgita*.

Discource 10

For the benefit of His devotees, the Lord gives in this discourse a glimpse of His divine manifestations.

THE LORD SAID :

1. Yet once more, O Mahabahu, here My supreme word, which I will utter to thee, gratified one, for thy benefit.

2. Neither the gods nor the great seers know My origin; for I am, every way, the origin of them both.

3. He who knows Me, the great lord of the worlds, as birthless and without beginning, he among mortals, undeluded, is released from sins.

4. Discernment, knowledge, freedom from delusion, .long suffering, truth, self-restraint, inward calm, pleasure, pain, birth, death, fear and fearlessness;

5. Non-violence, even-mindedness, contentment, austerity, beneficence, good and ill fame,—all these various attributes of creatures proceed verily from Me.

6. The seven great seers, the ancient four, and the Manus too were born of Me and of My mind, and of them were born all the creatures in the world.

7. He who knows in truth My immanence and My *yoga* becomes gifted with unshakable *yoga*; of this there is no doubt.

8. I am the source of all, all proceeds from me; knowing this, the wise worship Me with hearts full of devotion.

9. With me in their thoughts, their whole soul devoted to Me, teaching one another, with me ever on their lips, they live in contentment and joy,

10. To these, ever in tune with Me worshipping me with affectionate devotion, I give the power of selfless action, whereby they come to Me.

11. Out of every compassion for them, I who dwell in their hearts, destroy the darkness, born of ignorance, with the refulgent lamp of knowledge.

ARJUNA SAID:

12. Lord! Thou art the supreme *Brahman*, the supreme Abode, the supreme Purifier! Everlasting Celestial Being, the Primal God, Unborn, All-pervading.

13. Thus have all the seers—the divine seer Narada, Asita, Devala, *Vyasa*—declared Thee; and Thou Thyself dost tell me so.

14. All that Thou tellest me is true, I know, O Keshava, verily, Lord, neither the gods nor the demons know Thy manifestation.

15. Thyself alone Thou knowest by Thyself, O *Purushottama*, O Source and Lord of all beings, God of Gods, O Ruler of the universe.

16. Indeed Thou oughtest to tell me of all Thy manifestations, without a remainder, whereby Thou dost pervade the worlds.

17. O *Yogin*! Constantly meditating on Thee, how am I to know Thee? In what various aspects am I to think of Thee, O Lord?

18. Recount to me yet again, in full detail, Thy unique power and Thy immanence, O Janardana! For my ears cannot be sated with listening to Thy life-giving words.

THE LORD SAID :

19. Yea, I will unfold to thee, O Kurushreshtha, My divine manifestations,—the chiefest only; for there is no limit to their extent.

20. I am the *Atman*, O Gudakesha, seated in the heart of every being; I am the beginning, the middle and the end of all beings.

21. Of the *Adityas* I am Vishnu; of luminaries, the radiant Sun; of *Maruts*, I am Marichi; of constellations, the moon.

22. Of the Vedas I am the *Sama Veda*; of the gods Indra; of the senses I am the mind; of beings I am the consciousness.

23. Of *Rudras* I am Shankara; of *Yakshas* and *Rakshasas* Kubera; of Vasus I am the Fire; of mountains Meru.

24. Of priests, O Partha, know Me to be the chief Brihaspati; of army captains I am Kartikeya; and of waters the ocean.

25. Of the great seers I am Bhrigu; of words I am the one syllable '*AUM*'; of sacrifices I am the *Japa* sacrifice; of things immovable, the Himalaya.

26. Of all trees I am *Ashvattha*; of the divine seers, Narada; of the heavenly choir I am Chitraratha; of the perfected I am Kapila the ascetic.

27. Of horses, Know Me to be the Uchchaihshravas born with *Amrita*; of mighty elephants I am Airavata; of men, the monarch.

28. Of weapons, I am Vajra; of cows, Kamadhenu; I am Kandarpa, the god of generation; of serpants I am Vasuki.

29. Of cobras I am Anata; of water-dwellers I am Varuna; of the manes I am Aryaman; and of the chastisers, Yama.

30. Of demons I am Prahlada; of reckoners, the time; of beasts I am the lion; and of birds, Garuda.

31. Of cleansing agents I am the Wind; of wielders of weapons, Rama; of fishes I am the crocodile; of rivers the Ganges.

32. Of creations I am the beginning, end and middle, O Arjuna; of sciences, the science of spiritual knowledge; of debators, the right argument.

33. Of letters, the letter A; of compounds I am the *dvandva;* I am the imperishable Time; I am the creator to be seen everywhere.

34. All-seizing Death am I, as the source of things to be; in feminine virtues I am Kirti (glory), Shri (beauty), Vak (speech), Smriti (memory), Medha (intelligence), Dhriti (constancy) and Kshama (forgiveness).

35. Of *Saman* hymns I am Brihat *Saman*; of metres, Gayatri; of months I am Margashirsha; of seasons, the spring.

36. Of deceivers I am the dice-play; of the splendid the splendour; I am victory, I am resolution, I am the goodness of the good.

The 'dice-play of deceivers' need not alarm one. For the good and evil nature of things in not the matter in question, it is the directing and immanent power of God that is being described. Let the deceivers also know that they are under God's rule and judgment and put away their pride and deceit.

37. Of Vrishnis I am *Vasudeva*; of Pandavas Dhananjaya; of ascetics I am *Vyasa*; and of seers, Ushanas.

38. I am the rod of those that punish; the strategy of those seeking victory; of secret things I am silence, and the knowledge of those that know.

39. Whatever is the seed of every being, O Arjuna, that am I; there is nothing, whether moving or fixed, that can be without Me.

40. There is no end to my divine manifestations; what extent of them I have told thee now is only by way of illustration.

41. Whatever is glorious, beautiful and mighty know thou that all such has issued from a fragment of My splendour.

42. But why needest thou to learn this at great length, O Arjuna? With but a part of Myself I stand upholding this universe.

Thus ends the tenth discourse, entitled *'Vibhuti Yoga'* in the converse of Lord Krishna and Arjuna, on the science of *Yoga*, as part of the knowledge of *Brahman*, in the Upanishad called the *Bhagawadgita*.

Discource 11

In this discourse the Lord reveals to Arjuna's vision what Arjuna has heard with his ears—the Universal Form of the Lord. This discourse is a favourite with the Bhaktas. Here there is no argument, there is pure poetry. Its solemn music reverberates in one's ears and it is not possible to tire of reading it again and again.

ARJUNA SAID :

1. Out of Thy grace towards me, thou hast told me the supreme mystery revealing the knowledge of the Supreme; it has banished my delusion.

2. Of the origin and destruction of beings I have heard from Thee in full detail, as also Thy imperishable ajesty [sic], O Kamala-patraksha!

3. Thou art indeed as Thou hast described Thyself, *Parameshvara*! I do crave to behold, now, that form of Thine as *Ishvara*.

4. If, Lord, thou thinkest it possible for me to bear the sight, reveal to me, O Yogeshvara, Thy imperishable form.

THE LORD SAID :

5. Behold, O Partha, my forms divine in their hundreds and thousands, infinitely diverse, infinitely various in color and aspect.

6. Behold the *Adityas*, the Vasus, the *Rudras*, the two Ashwins, the *Maruts*; behold, O Bharata, numerous marvels never revealed before.

7. Behold today, O Gudakesha, in my body, the whole universe, moving and unmoving, all in one, and whatever else thou cravest to see.

8. But thou canst not see Me with these thine own eyes. I give thee the eye divine; behold My sovereign power!

SANJAYA SAID :

9. With these words, O King, the great Lord of *Yoga*, Hari, then revealed to Partha His supreme form as *Ishvara*.

10. With many mouths and many eyes, many wondrous aspects, many divine ornaments, and many brandished weapons divine.

11. Wearing divine garlands and vestments, annointed with divine perfumes, it was the form of God, all-marvellous [sic], infinite, seen everywhere.

12. Were the splendour of a thousand suns to shoot forth all at once in the sky that might perchance resemble the splendour of that Mighty One.

13. Then did Pandava see the whole universe in its manifold divisions gathered as one in the body of that God of gods.

14. Then Dhananjaya, wonderstruck and thrilled in every fibre of his being, bowed low his head before the Lord, addressing Him thus with folded hands.

ARJUNA SAID :

15. With Thy form, O Lord, I see all the gods and the diverse multitudes of beings, the Lord Brahma, on his lotus-throne and all the seers and serpents divine.

16. With many arms and bellies, mouths and eyes, I see Thy infinite form everywhere. Neither Thy end, nor middle, nor beginning, do I see, O Lord of the Universe, Universal-formed!

17. With crown and mace and disc, a mass of effulgence, gleaming everywhere I see Thee, so dazzling to the sight, bright with the splendour of the fiery sun blazing from all sides,—incomprehensible.

18. Thou art the Supreme Imperishable worthy to be known; Thou art the final resting place of this universe; Thou art the changeless guardian of the Eternal Dharma; Thou art, I believe, the Everlasting Being.

19. Thou hast no beginning, middle nor end; infinite is Thy might; arms innumerable; for eyes, the sun and the moon; Thy mouth a blazing fire, overpowering the universe with Thy radiance.

20. By Thee alone are filled the spaces between heaven and earth and all the quarters; at the sight of this Thy wondrous terrible form, the three worlds are sore oppressed, O Mahatman!

21. Here, too, the multitudes of gods are seen to enter Thee; some awe-struck praise Thee with folded arms; the hosts of great seers and siddhas, 'All Hail' on their lips, hymn Thee with songs of praise.

22. The *Rudras*, *Adityas*, Vasus, Sadhyas, all the gods, the twin Ashwins, *Maruts*, Manes, the hosts of Gandharvas, *Yakshas*, Asuras and Siddhas— all gaze on Thee in wonderment.

23. At the sight of thy mighty form, O Mahabahu, many-mouthed, with eyes, arms, thighs and feet innumerable, with many vast bellies, terrible with many jaws, the worlds feel fearfully oppressed, and so do I.

24. For as I behold Thee touching the sky, glowing, numerous-hued with gaping mouths and wide resplendent eyes, I feel oppressed in my innermost being; no peace nor quiet I find, O Vishnu!

25. As I see Thy mouths with fearful jaws, resembling the Fire of Doom, I lose all sense of direction, and find no relief. Be gracious, O Devesha, O Jagannivasa!

26. All the sons of Dhritarashtra, and with them the crowd of kings, Bhishma, Drona, and that Karna too, as also our chief warriors—

27. Are hastening into the fearful jaws of Thy terrible mouths. Some indeed, caught between Thy teeth, are seen, their heads being crushed to atoms.

28. As rivers, in their numerous torrents, run head-long to the sea, even so the heroes of the world of men rush into Thy flaming mouths.

29. As moths, fast-flying, plunge into blazing fire, straight to their doom, even so these rush headlong into Thy mouths, to their destruction.

30. Devouring all these from all sides, Thou lappest them with Thy flaming tongues; Thy fierce rays blaze forth, filling the whole universe with their lustre.

31. Tell me, Lord, who Thou art so dread of form! Hail to Thee, O Devavara! Be gracious! I desire to know Thee, Primal Lord; for I comprehend not what Thou dost.

THE LORD SAID :

32. Doom am I, full-ripe, dealing death to the worlds, engaged in devouring mankind. Even without slaying them not one of the warriors, ranged for battle against thee, shall survive.

33. Therefore, do thou arise, and win renown! Defeat thy foes and enjoy a thriving kingdom. By Me have these already been destroyed; be thou no more than an instrument, O Savyasachin!

34. Drona, Bhishma, Jayadratha and Karna, as also the other warrior chiefs—already slain by Me—slay thou! Fight! Victory is thine over the foes in the field.

SANJAYA SAID :

35. Hearing this world of Keshava, crown-wearer Arjuna folded his hands, and trembling made obeisance. Bowing and all hesitant, in faltering accents, he proceeded to address Krishna once more.

ARJUNA SAID :

36. Right proper it is, O Hrishikesha, that Thy praise should stir the world to gladness and tender emotion; the *Rakshasas* in fear fly to every quarter and all the hosts of Siddhas do reverent homage.

37. And why should they not bow down to Thee, O Mahatma? Thou art the First Creator, greater even than Brahma. O Ananta, O Devesha, O Jagannivasa, Thou art the Imperishable, Being, not-Being, and That which transcends even these.

38. Thou art the Primal God, the Ancient Being; Thou art the Final Resting Place of this Universe; Thou art the Knower, the 'to-be-known', the Supreme Abode; by Thee, O Myriad-formed, is the universe pervaded.

39. Thou art Vayu, Yama, Agni, Varuna, Shashanka, Prajapati, and Prapitamaha! All Hail to Thee, a thousand times all hail! Again and yet again all hail to Thee!

40. All hail to Thee from before and behind! all hail to Thee from every side, O All; Thy prowess is infinite, Thy might is measureless! Thou holdest all; therefore Thou art all.

41. If ever in carelessness, thinking of Thee as comrade, I addressed Thee saying, 'O Krishna!', 'O Yadava!' not knowing Thy greatness, in negligence or in affection.

42. If ever I have been rude to Thee in jest, whilst at play, at rest-time, or at meals, whilst alone or in company, O Achyuta, forgive Thou my fault—I beg of Thee, O Incomprehensible!

43. Thou art Father of this world, of the moving and the un-moving; thou art its adored, its worthiest, Master; there is none equal to Thee; how then any greater than Thee? Thy power is matchless in the three worlds.

44. Therefore, I prostrate myself before Thee, and beseech Thy grace, O Lord adorable! As father with son, as comrade with comrade, so shouldst Thou bear, beloved Lord, with me, Thy loved one.

45. I am filled with joy to see what never was seen before, and yet my heart is oppressed with fear. Show me that original form of Thine, O Lord! Be gracious, Devesha, O Jagannivasa!

46. I crave to see Thee even as Thou wast, with crown, with mace, and disc in hand; wear Thou, once more, that four-armed form, O thousand-armed Vishvamurti!

THE LORD SAID :

47. It is to favour thee, O Arjuna, that I have revealed to thee, by My own unique power, this My form Supreme, Resplendent, Universal, Infinite, Primal—which none save thee has ever seen.

48. Not by the study of the Vedas, not by sacrifice, not by the study of other scriptures, not by gifts, nor yet by performance of rites or of fierce austerities can I, in such a form, be seen by any one save thee in the world of men, O Kurupravira!

49. Be thou neither oppressed nor bewildered to look on this awful form of Mine. Banish thy fear, ease thy mind, and lo! behold Me once again as I was.

SANJAYA SAID :

50. So said *Vasudeva* to Arjuna, and revealed to him once more His original form. Wearing again His form benign, the Mahatma consoled him terrified.

ARJUNA SAID :

51. Beholding again thy benign human form I am come to myself and once more in my normal state.

THE LORD SAID :

52. Very hard to behold is that form of Mine which thou hast seen; even the gods always yearn to see it.

53. Not by the Vedas, not by penance, nor by gifts, nor yet by sacrifice, can any behold Me in the form that thou hast seen.

54. But by single-minded devotion, O Arjuna, I may in this form be known and seen, and truly entered into, O Parantapa!

55. He alone comes to me, O Pandava, who does My work, who has made Me his goal, who is My devotee, who has renounced attachment, who has ill-will toward none.

Thus ends the eleventh discourse, entitled
'Vishvarupadarshana Yoga' in the converse of Lord Krishna
and Arjuna, on the science of *Yoga* as part of the knowledge
of *Brahman* in the Upanishad called the *Bhagawadgita*.

Discource 12

Thus we see that vision of God is possible only through single-minded devotion. Contents of devotion must follow as a matter of course. This twelfth discourse should be learnt by hard even if all discourses are not. It is one of the shortest. The marks of a devotee should be carefully noted.

ARJUNA SAID :

1. Of the devotees who thus worship Thee, incessantly attached, and those who worship the Imperishable Unmanifest, which are the better *yogins*?

THE LORD SAID :

2. Those I regard as the best *yogins* who, riveting their minds on Me, ever attached, worship Me, with the highest faith.

3. But those who worship the Imperishable, the indefinable, the Unmanifest, the Omnipresent, the Unthinkable, the Rock-seated, the Immovable, the Unchanging,

4. Keeping the whole host of senses in complete control, looking on all with an impartial eye, engrossed in the welfare of all beings—these come indeed to Me.

5. Greater is the travail of those whose mind is fixed on the Unmanifest; for it is hard for embodied mortals to gain the Unmanifest—Goal.

Mortal man can only imagine the Unmanifest, the Impersonal, and as his language fails him he often negatively describes It as *'Neti', 'Neti'* (Not That, Not That). And so even iconoclasts are at bottom no better than idol-worshippers. To worship a book, to go to church, or to pray with one's face in a particular direction—all these are forms of worshipping the Formless in an image or idol. And yet, both the idol-breaker and the idol-worshipper cannot lose sight of the fact that there is something which is beyond all form, Unthinkable, Formless, Impersonal, Changeless. The highest goal of the devotee is to become one with the object of his devotion. The *bhakta* extinguishes himself and merges into, becomes, *Bhagvan*. This state can best be reached by devoting oneself to some form, and so it is said that the short cut to the Unmanifest is really the longest and the most difficult.

6. But those who casting all their actions on Me, making Me their all in all, worship Me with the meditation of undivided devotion,

7. Of such, whose thoughts are centered on Me, O Partha, I become ere long the Deliverer from the ocean of this world of death.

8. On Me set thy mind, on Me rest thy conviction; thus without doubt shalt thou remain only in Me hereafter.

9. If thou canst not set thy mind steadily on Me, then by the method of constant practice seek to win Me, O Dhananjaya.

10. If thou art also unequal to this method of constant practice, concentrate on service for Me; even thus serving Me thou shalt attain perfection.

11. If thou art unable even to do this, then dedicating all to Me, with mind controlled, abandon the fruit of action.

12. Better is knowledge than practice, better than knowledge is concentration, better than concentration is renunciation of the fruit of all action, from which directly issues peace. 'Practice' (abhyasa) is the practice of the *yoga* of meditation and control of psychic processes; 'knowledge' (*jnana*) is intellectual effort; 'concentration' (dhyana) is devoted worship. If as a result of all this there is no renunciation of the fruit of action, 'practice' is no 'practice', 'knowledge' is no 'knowledge', and 'concentration' is no 'concentration'.

13. Who has ill-will towards none, who is friendly and compassionate, who has shed all thought of 'mine' or 'I', who regards pain and pleasure alike, who is long-suffering;

14. Who is ever content, gifted with *yoga*, self-restrained, of firm conviction, who has dedicated his mind and reason to Me—that devotee (*bhakta*) of Mine is dear to Me.

15. Who gives no trouble to the world, to whom the world causes no trouble, who is free from exultation, resentment, fear and vexation,—that man is dear to Me.

16. Who expects naught, who is pure, resourceful, unconcerned, untroubled, who indulges in no undertakings,—that devotee of Mine is dear to Me.

17. Who rejoices not, neither frets nor grieves, who covets not, who abandons both good and ill—that devotee of Mine is dear to Me.

18. Who is same to foe and friend, who regards alike respect and disrespect, cold and heat, pleasure and pain, who is free from attachment;

19. Who weighs in equal scale blame and praise, who is silent, content with whatever his lot, who owns no home, who is of steady mind,—that devotee of Mine is dear to Me.

20. They who follow this essence of *dharma*, as I have told it, with faith, keeping Me as their goal,—those devotees are exceeding dear to Me.

Thus ends the twelfth discourse entitled *'Bhakti Yoga'* in
the converse of Lord Krishna and Arjuna, on the
science of *Yoga*, as part of the knowledge of *Brahman* in
the Upanishad called the *Bhagawadgita*.

Discource 13

This discourse treats of the distinction between the body (not-Self) and the Atman (the Self).

THE LORD SAID :

1. This body, O Kaunteya, is called the Field; he who knows it is called the knower of the Field by those who know.

2. And understand Me to be, O Bharata, the knower of the Field in all the Fields; and the knowledge of the Field and the knower of the Field, I hold, is true knowledge.

3. What the Field is, what its nature, what its modifications, and whence is what, as also who He is, and what His power—hear this briefly from Me.

4. This subject has been sung by seers distinctively and in various ways, in different hymns as also in aphoristic texts about *Brahman* well reasoned and unequivocal.

5. The great elements, Individuation, Reason, the Unmanifest, the ten senses, and the one (mind), and the five spheres of the senses;

6. Desire, dislike, pleasure, pain, association, consciousness, cohesion— this, in sum, is what is called the Field with its modifications.

    The great elements are Earth, Water, Fire, Air and Ether. 'Individuation' is the thought of I, or that the body is 'I'; the 'Unmanifest' is *prakriti* or maya; the ten senses are the five senses of perception— smell, taste, sight, touch and hearing, and the five organs of action,

189

viz.: the hands, the feet, the tongue, and the two organs of excretion. The five spheres or objects of the senses are smell, savour, form, touch, and sound. 'Association' is the property of the different organs to cooperate. Dhriti is not patience or constancy but cohesion, i.e. the property of all the atoms in the body to hold together; from 'individuation' springs this cohesion. Individuation is inherent in the unmanifest *prakriti*. The undeluded man is he who can cast off the individuation or ego, and having done so the shock of an inevitable thing like death and pairs of opposites caused by sense-contacts fail to affect him. The Field, subject to all its modifications, has to be abandoned in the end by the enlightened and the unenlightened alike.

7. Freedom from pride and pretentiousness, nonviolence, forgiveness, uprightness, service of the Master, purity, steadfastenes, self-restraint;

8. Aversion from sense-objects, absence of conceit, realization of the painfulness and evil of birth, death, age and disease;

9. Absence of attachment, refusal to be wrapped up in one's children, wife, home and family, even-mindedness whether good or ill befall;

10. Unwavering and all-exclusive devotion to Me, resort to secluded spots, distaste for the haunts of men;

11. Settled conviction of the nature of the *Atman*, perception of the goal of the knowledge of Truth,—

    All this is declared to be Knowledge and the reverse of it is ignorance.

12. I will (now) expound to thee that which is to be known and knowing which one enjoys immortality; it is the supreme *Brahman* which has no beginning, which is called neither Being nor non-Being.

    The Supreme can be described neither as being nor as non-Being. It is beyond definition or description, above all attributes.

13. Everywhere having hands and feet, everywhere having eyes, heads, mouths, everywhere having ears, It abides embracing everything in the universe.

14. Seeming to possess the functions of the senses, It is devoid of all the senses; It touches naught, upholds all; having no *gunas*, It experiences the *gunas*.

15. Without all beings, yet within; immovable yet moving, so subtle that It cannot be perceived; so far and yet so near It is.

    He who knows It is within It, close to It; mobility and immobility, peace and restlessness, we owe to It, for It has motion and yet is motionless.

16. Undivided, It seems to subsist divided in all beings; this *Brahman*— That which is to be known as the Sustainer of all, yet It is their Devourer and Creator.

17. Light of all lights, It is said to be beyond darkness; It is knowledge, the object of knowledge, to be gained only by knowledge; It is seated in the hearts of all.

18. Thus have I expounded in brief the Field, Knowledge and That which is to be known; My devotee, when he knows this, is worthy to become one with Me.

19. Know that *Prakriti* and *Purusha* are both without beginning; know that all the modifications and *gunas* are born of *Prakriti*.

20. *Prakriti* is described as the cause in the creation of effects from causes; *Purusha* is described as the cause of the experiencing of pleasure and pain.

21. For the *Purusha*, residing in *Prakriti*, experiences the *gunas* born in *Prakriti*; attachment to these *gunas* is the cause of his birth in good or evil wombs.

    Prakriti in common parlance is *Maya*. *Purusha* is the *Jiva*. *Jiva* acting in accordance with his nature experiences the fruit of actions arising out of the three *gunas*.

22. What is called in this body the Witness, the Assentor, the Sustainer, the Experiencer, the Great Lord and also the Supreme *Atman*, is Supreme Being.

23. He who thus knows *Purusha* and *Prakriti* with its *gunas*, is not born again, no matter how he live and move.

    Read in the light of discourses II, IX and XII this *shloka* may not be taken to support any kind of libertinism. It shows the virtue of self-surrender and selfless devotion. All actions bind the self, but if all are dedicated to the Lord they do not bind, rather they release him.

He who has thus extinguished the 'self or the thought of 'I' and who acts as ever in the great witness' eye, will never sin nor err. The self-sense is at the root of all error or sin. Where the 'I' has ben extinguished, there is no sin. This *shloka* shows how to steer clear of all sin.

24. Some through meditation hold the *Atman* by themselves in their own self; others by *Sankhya Yoga*, and others by *Karma Yoga*.

25. Yet others, not knowing (Him) thus, worship (Him) having heard from others; they too pass beyond death, because of devoted adherence to what they have heard.

26. Wherever something is born, animate or inanimate, know thou *Bharatarshabha*, that it issues from the union of the Field and the Knower of the Field.

27. Who sees abiding in all beings the same *Parameshvara*, imperishable in the perishable, he sees indeed.

28. When he sees the same *Ishvara* abiding everywhere alike, he does not hurt himself by himself and hence he attains the highest goal.

    He who sees the same God everywhere merges in Him and sees naught else; he thus does not yield to passion, does not become his own foe and thus attains Freedom.

29. Who sees that it is *Prakriti* that performs all actions and thus (knows) that *Atman* performs them not, he sees indeed.

    Just as, in the case of a man who is asleep, his "Self" is not the agent of sleep, but *Prakriti*, even so the enlightened man will detach his "Self" from all activities. To the pure everything is pure. *Prakriti* is not unchaste, it is when arrogant man takes her as wife that of these twain passion is born.

30. When he sees the diversity of beings as founded in unity and the whole expanse issuing therefrom, then he attains to *Brahman*.

    To realize that everything rests in *Brahman* is to attain to the state of *Brahman*. Then *Jiva* becomes Shiva.

31. This imperishable Supreme *Atman*, O Kaunteya, though residing in the body, acts not and is not stained, for he has no beginning and no *gunas*.

.

32. As the all-pervading ether, by reason of its subtlety, is not soiled even so *Atman* pervading every part of the body is not soiled.

33. As the one Sun illumines the whole universe, even so the Master of the Field illumines the whole field, O Bharata!

34. Those who, with the eyes of knowledge, thus perceive the distinction between the Field and the Knower of the Field, and (the secret) of the release of beings from *Prakriti*, they attain to the Supreme.

Thus ends the thirteenth discourse, entitled *'Kshetra-kshetrajnavibhaga Yoga'* in the converse of Lord Krishna and Arjuna, on the science of *Yoga*, as part of the knowledge of *Brahman* in the Upanishad called the *Bhagawadgita*.

Discource 14

The description of Prakriti naturally leads on to that of its constituents, the Gunas, which from the subject of this discourse. And that, in turn, leads to a description of the marks of him who has passed beyond the three gunas. These are practically the same as those of the man of secure understanding (II. 54-72) as also those of the ideal Bhakta (XII. 12-20).

THE LORD SAID :

1. Yet again I will expound the highest and the best of all knowledge, knowing which all the sages passed hence to the highest perfection.

2. By having recourse to this knowledge they became one with Me. They need not come to birth even at a creation, nor do they suffer at a dissolution.

3. The great *prakriti* is for me the womb in which I deposit the germ; from it all beings come to birth, O Bharata.

4. Whatever forms take birth in the various species, the great *prakriti* is their Mother and I the seed-giving Father.

5. *Sattva, rajas* and *tamas* are the *gunas* sprung from *prakriti;* it is they, O Mahabahu, that keep the imperishable Dweller bound to the body.

6. Of these *sattva*, being stainless, is light-giving and healing; it binds with the bond of happiness and the bond of knowledge, O sinless one.

7. *Rajas*, know thou, is of the nature of passion, the source of thirst and attachment; it keeps man bound with the bond of action.

8. *Tamas*, know thou, born of ignorance, is mortal man's delusion; it keeps him bound with heedlessness, sloth and slumber, O Bharata.

9. *Sattva* attaches man to happiness, *rajas* to action, and *tamas*, shrouding knowledge, attaches him to heedlessness.

10. *Sattva* prevails, O Bharata, having overcome *rajas* and *tamas*; *rajas*, when it has overpowered *sattva* and *tamas*; likewise *tamas* reigns when *sattva* and *rajas* are crushed.

11. When the light—knowledge—shines forth from al the gates of this body, then it may be known that the *sattva* thrives.

12. Greed, activity, assumption of undertakings, restlessness, craving — these are in evidence when *rajas* flourishes, O Bharatarshabha.

13. Ignorance, dullness, heedlessness, and delusion—these are in evidence when *tamas* reigns, O Kurunandana.

14. If the embodied one meets his end whilst *sattva* prevails, then he attains to the spotless worlds of the knowers of the Highest.

15. If he dies during the reign within him of *rajas*, he is born among men attached to action; and if he dies in *tamas*, he is born in species not endowed with reason.

16. The fruit of *sattvika* action is said to be stainless merit. That of *rajas* is pain and that of *tamas* ignorance.

17. Of *sattva* knowledge is born, of *rajas*, greed; of *tamas* heedlessness, delusion and ignorance.

18. Those abiding in *sattva* rise upwards, those in *rajas* stay midway, those in *tamas* sink downwards.

19. When the seer perceives no agent other than the *gunas*, and knows Him who is above the *gunas*, he attains to My being.

As soon as a man realizes that he is not the doer, but the *gunas* are the agent, the 'self' vanishes, and he goes through all his actions spontaneously, just to sustain the body. And as the body is meant to subserve the highest end, all his actions will even reveal detachment and dispassion. Such a seer can easily have a glimpse of the One who is above the *gunas* and offer his devotion to Him.

20. When the embodied one transcends these three *gunas* which are born of his contact with the body, he is released from the pain of birth, death and age and attains deathlessness.

ARJUNA SAID :

21. What, O Lord, are the marks of him who has transcended the three *gunas*? How does he conduct himself? How does he transcend the three *gunas*?

THE LORD SAID :

22. He, O Pandava, who does not disdain light, activity, and delusion when they come into being, nor desires them when they vanish;

23. He, who seated as one indifferent, is not shaken by the *gunas*, and stays still and moves not, knowing it is *gunas* playing their parts;

24. He who holds pleasure and pain alike, who is sedate, who regards as same earth, stone and gold, who is wise and weighs in equal scale things pleasant and unpleasant, who is even-minded in praise and blame;

25. Who holds alike respect and disrespect, who is the same to friend and foe, who indulges in no undertakings—That man is called *gunatita*.

Shls. 22-25 must be read and considered together. Light activity and delusion, as we have seen in the foregoing *shlokas*, are the products or indications of *sattva*, *rajas* and *tamas* respectively. The inner meaning of these verses is that he who has transcended the *gunas* will be unaffected by them. A stone does not desire light, nor does it disdain activity or inertness; it is still, without having the will to be so. If someone puts it into motion, it does not fret; if again, it is allowed to lie still, it does not feel that inertness or delusion has seized it. The difference between a stone and a *gunatita* is that the latter has full consciousness and with full knowledge he shakes himself free from the bonds that bind an ordinary mortal. He has, as a result of his knowledge, achieved the purpose of a stone. Like the stone he is witness, but not the doer, of the activities of the *gunas* or *prakriti*. Of such *jnani* one may say that he is sitting still, unshaken in the knowledge that it is the *gunas* playing their parts. We who are every moment of our lives acting as though we are the doers can only imagine the state, we can hardly experience it. But we can hitch our waggon to that star and work our way closer and closer towards it by gradually withdrawing the self from our actions. A *gunatita* has experience of his own condition but he cannot describe it, for he who can describe it ceases to be one. The moment he proceeds to do so, 'self' peeps in. The peace and light and bustle and inertness of our common experience are illusory. The *Gita* itself has made it clear in so many words that the *sattvika* state is the one nearest that of a *gunatita*. Therefore everyone should strive to develop more and more *sattva* in himself, believing that some day he will reach the goal of the state of *gunatita*.

26. He who serves me in an unwavering and exclusive *bhaktiyoga* transcends these *gunas* and is worthy to become one with *Brahman*.

27. For I am the very image of *Brahman*, changeless and deathless, as also of everlasting *dharma* and perfect bliss.

Thus ends the fourteenth discourse, entitled
'Gunatrayavibhaga Yoga' in the converse of Lord Krishna and
Arjuna, on the science of *Yoga*, as part of the knowledge of
Brahman, in the Upanishad called the *Bhagawadgita*.

Discource 15

This discourse deals with the supreme form of the Lord, transcending Kshara (perishable) and Akshara (imperishable).

THE LORD SAID :

1. With the root above and branches below, the *ashvattha* tree, they say, is impossible; it has Vedic hymns for its leaves; he who knows it knows the Vedas.

    Shvah means tomorrow, and *ashvattha* (*na shvopi sthata*) means that which will not last even until tomorrow, i.e. the world of sense which is every moment in a state of flux. But even though it is perpetually changing, as its root is *Brahman* or the Supreme, it is imperishable. It has for its protection and supports the leaves of the Vedic hymns, i.e. *dharma*. He who knows the world of sense as such and who knows *dharma* is the real *jnani*, that man has really known the Vedas.

2. Above all and below its branches spread, blossoming because of the *gunas*, having for their shoots the sense-objects; deep down in the world of men are ramified its roots, in the shape of the consequences of action.

    This is the description of the tree of the world of sense as the unenlightened see it. They fail to discover its Root above in *Brahman* and so they are always attached to the objects of sense. They water the tree with the three *gunas* and remain bound to *Karman* in the world of men.

3. Its form as such is not here perceived, neither is its end, nor beginning, nor basis. Let man first hew down this deep-rooted *Ashvattha* with the sure weapon of detachment;

4. Let him pray to win to that haven from which there is no return and seek to find refuge in the primal Being from whom has emanated this ancient world of action.

   'Detachment in *shl.* 3 here means dispassion, aversion to the objects of the senses. Unless man is determined to cut himself off from the temptations of the world of sense he will go deeper into the mire every day. These verses show that one dare not play with the objects of the senses with impunity.

5. To that imperishable haven those enlightened souls go—who are without pride and delusion, who have triumphed over the taints of attachment, who are ever in tune with the Supreme, whose passions have died, who are exempt from the pairs of opposites, such as pleasure and pain.

6. Neither the sun, nor the moon, nor fire illumine it; men who arrive there return not—that is My supreme abode.

7. As part indeed of Myself which has been the eternal *Jiva* in this world of life, attracts the mind and the five senses from their place in *prakriti*.

8. When the master (of the body) acquires a body and discards it he carries these with him wherever he goes, even as the wind carries scents from flower beds.

9. Having settled himself in the senses—ear, eye, touch, taste, and smell—as well as the mind, through them he frequents their objects.

   These objects are the natural objects of the senses. The frequenting or enjoyment of these would be tainted if there were the sense of 'I' about it; otherwise it is pure, even as a child's enjoyment of these objects is innocent.

10. The deluded perceive Him not as He leaves or settles in (a body) or enjoys (sense objects) in association with the *gunas*; it is those endowed with the eye of knowledge who alone see Him.

11. *Yogins* who strive see Him seated in themselves; the witless ones who have not cleansed themselves to see Him not, even though they strive.

This does not conflict with the covenant that God has made even with the sinner in discourse 9. *Akritatman* (who has not cleansed himself) means one who has no devotion in him, who has not made up his mind to purify himself. The most confirmed sinner, if he has humility enough to seek refuge in surrender to God, purifies himself and succeeds in finding Him. Those who do not care to observe the cardinal and the casual vows and expect to find God through bare intellectual exercise are witless, Godless; they will not find Him.

12. The light in the sun which illumines the whole universe and which is in the moon and in fire—that light, know thou, is Mine;

13. It is I, who penetrating the earth uphold all beings with My strength, and becoming the moon—the essence of all sap—nourish all the herbs;

14. It is I who becoming the Vaishvanara Fire and entering the bodies of all that breathe, assimilate the four kinds of food with the help of the outward and the inward breaths.

15. And I am seated in the hearts of all, from Me proceed memory, knowledge and the dispelling of doubts; it is I who am to be known in all the Vedas, I, the author of Vedanta and the knower of the Vedas.

16. There are two Beings in the world: *kshara* (perishable) and *akshara* (imperishable). *Kshara* embraces all creatures and their permanent basis is *akshara*.

17. The Supreme Being is surely another—called *Paramatman* who is the Imperishable *Ishvara* pervades and supports the three worlds.

18. Because I transcend the *kshara* and am also higher than the *akshara*, I am known in the world and in the Vedas as *Purushottama* (the Highest Being).

19. He who, undeluded, knows Me as *Purushottama*, knows all, he worships Me with all his heart, O Bharata.

20. Thus I have revealed to thee, sinless one, this most mysterious *shastra*; he who understands this, O Bharata, is a man of understanding, he has fulfilled his life's mission.

Thus ends the fifteenth discourse, entitled *'Purushottama Yoga'* in the converse of Lord Krishna and Arjuna, on the science of *Yoga*, as part of the knowledge of *Brahman* in the Upanishad called the *Bhagawadgita*.

Discource 16

This discourse treats of the divine and the devilish heritage.

THE LORD SAID :

1. Fearlessness, purity of heart, steadfastness in *jnana* and *yoga*— knowledge and action, beneficence, self-restraint, sacrifice, spiritual study, austerity, and uprightness;

2. Non-violence, truth, slowness to wrath, the spirit of dedication, serenity, aversion to slander, tenderness to all that lives, freedom from greed, gentleness, modesty, freedom from levity;

3. Spiritedness, forgiveness, fortitude, purity, freedom from ill-will and arrogance—these are to be found in one born with the divine heritage, O Bharata.

4. Pretentiousness, arrogance, self-conceit, wrath, coarseness, ignorance—these are to be found in one born with the devilish heritage.

5. The divine heritage makes for Freedom, the devilish for bondage. Grieve not, O Partha; thou art born with a divine heritage.

6. There are two orders of created beings in this world—the divine and the devilish; the divine order has been described in detail, hear from Me now of the devilish, O Partha.

7. Men of the devil do not know what they may do and what they may not do; neither is there any purity, nor right conduct, nor truth to be found in them.

8. 'Without truth, without basis, without God is the universe,' they say; 'born of the union of the sexes, prompted by naught but lust.'

9. Holding this view, these depraved souls, of feeble understanding and of fierce deeds, come forth as enemies of the world to destroy it.

10. Given to insatiable lust, possessed by pretentiousness, arrogance and conceit, they seize wicked purposes in their delusion, and go about pledged to uncleaned deeds.

11. Given to boundless cares that ends only with their death, making indulgence or lust their sole goal, convinced that that is all;

12. Caught in a myriad snares of hope, slaves to lust and wrath, they speak unlawfully to amass wealth for the satisfaction of their appetites.

13. 'This have I gained today; this aspiration shall I now attain; this wealth is mine; this likewise shall be mine hereafter;

14. 'This enemy I have already slain, others also I shall slay; lord of all am I; enjoyment is mine, perfection is mine, strength is mine, happiness is mine;

15. 'Wealthy am I, and high-born. What other is like unto me? I shall perform a sacrifice! I shall give alms! I shall be merry!' Thus think they, by ignorance deluded;

16. And tossed about by diverse fancies, caught in the net of delusion, stuck deep in the indulgence of appetites, into foul hell they fall.

17. Wise in their own conceit, stubborn, full of the intoxication of pelf and pride, they offer nominal sacrifices for show, contrary to the rule.

18. Given to pride, force, arrogance, lust and wrath they are deriders indeed, scorning Me in their own and other' bodies.

19. These cruel scorners, lowest of mankind and vile, I hurl down again and again, into devilish wombs.

20. Doomed to devilish wombs, these deluded ones, far from ever coming to Me, sink lower and lower in birth after birth.

21. Three-fold is the gate of hell, leading man to perdition—Lust, Wrath, and Greed; these three, therefore, should be shunned.

22. The man who escapes these three gates of Darkness, O Kaunteya, works out his welfare and thence reaches the highest state.

23. He who forsakes the rule of *shastra* and does but the bidding of his selfish desires, gains neither perfection, nor happiness, nor the highest state.

Shastra does not mean the rites and formulae laid down in the so-called *dharmashastra*, but the path of self-restraint laid down by the seers and the saints.

24. Therefore let *shastra* be thy authority for determining what ought to be done and what ought not to be done; ascertain thou the rule of the *shastra* and do thy task here (accordingly).

Shastra here too has the same meaning as in the preceding *shloka*. Let no one be a law unto himself, but take as his authority the law laid down by men who have known and lived religion.

Thus ends the sixteenth discourse, entitled 'Daivasurasampadvibhaga Yoga' in the converse of Lord Krishna and Arjuna, on the science of *Yoga*, as part of the knowledge of *Brahman* in the Upanishad called the *Bhagawadgita*.

Discource 17

On being asked to consider Shastra (conduct of the worthy) as
the authority, Arjuna is faced with a difficulty. What is the position of those who may not be able to accept the authority of
Shastra but who may act in faith? An answer to the question is
attempted in this discourse. Krishna rests content with pointing
out the rocks and shoals on the path of the one who forsakes
the beacon light of Shastra (conduct of the worthy). In doing so
he deals with the faith and sacrifice, austerity and charity,
performed with faith, and their divisions according to the spirit
in which they are performed. He also sings the greatness of the
mystic syllables AUM TAT SAT—a formula of dedication of all
work to God.

ARJUNA SAID :

1. What, then, O Krishna, is the position of those who forsake the rule
   of *Shastra* and yet worship with faith? Do they act from *sattva* or *rajas*
   or *tamas*?

THE LORD SAID:

2. Threefold is the faith of men, an expression of their nature in each
   case; it is *sattvika*, *rajas* or *tamasa*. Hear thou of it.
3. The faith of every man is in accord with his innate character; man is
   made up of faith; whatever his object of faith, even so is he.

4. *Sattvika* persons worship the gods; *rajas* ones, the *Yakshas* and *Rakshasas*; and others—men of *tamas*—worship manes and spirits.

5. Those men who, wedded to pretentiousness and arrogance, possessed by the violence of lust and passion, practice fierce austerity not ordained by *shastra*;

6. They, whilst they torture the several elements that make up their bodies, torture Me too dwelling in them; know them to be of unholy resolves.

7. Of three kinds again is the food that is dear to each; so also are sacrifice, austerity, and charity. Hear how they differ.

8. Victuals that add to one's years, vitality, strength, health, happiness and appetite; are savoury, rich, substantial and inviting, are dear to the *sattvika*.

9. Victuals that are bitter, sour, salty, over-hot, spicy, dry, burning, and causing pain, bitterness and disease, are dear to *rajasa*.

10. Food which has become cold, insipid, putrid, stale, discarded and unfit for sacrifice, is dear to the *tamasa*.

11. That sacrifice is *sattvika* which is willingly offered as a duty without desire for fruit and according to the rule.

12. But when sacrifice is offered with an eye to fruit and for vain glory, know, O Bharatashreshtha, that it is *rajasa*.

13. Sacrifice which is contrary to the rule, which produces no food, which lacks the sacred text, which involves no giving up, which is devoid of faith is said to be *tamasa*.

14. Homage to the gods, to *Brahmanas*, to gurus and to wise men; cleanliness, uprightness, *brahmacharya* and non-violence—these constitute austerity (tapas) of the body.

15. Words that cause no hurt, that are true loving and helpful, and spiritual study constitute austerity of speech.

16. Serenity, benignity, silence, self-restraint, and purity of the spirit — these constitute austerity of the mind.

17. This threefold austerity practiced in perfect faith by men not desirous of fruit, and disciplined, is said to be *sattvika*.

18. Austerity which is practiced with an eye to gain praise, honour and homage and for ostentation is said to be *rajasa;* it is fleeting and unstable.

19. Austerity which is practiced from any foolish obsession, either to torture oneself or to procure another's ruin, is called *tamasa.*

20. Charity, given as a matter of duty, without expectation of any return, at the right place and time, and to the right person is said to be *sattvika.*

21. Charity, which is given either in hope of receiving in return, or with a view of winning merit, or grudgingly, is declared to be *rajasa.*

22. Charity given at the wrong place and time, and to the undeserving recipient disrespectfully and with contempt is declared to be *tamasa.*

23. *AUM TAT SAT* has been declared to be the threefold name of *Brahman* and by that name were created of old the *Brahmanas*, the Vedas and sacrifices.

24. Therefore, with *AUM* ever on their lips, are all the rites of sacrifice, charity and austerity, performed always to the rule, by Brahmavadins.

25. With the utterance of *TAT* and without the desire for fruit are the several rites of sacrifice, austerity and charity performed by those seeking Freedom.

26. *SAT* is employed in the sense of 'real' and 'good'; O Partha, *SAT* is also applied to beautiful deeds.

27. Constancy in sacrifice, austerity and charity, is called *SAT*; and all work for those purposes is also *SAT*.

    The substance of the last four *shlokas* is that every action should be done in a spirit of complete dedication to God. For *AUM* alone is the only Reality. That only which is dedicated to It counts.

28. Whatever is done, O Partha, by way of sacrifice, charity or austerity or any other work, is called *Asat* if done without faith. It counts for naught hereafter as here.

Thus ends the seventeenth discourse, entitled
'*Sharaddhatrayavibhaga Yoga*' in the converse of Lord Krishna
and Arjuna, on the science of *Yoga*, as part of the knowledge of
Brahman in the Upanishad called the *Bhagawadgita*.

Discource 18

This concluding discourse sums up the teaching of the Gita. It may be said to be summed up in the following: "Abandon all duties and come to Me, the only Refuge" (66). That is true renunciation. But abandonment of all duties does not mean abandonment of actions; it means abandonment of the desire for fruit. Even the highest act of service must be dedicated to Him, without the desire. That is Tyaga (abandonment), that is Sannyasa (renunciation).

ARJUNA SAID :

1. Mahabahu! I would fain learn severally the secret of *sannyasa* and of *tyaga*, O Hrishikesha, O Keshinishudana.

THE LORD SAID :

2. Renunciation of actions springing from selfish desire is known as *sannyasa* by the seers; abandonment of the fruit of all action is called *tyaga* by the wise.

3. Some thoughtful persons say: 'All action should be abandoned as an evil'; others say: 'Action for sacrifice, charity and austerity should not be relinquished'.

4. Hear my decision in this matter of *tyaga*, O Bharatasattama; for *tyaga*, too, O mightiest of men, has been described to be of three kinds.

5. Action for sacrifice, charity and austerity may not be abandoned; it must needs be performed. Sacrifice, charity and austerity are purifiers of the wise.

6. But even these actions should be performed abandoning all attachment and fruit; such, O Partha, is my best and considered opinion.

7. It is not right to renounce one's allotted task; its abandonment, from delusion, is said to be *tamasa*.

8. He who abandons action, deeming it painful and for fear of straining his limbs, he will never gain the fruit of abandonment, for his abandonment is *rajasa*.

9. But when an allotted task is performed from a sense of duty and with abandonment of attachment and fruit, O Arjuna, that abandonment is deemed to be *sattvika*.

10. Neither does he disdain unpleasant action, nor does he cling to pleasant action—this wise man full of *sattva*, who practices abandonment, and who has shaken off all doubts.

11. For the embodied one cannot completely abandon action; but he who abandons the fruit of action is named a *tyagi*.

12. To those who do not practice abandonment accrues, when they pass away, the fruit of action which is of three kinds: disagreeable, agreeable, mixed; but never to the *sannyasin*s.

13. Learn, from me, O Mahabahu, the five factors mentioned in the *Sankhyan* doctrine for the accomplishment of all action:

14. The field, the doer, the various means, the several different operations, the fifth and the last, the Unseen.

15. Whatever action, right or wrong, a man undertakes to do with the body, speech or mind, these are the five factors thereof.

16. This being so, he who, by reason of unenlightened intellect, sees the unconditioned *Atman* as the agent—such a man is dense and unseeing.

17. He who is free from all sense of 'I', whose motive is untainted, slays not nor is bound, even though he slay all these worlds.

This *shloka* though seemingly somewhat baffling is not really so. The *Gita* on many occasions presents the ideal to attain which the aspirant has to strive but which may not be possible completely to realize in the world. It is like definitions in geometry. A perfect straight line does not exist, but it is necessary to imagine it in order to prove the various propositions. Even so, it is necessary to hold up ideals of this nature as standards for imitation in matters of conduct. This then would seem to be the meaning of this *shloka*: He who has made ashes of 'self', whose motive is untainted, may slay the whole world, if he will. But in reality he who has annihilated 'self' has annihilated his flesh too, and he whose motive is untainted sees the past, present and future. Such a being can be one and only one—God. He acts and yet is no doer, slays and yet is no slayer. For mortal man and royal road— the conduct of the worthy—is ever before him, viz. *ahimsa*—holding all life sacred.

18. Knowledge, the object of knowledge, and the knower compose the threefold urge to action; the means, the action and the doer compose the threefold sum of action.

19. Knowledge, action, and the doer are of three kinds according to their different *gunas*; hear thou these, just as they have been described in the science of the *gunas*.

20. Know that knowledge whereby one sees in all beings immutable enti- ty—a unity in diversity—to be *sattvika*.

21. That knowledge which perceives separately in all beings several enti- ties of diverse kinds, know thou to be *rajasa*.

22. And knowledge which, without reason, clings to one single thing, as though it were everything, which misses the true essence and is super- ficial is *tamasa*.

23. That action is called *sattvika* which, being one's allotted task, is performed without attachment, without like or dislike, and without a desire for fruit.

24. That action which is prompted by the desire for fruit, or by the thought of 'I', and which involves much dissipation of energy is called *rajasa*.

25. That action which is blindly undertaken without any regard to capac- ity and consequences, involving loss and hurt, is called *tamasa*.

26. That doer is called *sattvika* who has shed all attachment, all thought of 'I', who is filled with firmness and zeal, and who recks neither success nor failure.

27. That doer is said to be *rajasa* who is passionate, desirous of the fruit of action, greedy, violent, unclean, and moved by joy and sorrow.

28. That doer is called *tamasa* who is undisciplined, vulgar, stubborn, knavish, spiteful, indolent, woebegone, and dilatory.

29. Hear now, O Dhananjaya, detailed fully and severally, the threefold division of understanding and will, according to their *gunas*.

30. That understanding, O Partha, is *sattvika* which knows action from inaction, what ought to be done from what ought not to be done, fear from fearlessness and bondage from release.

31. That understanding, O Partha, is *rajasa*, which decides erroneously between right and wrong, between what ought to be done and what ought not to be done.

32. That understanding, O Partha, is *tamasa*, which, shrouded in darkness, thinks wrong to be right and mistakes everything for its reverse.

33. That will, O Partha, is *sattvika* which maintains an unbroken harmony between the activities of the mind, the vital energies and the senses.

34. That will, O Partha, is *rajasa* which clings, with attachment, to righteousness, desire and wealth, desirous of fruit in each case.

35. That will, O Partha, is *tamasa*, whereby insensate man does not abandon sleep, fear, grief, despair and self-conceit.

36. Hear now from Me, O Bharatarshabha, the three kinds of pleasure.

    Pleasure which is enjoyed only by repeated practice, and which puts an end to pain,

37. Which, in its inception, is as poison, but in the end as nectar, born of the serene realization of the true nature of *Atman*—that pleasure is said to be *sattvika*.

38. That pleasure is called *rajasa* which, arising from the contact of the senses with their objects, is at first as nectar but in the end like poison.

39. That pleasure is called *tamasa* which arising from sleep and sloth and heedlessness, stupefies the soul both at first and in the end.

40. There is no being, either on earth or in heaven among the gods, that can be free from these three *gunas* born of *prakriti*.

41. The duties of *Brahmanas, Kshatriyas, Vaishyas,* and *Shudras,* are distributed according to their innate qualifications, O Parantapa.

42. Serenity, self-restraint, austerity, purity, forgiveness, uprightness, knowledge and discriminative knowledge, faith in God are the *Brahmana's* natural duties.

43. Valour, spiritedness, constancy, resourcefulness, not fleeing from battle, generosity, and the capacity to rule are the natural duties of a *Kshatriya*.

44. Tilling the soil, protection of the cow and commerce are the natural functions of a *Vaishya*, while service is the natural duty of a *Shudra*.

45. Each man, by complete absorption in the performance of his duty, wins perfection. Hear now how he wins such perfection by devotion to that duty.

46. By offering the worship of his duty to Him who is the moving spirit of all beings, and by whom all this is pervaded, man wins perfection.

47. Better one's own duty, though uninviting, than another's which may be more easily performed; doing duty which accords with one's nature, one incurs no sin.

     The central teaching of the *Gita* is detachment—abandonment of the fruit of action. And there would be no room for this abandonment if one were to prefer another's duty to one's own. Therefore one's own duty is said to be better than another's. It is the spirit in which duty is done that matters, and its unattached performance is its own reward.

48. One should not abandon, O Kaunteya, that duty to which one is born, imperfect though it be; for all action, in its inception, is enveloped in imperfection, as fire in smoke.

49. He who has weaned himself of all kinds, who is master of himself, who is dead to desire, attains through renunciation the perfection of freedom from action.

50. Learn now from Me, in brief, O Kaunteya, how he who has gained this perfection, attains to *Brahman*, the supreme consummation of knowledge.

51. Equipped with purified understanding, restraining the self with firm will, abandoning sound and other objects of the senses, putting aside likes and dislikes,

52. Living in solitude, spare in diet, restrained in speech, body and mind, ever absorbed in *dhyanayoga*, anchored in dispassion,

53. Without pride, violence, arrogance, lust, wrath, possession, having shed all sense of 'mine' and at peace with himself, he is fit to become one with *Brahman*.

54. One with *Brahman* and at peace with himself, he grieves not, nor desires; holding all beings alike, he achieves supreme devotion to Me.

55. By devotion, he realizes in truth how great I am, who I am; and having known Me in reality he enters into Me.

56. Even whilst always performing actions, he who makes Me his refuge wins, by My grace, the eternal and imperishable haven.

57. Casting, with thy mind, all actions on Me, make Me thy goal, and resorting to the *yoga* of even-mindedness fix thy thought ever on Me.

58. Fixing his thy thought on Me, thou shalt surmount all obstacles by My grace; but if possessed by the sense of 'I' thou listen not, thou shalt perish.

59. If obsessed by the sense of 'I', thou thinkest, 'I will not fight', vain is thy obsession; (thy) nature will compel thee.

60. What thou wilt not do, O Kaunteya, because of thy delusion, thou shalt do, even against thy will, bound as thou art by the duty to which thou art born.

61. God, O Arjuna, dwells in the heart of every being and by His delusive mystery whirls them all, (as though) set on a machine.

62. In Him alone seek thy refuge with all thy heart, O Bharata. By His grace shalt thou win to the eternal haven of supreme peace.

63. Thus have I expounded to thee the most mysterious of all knowledge; ponder over it fully, then act as thou wilt.

64. Hear again My supreme word, the most mysterious of all; dearly beloved thou art of Me, hence I desire to declare thy welfare.

65. On Me fix thy mind, to Me bring thy devotion, to Me offer thy sacrifice, to Me make thy obeisance; to Me indeed shalt thou come— solemn is My promise to thee, thou art dear to Me.

66. Abandon all duties and come to Me the only refuge. I will release thee from all sins; grieve not!

67. Utter this never to him who knows no austerity, has no devotion, nor any desire to listen, nor yet to him who scoffs at Me.

68. He who will propound this supreme mystery to My devotees, shall, by that act of highest devotion to Me, surely come to Me.

69. Nor among men is there any who renders dearer service to Me than he; nor shall there be on earth any more beloved by Me than he.

It is only he who has himself gained the knowledge and lived it in his life that can declare it to others. These two *shlokas* cannot possibly have any reference to him, who no matter how he conducts himself, can give flawless reading and interpretation of the *Gita*.

70. And whoso shall study this sacred discourse of ours shall worship Me with the sacrifice of knowledge. That is My belief.

71. And the man of faith who, scorning not, will but listen to it,—even he shall be released and will go to the happy worlds of men of virtuous deeds.

72. Hast thou heard this, O Partha, with a concentrated mind? Has thy delusion, born of ignorance, been destroyed, O Dhananjaya?

ARJUNA SAID :

73. Thanks to Thy grace, O Achyuta, my delusion is destroyed, my understanding has returned. I stand secure, my doubts all dispelled; I will do thy bidding.

SANJAYA SAID :

74. Thus did I hear this marvellous and thrilling discourse between *Vasudeva* and the great-souled Partha.

75. It was by Vyasa's favor that I listened to this supreme and mysterious *Yoga* as expounded by the lips of the Master of *Yoga*, Krishna Himself.

76. O King, as often as I recall that marvellous and purifying discourse between Keshava and Arjuna, I am filled with recurring rapture.

77. And as often as I recall that marvellous form of Hari, my wonder knows no bounds and I rejoice again and again.

78. Wheresoever Krishna, the Master of *Yoga*, is, and wheresoever is Partha the Bowman, there rest assured are Fortune, Victory, Prosperity, and Eternal Right.

Thus ends the eighteenth discourse, entitled '*Sannyasa Yoga*' in the converse of Lord Krishna and Arjuna, on the science of *Yoga*, as part of the knowledge of *Brahman* in the Upanishad called the *Bhagawadgita*.

THE POWER OF YOUR
SUBCONSCIOUS MIND
by Dr. Joseph Murphy

Pages : 242
Size : 8.5x5.5 inches
Binding : Hardback
Language : English
Subject : Self-Help
ISBN : 9789387669222

'The Power of Your Subconscious Mind' has been a bestseller since its first publication in 1963, selling many millions of copies since its original publication. It is one of the most brilliant and beloved spiritual self-help works of all time which can help you heal yourself, banish your fears, sleep better, enjoy better relationships and just feel happier. The techniques are simple and results come quickly. You can improve your relationships, your finances, your physical well-being.

Dr Joseph Murphy explains that life events are actually the result of the workings of your conscious and subconscious minds. He suggests practical techniques through which one can change one's destiny, principally by focusing and redirecting this miraculous energy. Years of research studying the world's major religions convinced him that some Great Power lay behind all spiritual life and that this power is within each of us.

'The Power of Your Subconscious Mind' will open a world of success, happiness, prosperity, and peace for you.

OTHER HARDBACK BOOKS

- 1984 by George Orwell
  Fiction/Classics, ISBN: 9788193545836

- Abraham Lincoln by Lord Charnwood
  Biographies/Leaders, ISBN: 9789387669147

- Alice's Adventures in Wonderland by Lewis Carroll
  Children's/Classics, ISBN: 9789387669055

- Animal Farm by George Orwell
  Fiction/Classics, ISBN: 9789387669062

- Anthem by Ayn Rand
  Fiction/Classics, ISBN: 9789389157178

- As a Man Thinketh by James Allen
  Fiction/Classics, ISBN: 9789388118422

- Awakened Imagination by Neville Goddard
  Religion & Spirituality, ISBN: 9789389157185

- Be What You Wish by Neville Goddard
  Mind, Body & Spirit, ISBN: 9789388118163

- Becoming a Writer by Dorothea Brande
  Self Help/General, ISBN: 9789389157192

- Believe in Yourself by Joseph Murphy
  Mind, Body & Spirit, ISBN: 9789388118439

- Black Beauty by Anna Sewell
  Children's/Classics, ISBN: 9789388118262

- Civilization and Its Discontents by Sigmund Freud
  Social Sciences/General, ISBN: 9789388118279

- Demian by Hermann Hesse
  Fiction/Classics, ISBN: 9789388118170

- Feeling is the Secret by Neville Goddard
  Religion & Spirituality, ISBN: 9789389157208

OTHER HARDBACK BOOKS

- Gitanjali by Rabindranath Tagore
  Fiction/Poems, ISBN: 9789387669079

- Great Speeches of Abraham Lincoln by Abraham Lincoln
  History/United States, ISBN: 9789387669154

- How to Attract Money by Joseph Murphy
  Self Help/Success, ISBN: 9789388118446

- How to be Filled with the Holy Spirit by A.W. Tozer
  Religion/Christianity, ISBN: 9789389157215

- How to Enjoy Your Life and Your Job by Dale Carnegie
  Self Help/General, ISBN: 9789388118293

- Illust. Biography of William Shakespeare by Manju Gupta
  Biographies/Authors, ISBN: 9789387669246

- Madhubala by Manju Gupta
  Biographies/Cinems, ISBN: 9789387669253

- Mansarover 1 (Hindi) by Premchand
  Fiction/Short Stories, ISBN: 9789387669086

- Meditations by Marcus Aurelius
  Non Fiction/Philosopy, ISBN: 9789388118781

- My Inventions: The Autobio. of Nikola Tesla by Nikola Tesla
  Autobiographies/Scientists, ISBN: 9789388118187

- Selected Stories of Rabindranath Tagore by Rabindranath Tagore
  Fiction/Short Stories, ISBN: 9789387669307

- Sense and Sensibility by Jane Austen
  Fiction/Classics, ISBN: 9789387669109

- Siddhartha by Hermann Hesse
  Fiction/Classics, ISBN: 9789387669116

- Tales from India by Rudyard Kipling
  Fiction/Short Stories, ISBN: 9789387669123

OTHER HARDBACK BOOKS

- Tales from Shakespeare by Charles Lamb, Mary Lamb
  Fiction/Short Stories, ISBN: 9789387669314

- The Alchemy of Happiness by Al-Ghazzali
  Religion & Spirituality, ISBN: 9789388118309

- The Art of Public Speaking by Dale Carnegie
  Self Help/General, ISBN: 9789388118477

- The Autobiography of a Yogi by Paramahansa Yogananda
  Autobiographies/General, ISBN: 9789387669192

- The Dynamic Laws of Prosperity by Catherine Ponder
  Mind, Body & Spirit, ISBN: 9789388118194

- The Elements of Style by William Strunk
  Non Fiction/Skill, ISBN: 9789389157222

- The Game of Life and How to Play It by Florence Scovel Shinn
  Mind, Body & Spirit, ISBN: 9789388118316

- The Imitation of Christ by Thomas À Kempis
  Religion/Christianity, ISBN: 9789388118200

- The Jungle Book by Rudyard Kipling
  Children's/Classics, ISBN: 9789387669338

- The Knowledge of the Holy by A.W. Tozer
  Religion/Christianity, ISBN: 9789389157239

- The Light of Asia by Sir Edwin Arnold
  Fiction/Poetry, ISBN: 9789387669130

- The Magic of Faith by Joseph Murphy
  Mind, Body & Spirit, ISBN: 9789388118712

- The Origin of Species by Charles Darwin
  Sciences/Life Sciences, ISBN: 9789387669345

- The Path of Prosperity by James Allen
  Mind, Body & Spirit, ISBN: 9789388118323

OTHER HARDBACK BOOKS

- The Power of Awareness by Neville Goddard
  Mind, Body & Spirit, ISBN: 9789388118330

- The Power of Concentration by Theron Q. Dumont
  Self Help/General, ISBN: 9789388118224

- The Power of Positive Thinking by Norman Vincent Peale
  Mind, Body & Spirit, ISBN: 9789388118729

- The Prophet by Kahlil Gibran
  Fiction/Classics, ISBN: 9789388118453

- The Psychopathology of Everyday Life by Sigmund Freud
  Non Fiction/Psychology, ISBN: 9789388118231

- The Pursuit of God by A.W. Tozer
  Religion/Christianity, ISBN: 9789389157246

- The Quick and Easy Way to Effec. Speaking by Dale Carnegie
  Self Help/General, ISBN: 9789388118347

- The Science of Getting Rich by Wallace D. Wattles
  Self Help/Success, ISBN: 9789387669239

- The Seven Laws of Teaching by John Milton Gregory
  Self Help/General, ISBN: 9789388118460

- The Upanishads by Swami Paramananda
  Religion/Hinduism, ISBN: 9789388118774

- The World as I See It by Albert Einstein
  Non Fiction/Philosopy, ISBN: 9789388118248

- Thought Vibration by William Walker Atkinson
  Non Fiction/Philosopy, ISBN: 9789389157253

- Wake Up and Live! by Dorothea Brande
  Mind, Body & Spirit, ISBN: 9789388118255

- Your Faith is Your Fortune by Neville Goddard
  Religion & Spirituality, ISBN: 9789389157260